How to Have a Great Sunday School

by

Wes and Sheryl Haystead

Gospel Light

Gospel Light is an evangelical Christian publisher dedicated to serving the local church. We believe God's vision for Gospel Light is to provide church leaders with biblical, user-friendly materials that will help them evangelize, disciple and minister to children, youth and families.

We hope this Gospel Light resource will help you discover biblical truth for your own life and help you minister to youth. God bless you in your work.

For a free catalog of resources from Gospel Light please contact your Christian supplier or contact us at 1-800-4-GOSPEL.

PUBLISHING STAFF
William T. Greig, Publisher
Dr. Elmer L. Towns, Senior Consulting Publisher
Dr. Gary S. Greig, Senior Consulting Editor
Pam Weston, Editor
Patti Pennington Virtue, Assistant Editor
Christi Goeser, Editorial Assistant
Kyle Duncan, Associate Publisher
Bayard Taylor, M.Div., Senior Editor, Theological and Biblical Issues
Kevin Parks, Cover Designer
Debi Thayer, Designer
Rob Williams, Designer
Aimee Denzel, Illustrator
Tom Stephen, M. Div., Youth Consultant

ISBN 0-8307-1826-5
© 2000 by Gospel Light
All rights reserved.
Printed in U.S.A.

How to Make Clean Copies
from This Book

Contents

Chapter One

How to Make This Book Work for You

Before you plunge into this book, first consider several various approaches you can take to the information here, fitting the book to your specific needs and interests. In this way, you will find useful guidance in evaluating and improving Sunday School and other teaching ministries of your church. As you use this book, focus on the topics that address your specific situation.

What This Chapter Tells You

- Your church has unique strengths and weaknesses that color how your teaching ministries can operate effectively.
- Sunday School is the most familiar teaching ministry and a useful model for leaders of other programs to consider.

What This Chapter Shows You

- How to get an overview of a thoughtfully planned and effectively operated Sunday School;
- How to identify topics that address your church, your role, your areas of concern;
- Tips for sharing this book (in whole or in part) with others who can benefit from its insights;
- What to do after you've reviewed this chapter.

Get the Big Picture

Improvement and growth results from a decision to start and a commitment to keep at it. Just because we've always done something one way is no reason to keep doing it that way. As you approach this book, start with the attitude that with God's help, your Sunday School can improve. As you read through the following pages, set your heart and mind to look for ideas that you can implement. Set out for yourself both long-term and short-term goals. Envision what your Sunday School can become through consistent effort over time as well as immediate actions that can make a positive difference in coming weeks.

Consider the benefits that will result from not settling for the status quo:

- You will gain increased vision for ways that God can work through your Sunday School to make positive changes in individual lives as well as the total church.
- Your enthusiasm will stimulate others, multiplying your vision and efforts.
- Developing a plan for improvement will give you tools to evaluate progress, helping you and other leaders "stay on track" in ministry efforts.

Take a Fresh Look

While millions of people continue to benefit from it, for decades the Sunday School has received a steady dose of criticism. It has been popular to belittle the Sunday School, almost gleefully pointing out its flaws. You may be coming to this book somewhat less than enthusiastically, perhaps because you have questions about how, and even whether, your church can effectively conduct its teaching ministry.

Sunday School and other teaching ministries really can strengthen and enrich your church. Regardless of the size of your church, your specific leadership role or the age level(s) you direct, you can make a positive difference in the quality of teaching your church provides.

A REFERENCE FOR ALL TEACHING MINISTRIES

Many churches conduct a great deal of their teaching ministry through programs other than the Sunday School. Whatever the variations among these programs—and they are almost endless—there are some essential components (principles, standards, goals, etc.) of any effective teaching ministry. This book uses the Sunday School as its prime example and reference point, but it deals with issues that apply to any program that pursues the awesome ministry of making disciples of Christ.

"There are three keys to a successful Sunday School:

1. Plan your work.
2. Work your plan.
3. Pray for numbers one and two!"

Look at Where You Are

The rest of this chapter will help you identify the parts of this book where you need to focus your attention.

Focus on Characteristics

CHARACTERISTIC 1: CHURCH SIZE

Choose strategies that fit your church.

Teaching and ministry principles are the same regardless of church size, but they must be carried out in varying ways to fit the number of people involved.

Think About It

1. What are some ways that the size of your church impacts your teaching ministries?
   - What *advantages* does your church size have for effective teaching?
   - What are the *limitations* to effective teaching?
2. In what ways do your present teaching ministries impact the size of your church?
   - What evidence is there that your Sunday School *encourages* and/or sustains attendance growth?
   - What evidence is there that growth is *hindered*?
   - What might be hindering growth?

CHARACTERISTIC 2: LEADERSHIP ROLE

Focus on your own leadership role.

Effective leadership is essential if teaching ministries are to improve. People in widely different leadership roles are often the ones who provide the positive guidance needed.

Think About It

- How does your job status (full-time or part-time, paid staff or volunteer) impact your leadership role?
- What do you like about your present position?
- What changes might make your leadership more effective?
- What aspects of your leadership role are largely independent of your job status?

"That will never work in our church because we're too (small, big, etc.)."

Tip: It's easy to discount ideas or experiences from churches that are much larger or smaller than yours. However, the wise leader always considers how to adapt new ideas to his or her own church situation. Your answers to the questions in the "Think About It" section can prepare you to use this book to meet the special needs and opportunities of your church.

"The Sunday School hour is the most wasted hour of the week only for the people who aren't there."

"That's not my job."

Tip: Some people look through a manual like this and notice all the things that aren't part of their job descriptions. Others are overwhelmed by discovering that everything in here IS their responsibility. In either case, it's best to actively look for a few things that you can begin to address.

CHARACTERISTIC 3:
AGE LEVEL

Apply principles and instructions to the age level(s) you serve.

Some people assume that a book that deals with all age levels has limited value for any specific age group. (*How can a book that deals with preschoolers and senior citizens say anything worthwhile about teenagers?*)

A four-year-old, a fourteen-year-old and a forty-year-old are obviously different from each other in many ways. But they are all human beings, and they have much more in common than we often realize.

Think About It

1. What are needs and interests that distinguish people in the age level(s) you serve?
   - What are some special *pleasures* gained by ministry to these people?
   - What are *challenges*?
2. What are needs and interests shared in common with other age groups?

CHARACTERISTIC 4:
PROGRAM

Adapt information to the specific ministry in which you work.

Programs are organized vehicles with which to accomplish ministry objectives. This book contains ideas, guidelines and examples that may at first glance seem far removed from the program(s) you are involved with. We encourage you to linger for a few moments over paragraphs that seem aimed at vastly different programs than yours and to consider what you can do to adapt the information to fit your program(s).

Think About It

1. What are some strengths of the program(s) you lead?
   - In what ways are the present leaders making a positive impact on participants?
   - What do participants indicate that they like about the program(s)?

Tip: *"That'll never work here"* is a familiar response to many proven ideas. Rather than discount something that worked in a different program, open your mind to explore possible ways to modify and implement ideas to fit your program or perhaps modify your program to fit some new ideas.

- Why do they continue to attend?
2. What are some challenges faced by the program(s) you lead?
   - What are some concerns that other people have expressed to you?
   - What problems or weaknesses have you noticed?

APPROACH 1:
ONWARD AND UPWARD

Move on to chapter 2 and keep on until you come to the end.

This approach assumes that the writers had a plan in mind in how the book is organized, so why not just follow the plan? Some things you discover in an early chapter may actually be foundational for concepts presented in a later chapter.

APPROACH 2:
FOLLOW THE TOPIC

Look up topics of interest and see where they lead.

This approach assumes you would never have picked up this book if you did not have some specific questions or problems related to improving your church's teaching ministry. So check out the table of contents in the front of the book, the detailed index in the back or the Where Do I Start? listings at the front of each chapter to locate information on any topics of concern. You might have to go back and read some information you skipped, but that's OK. This is not a novel—you won't spoil the ending by reading ahead.

Look at Where You Are
Now that you have reviewed some important characteristics of your church's ministries, consider these options for approaching the rest of this book.

Bonus Idea for Implementing Change: Always involve as many people as possible in any decision for change. People accept change more readily when they have a part in the decision-making process. Test a new idea out on several people before presenting it to a larger group. This is a good way of getting the support of others, and it helps make it "our" idea rather than "my" idea. *Willamae Myers, Grace Bible Fellowship, Pinellas Park, Florida*

APPROACH 3:
POINT AND PICK

Close your eyes, flip the pages, stab your finger at the text, open your eyes and start reading.

This is not recommended if you desire to build a teaching ministry of substance. It could be fun if you're just looking for a few random ideas to graft onto whatever you're already doing, however.

APPROACH 4:
TUNNEL VISION

Target your reading on topics that fit your situation—facilities, recruiting, job descriptions, outreach, etc.—and ignore the rest.

Use the table of contents and index, or just flip through pages, looking for information directed specifically for your situation or need. Then go back through the rest of the book to discover how almost everything else also applies to you!

APPROACH 5:
TEAMWORK

Study this book with several other people who care about the quality of teaching in your church.

Building a solid teaching ministry is never a one-person operation. So get together a group of people whose support and inspiration you know you need, including the board or committee already involved. Then, over a period of months or at a weekend planning retreat, try one of the following approaches:

- Assign each person a different chapter to study; then lead the group in discussion.
- Give each person a copy of the manual. Assign one chapter to be read by everyone in advance of every meeting. Then discuss the assigned chapter.

In either case, keep the discussions focused on exploring practical ways to implement or modify the ideas in the chapter. Planning for the future needs to happen on a regular if not yearly basis.

Visual Directory

(Here's What the Little Pictures Mean!)

CHAPTER ELEMENTS

 Look at Where You Are
Provides information that will help you evaluate your present situation.

 Get the Big Picture
States the overall focus of the chapter

 **Look to the Future**
Rate your church's progress toward meeting improvement goals and list actions to reach each goal.

✔ **Action Checklist**

Provides step-by-step procedures for taking action on specific goals.

AGE-LEVEL ICONS

 Early Childhood
Indicates information, forms, guidelines, etc. intended for use with children from infants to 5 years old.

 Nursery
Although information for infants through $2^1/_2$ will generally be found in the Early Childhood section, there are a few incidents where ideas, forms, etc. pertain to nursery classes only. In those cases the Nursery icon will be used.

 Bonus Idea:
Provides practical suggestions from fellow Sunday School workers throughout North America.

 Children
Indicates information, forms, guidelines, etc. intended for use with children in kindergarten through fifth or sixth grades.

 Youth
Indicates information, forms, guidelines, etc. intended for use with children from middle school through high school.

College/Career

Although not used often, this icon indicates information, forms, guidelines, etc. intended for use with young adults from 18 to approximately 25 years of age.

Adult

Indicates information, forms, guidelines, etc. intended for use with adults.

Chapter Two

The Insider's Guide to Sunday School

Why should a car have an engine? Why should an airplane have wings? Why should a computer have a keyboard? Obviously, a car with no engine won't run; an airplane with no wings won't fly; and a computer with no keyboard might compute, but it will not be very useful. Likewise, a church with no consistent teaching ministry for all age groups is ill equipped to fulfill what a church is called to do—to equip believers to grow in faith and to serve God and others.

If you are already convinced that a healthy teaching ministry—regardless of what you call it or when it meets—is vitally important to the mission of your church, you can skip this chapter, unless you'd like a little information to aim at folks who feel they can get along without Sunday School. In that case, you may want to take notes.

If you are among those who wonder if putting time and energy into the Sunday School is really worth it, this chapter is for *you*! Do not skip to chapter 3. Do not pass Go. Do not collect $200. Start reading now!

What This Chapter Tells You

- A well-run Sunday School provides rich benefits for a church, helping the congregation in fulfilling its ministry goals.
- The purpose of the Sunday School is far more than religious child care for children or indoctrination in Bible history or theology for youth and adults.

What This Chapter Shows You

- How other teaching ministries compare and/or contrast with Sunday School;
- How to communicate the Sunday School's purpose to church leaders and the congregation;
- Tips for writing a mission/vision statement that provides a focused direction for your Sunday School.

Where Do I Start?

> "I still remember my first Sunday School teacher's name—Mrs. Baldwin. She loved me! She was the first person to tell me about Jesus. She told me that He loved me and that He knew me by name.... There's a place in a Sunday School class for crafts, for clay modeling, for coloring and other activities. But we must not forget the purpose for our teaching. It is to introduce children to Jesus."
> *Shirley Dobson*[1]

> *"Start off by dumping the name 'Sunday School.'" Gina Bolenbaugh*
> *Pasadena, California*

Beyond Sunday School

Yes, we know there are other important and valuable teaching ministries in addition to Sunday School. Many churches seeking to keep their teaching ministry vital have tried to come up with a contemporary name to replace "Sunday School." But this particular chapter, even more than the rest of this book, focuses on the Sunday School because, for the great majority of churches, it involves more age levels and people than any other program—and it tends to meet more consistently and be more coordinated in the content it studies.

No matter what this ministry is called, whether it meets Sunday morning before the worship service; Sunday morning at the same time as the worship service; Sunday morning after the worship service; Sunday afternoon or evening (often the plan for congregations that use a shared facility); Saturday night (becoming popular with churches extending their outreach); or weeknights, the whole point of this chapter is to encourage churches to begin or maintain and improve a ministry with a place for all ages that achieves the benefits and purposes listed here.

> *"A rose by any other name."*
> *William Shakespeare*

Get the Big Picture

Sunday School provides a rich treasure of benefits when its intended purposes are fulfilled.

BENEFITS OF A WELL-RUN SUNDAY SCHOOL
- People of all ages grow in faith, knowledge and vision.
- People, including seekers and others new to the church, find acceptance.
- People at all levels of maturity discover new ways to serve God and others.
- The total church is strengthened in all areas of its ministry.

PURPOSES OF THE SUNDAY SCHOOL
- Bible learning—guiding people in discovering and applying Bible truth;
- Fellowship—providing positive interaction that provides encouragement and support;
- Service—promoting opportunities to serve God and minister to others;
- Outreach—equipping and motivating teachers and students to reach people for Christ and incorporate them into the life of the church.

Focus on the Benefits

BENEFIT 1:
PEOPLE GROW

People of all ages grow in faith, knowledge and vision.

Whether a person is two or twenty-two—or even ninety-two—Sunday School is a place for personal and spiritual growth. Frankly, it's pretty hard not to grow after spending an hour with a peer group focused on exploring the Bible and applying it to daily life!

Musings

Church leaders are often quick to claim that they provide a place for everyone. But after giving it some thought, there are almost always some groups who are missing out. Sometimes a church misses the chance to effectively nurture the youngest children, providing only minimal child care instead of age-appropriate Bible learning. Or it may be the adults who are left without opportunities to study and grow and the church excuses its lack because "everyone's so busy, and it's too hard to get people to come and besides, they get a chance to hear a sermon every week in church."

Think About It

1. What opportunities for personal and spiritual growth are now provided through your church for...
   * Preschool children?
   * Elementary school children?
   * Youth?
   * Young adults?
   * Middle adults?
   * Senior adults?
2. What percentage of the following people in each age group are currently involved in one or more of these growth opportunities?
   * Preschool children
   * Elementary school children
   * Youth
   * Young adults
   * Middle adults
   * Senior adults

 Bonus Idea for Communicating the Purpose of Sunday School: Communicate clearly to parents and church leaders the role of Sunday School as it relates to other teaching ministries. To create appropriate expectations for Sunday School, we proclaim its major purposes:
* To teach Bible knowledge and build skills in using the Bible;
* To apply that knowledge to life experiences;
* To build lasting personal relationships within the church family.

We also have a children's church that exists primarily to teach children about worship and involve them in worship experiences. Our midweek club program exists for yet other reasons: evangelism, Bible memory and fun recreational activities.

So I work hard to cast the vision of how all of these emphases are carefully coordinated to provide a balanced ministry. *Jody Burgin, Vineyard Community Church, Cincinnati, Ohio*

Ideas for Kid-Friendly Names for Sunday School

Discovery Station
Sonship for Kids
Sonland for Kids
Power Plant
Sunday Morning Live
Kids' University
Promiseland Park
Shining Stars
Kids' Community
Celebration Kids' Club

3. Based on those percentages, which of the following age levels seem to be most effective at involving people? Least effective? Why?
- Preschool children
- Elementary school children
- Youth
- Young adults
- Middle adults
- Senior adults

The Men and the Women and the Boys and the Girls

How many places are there, besides Sunday School...
- That provide a warm, friendly environment?
- Where people of all ages participate in groups designed for their unique needs and interests?
- Everyone is encouraged to learn, build friendships and to serve others?

Write your list here:

- _____
- _____
- _____

BENEFIT 2:
PEOPLE FIND ACCEPTANCE

**People, including seekers and others new
to the church, find acceptance.**

People experience growth in settings where they are warmly accepted, even with their imperfections. It may seem contradictory to tolerate immaturity while being committed to maturation. But if there is anyplace on God's green earth where imperfect people should be welcomed, it's in a Sunday School class where they can enjoy the opportunity to have God's Word speak directly to them.

> *"Accept one another, then, just as Christ accepted you, in order to bring praise to God."*
> *Paul*
> *(Romans 15:7)*

Think About It

1. What is the best way to get acquainted in your church for a new person who is a(n)...
   - Preschool child?
   - Elementary school child?
   - Youth?
   - Young adult?
   - Middle adult?
   - Senior adult?

2. What barriers exist to inhibit a new person from feeling a sense of belonging in your church's programs for...
   - Preschool children?
   - Elementary school children?
   - Youth?
   - Young adults?
   - Middle adults?
   - Senior adults?

3. What factors contribute to a sense of belonging for a new person who is a(n)...
   - Preschool child?
   - Elementary school child?
   - Youth?
   - Young adult?
   - Middle adult?
   - Senior adult?

BENEFIT 3: PEOPLE LEARN TO SERVE

People at all levels of maturity discover new ways to serve God and others.

Observation

There's a school of thought that learning must follow these steps:

1. Gain new information;
2. Come to understand its meaning;
3. Develop attitudes and beliefs about that meaning; and finally
4. Put it into practice.

In real life, especially with young children, a great deal of learning occurs almost in reverse. The process begins by doing something; then out of that experience comes attitudes, beliefs, insights and information.

Either way, an effective teaching ministry consistently emphasizes putting truth into action. And what better action can there be than serving God by reaching out to others?

A child eagerly joins in picking up blocks and putting them back on the shelf, all while singing "Let's put our toys away...I will help and so can you" to the tune of "Farmer in the Dell"; a class of fifth graders carefully stamps the insides of books that will be given to prisoners; a high school class plans a time to serve food to homeless people; or an adult class collects baby items for a single mother.

What do these scenes have in common, beside teachers who intentionally guide their classes in practical, meaningful acts of service? They reflect groups that are learning to develop an outward focus—caring for the needs of others, not just seeking what they can get for themselves. In today's world, what church couldn't use more people who have learned the joy of serving?

Think About It

1. In the average group in your church, who does most of the serving:
   - Leaders and teachers?
   - A few willing volunteers?
   - A few reluctant volunteers?
   - Most of the group members?
2. Think about the most recent Bible study group in which you participated.
   - What would have been the result if everyone there actually put into practice something from that session?
   - In what ways could participants in the group have better served one another?
   - What opportunities to put lesson content into practice are provided in the typical session?
3. What would be the impact on a group if its members really were growing in their service to God and others?
   - How would attendance be impacted?
   - What would happen to leader/teacher recruitment?

BENEFIT 4:
THE CHURCH IS STRENGTHENED

The total church is strengthened in all areas of its ministry.

Imagine that throughout your church, individuals and groups are growing stronger in knowledge, faith and service. Got the picture? Great! Now zoom out to gain a view of the entire congregation. Looks pretty healthy, doesn't it? When provision for growth is made at all age levels, the church as a whole gains noticeably.

Sometimes people who serve in the church's teaching ministry feel isolated, forgotten in their little corner. Does it really matter to your church that someone is lovingly teaching three-year-olds about Jesus? Does patiently putting up with a room full of middle schoolers make a difference in the life of the church? Does teaching a class of elderly widows help the church fulfill its mission? The answer to all three questions is: Of course! To paraphrase the apostle Paul: "If one part of the body grows, every part grows with it" (see Ephesians 4:16).

Think About It

1. What teachers have influenced your growth in the Christian life?
   • What did they do that contributed to your growth?
   • Who else did they influence?
   • What might your church be lacking now if not for their ministry to you and others?
2. In your church, who are some people you see contributing to the growth of others?
   • What differences do those people's ministries make in the life of your church?

An Example of Dedication
Mabelle Sloan taught babies. And toddlers. And parents. And other teachers. And youth helpers. She taught about love and patience and being faithful. She taught the value of prayer and reading God's Word. She taught about being cheerful in hard times and about being willing to help wherever there's a need. She taught about all these things, and more, by her quiet example, influencing without preaching, spreading an attitude of caring. She kept teaching all this well into her 80s, right up to her last day on earth—a day spent teaching babies at Vacation Bible School.

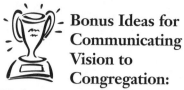

Bonus Ideas for Communicating Vision to Congregation:
We have a ministry parade during the morning service. Everyone involved in an area of ministry carries a banner with the name of the ministry. As the banners are paraded, the pastor gives a brief statement about each, including how to become a part of it. *Hailey Armoogan, Waterloo Pentecostal Assembly, Waterloo, Ontario, Canada*

- Blow up photos of classes to poster size and display around church.
- Put up a tent or canopy outside, serve cake and punch, and distribute information on Sunday School.
- Pick a visual theme (e.g., rainbows) to decorate church (rainbows of balloons), serve refreshments (rainbow sugar cookies) and tie to printed information on Sunday School.
- Show a video of classes in action.
- Have a committed teacher tell of the importance of teaching in his or her life and conclude by having his or her students come forward and escort their teacher back to class. *Ivy Beckwith, Ventura, California*

Sunday School and the Pastor: From the earliest days of the Church, one of the central tasks of the pastor has been to teach. Thus, pastors and Sunday Schools should be an ideal match, right? Not always. Far too many pastors recount stories in which the Sunday School seemed more of a hindrance than a help to an effective teaching ministry. And a great many Sunday School teachers tell of not being able to get their pastor to care about the Sunday School.

On the assumption that this book is more likely to be read by Sunday School teachers than by pastors, here are a few tips for getting and keeping the pastor's support:

1. Pray for your pastor and his or her ministry, not just asking that the pastor will come around to your point of view about Sunday School.
2. Share positive things from Sunday School with your pastor: leave a photo of a Sunday School class in action on the pastor's desk, tell the pastor a story of how someone has benefited from a Sunday School class, etc.
3. Repeat Steps 1 and 2 regularly.
4. Invite the pastor to participate in ways that utilize personal strengths and interests, not just a position of leadership. Making an appeal for additional teachers might not be part of pastoral responsibility, but barbecuing steaks or baking a cake for those who have served faithfully could be something a pastor might thoroughly enjoy.
5. Ask for the pastor's insights in dealing with opportunities, challenges and problems. Then give those insights due consideration in planning appropriate actions.

Focus on the Purposes

The words "discovering" and "applying" were carefully chosen for this statement.

- *Discovering* goes beyond the idea of passively listening to someone talk about the Bible. It conveys the idea that people at every age need to be actively involved in exploring the Bible themselves, looking for insights and answers.

- *Applying* is the other side of the learning coin. Just as it is often said that the teacher hasn't taught until the student has learned, it should also be emphasized that the student hasn't learned until information and insights have been applied.

Oh, and don't overlook the word "guide" at the beginning of the statement. Learning (encompassing both discovery and application) is not a force-feeding process. It really does not work, especially in Christian education, to...

Ram it in,
Cram it in,
Children's heads are hollow.
Ram it in,
Cram it in,
There's plenty more to follow.

✔ Action Checklist

- ❑ Read a lesson in the teaching materials your church provides for teachers and identify the learning objectives for the lesson.
- ❑ Observe a class in action and identify the learning objectives.
- ❑ Ask a few participants in a group what they feel they are learning by attending the group sessions.

Tip: A Sunday School teacher who complains about having to teach the "same old boring lessons year after year" has obviously stopped finding fresh insights in familiar parts of Scripture. A truly effective teaching ministry is not really built on an efficient organization or even a solid educational philosophy. Effective teaching grows out of a deep conviction that God's Word speaks to our lives today.

Every **child**, every Sunday, should have a one-on-one encounter with a friendly adult who loves kids and loves Jesus. **Teens** love to discuss, even debate, an endless stream of topics. But they crave the friendship of adults and peers who accept them just as they are. Why will busy **adults** come back to Sunday School week after week after week? Perhaps to learn, but always to meet again with people who love them.

Tip: People other than committed church members will gladly participate in Sunday School classes where they find a genuine acceptance, freedom to ask questions and make comments and the opportunity to see what the Bible really does say about life issues.

PURPOSE 2: FELLOWSHIP

Provide positive interaction that provides encouragement and support.

There were occasions in Scripture when God pulled a person aside for some intensive one-on-one instruction, but most of the instruction we see in both the Old and New Testaments was done in group settings. As we look at these situations, it becomes very evident that the purpose of teaching in groups was not simply a mechanism to speed up the dissemination of information. Jesus did not choose 12 disciples so that He could expand His impact 12 times faster than if He had simply focused on Peter or John or one of the others.

Repeatedly we see that group teaching provides a setting for living out what was being learned. It is precisely because God's people have always been called to love Him and each other that learning so often takes place among those we are called to love. Thus, we see that a central purpose of the Sunday School must be to foster opportunities for building friendships and for growing in practical demonstrations of God's love.

✔ Action Checklist

❏ Ask several people how they would rate the friendship level of a class they have attended, using the following guidelines:
  • Include some children and teenagers in your survey;
  • Include a few nonattenders, absentees, dropouts and visitors;
  • Ask each person, "What would help make that class a friendlier group?"
❏ Recall the session you observed for Purpose 1 or a recent class you've attended.
  • How much of the class involved interaction between group members?
  • How do you think a new visitor would have felt in that group?
  • Did you notice anyone who seemed isolated from the others?
  • Did you notice any intentional actions to encourage friendship among group members?

PURPOSE 3:
SERVICE

Promote opportunities to serve God and minister to others.

The goal of any teaching ministry is to ensure that people continue to grow, so they do not stagnate or regress; however, teaching by itself will never accomplish that goal. Gaining new information or deeper insights is not an automatic harbinger of growth, any more than eating more food, even healthy food, will produce strength and stamina. In producing both spiritual and physical health and energy, exercise is required.

Teaching that does not result in action, as bluntly stated by James (see James 2:17), is dead. Thus, the effective Sunday School provides varied opportunities for people to get involved, not in busy work, but in tasks that get to the heart of what the Christian life is all about—studying and sharing God's Word, caring for others and reaching people in need.

✔ Action Checklist

❏ Evaluate opportunities for service provided through your Sunday School.
  • Is teaching a class viewed as a burdensome duty or a joyous privilege?
  • Are group members encouraged to work together to make an impact?
❏ Encourage classes to take on service projects that help others beyond their own circles.

The fellowship hall was filled with teenagers and their parents. And a few grandparents. And siblings. Plus a goodly number of church members with no obvious connection to anyone in the youth group. They were gathered together to hear a report from the teenagers of a mission trip taken during spring break.

Everyone enjoyed the home video and the slide/music show with narration. The teens who stood up to tell of what they had learned through the project were greeted with enthusiastic applause. Everyone went home commenting on how great it was to be around a group of young people who had volunteered to give up a week of vacation to dig ditches, build a shed and teach Vacation Bible School. Imagine, Christian teens who took it for granted that the truths they had been taught were actually supposed to be put into action!

PURPOSE 4: OUTREACH

Equip and motivate teachers and students to reach people for Christ and incorporate them into the life of the church.

During the first century of its existence, the Sunday School was primarily seen as a means to reach those who needed to know Christ. Gradually, in many circles, the Sunday School shifted its purpose away from outreach to one of nurturing those already in the church. Often this change was accompanied by church leaders contending that other ministries were better suited for the purpose of outreach. Sadly, no other agency ever became as effective in outreach as the Sunday School had been. Most other outreach-oriented programs lacked the Sunday School's...

- **Consistency,** in which week after week after week, people were encouraged to learn and grow and bring their friends along;
- **Involvement,** as the majority of the church participated, not just an "elite, dedicated" few;
- **Incorporation,** in which new people could be folded into friendly groups that served as entry points into the life of the church.

None of this evaluation is intended to criticize other approaches, but to point out that when a church stops viewing the Sunday School as a means of reaching and winning people, both the Sunday School and the church are weakened. (See chapter 10 for specific outreach ideas.)

✔ Action Checklist

❑ In light of these four purposes, write a purpose statement for the teaching ministry of your Sunday School.
- If your church has developed a mission statement, use it as a framework, stating how your teaching ministry is intended to help fulfill the mission of your church.
- If your church has not developed a mission statement, write a declaration of why your teaching ministry needs to exist and flourish.

A few guidelines in writing a purpose statement:
- Keep the statement as brief as possible so that people can remember it.
- Focus on the most essential issues.

❑ After writing the statement, write four to six specific, measurable objectives that would indicate progress in achieving your purpose, such as enrollment and attendance goals.

Clarify Your Purpose

Many church leaders have gone through the healthy exercise of writing a declaration of purpose (or a mission statement) for their church. Unfortunately, too often these statements never get transformed into meaningful action in the life of the church. Many times this is a result of unclear definitions by the leadership of different ministry areas for how that purpose is to be carried out through their ministries. (See page 160 in chapter 7 for additional creative ideas in presenting the value of your Sunday School to church leaders and the congregation.)

SAMPLE VISION/MISSION STATEMENTS

For Children: The goal of our children's Sunday School is to provide a safe and loving environment where children find and love God, explore His Word, build relationships with His family and discover their own God-given uniqueness.

For Youth: Our youth Sunday School classes provide a balanced approach to knowing and sharing God's Word, encouraging a sense of community, giving service in the name of Jesus and experiencing a growing relationship with Jesus Christ.

For Adults: Our adult Sunday School provides an entry point for visitors into the congregation, a life-related education in the Scriptures, opportunities for meaningful fellowship with others and encouragement for every adult to use his/her special gifts to glorify God's kingdom.

Look to the Future

Complete "The Value of Your Sunday School" worksheet (pp. 29-30) to determine how to begin working to meet the purposes stated in this chapter.

Bonus Idea for Purpose Statement: When we wrote our purpose statement, we followed a format from Nehemiah Ministry and established three levels of measurable objectives for each statement: minimum, acceptable and exceptional. For example, one statement was "to develop an increased atmosphere of warmth in the classrooms, showing God's love through love, acceptance, fun and building personal relationships." The minimum objective was "to greet students at the door with a smile, to plan time for interaction with other students and to maintain acceptable class sizes." The acceptable objective was for teachers to "prepare mixers for students to get to know each other, to contact children during the week through letters and phone calls and to pray for students by name," while the exceptional objective was for teachers "to invite students to their homes and to attend sport and music events of students." *Connie Wellik, Bible Fellowship Church, Ventura, California*

Note
1. Wes and Sheryl Haystead, eds.; *Sunday School Smart Pages* (Ventura, CA: Gospel Light, 1992), p. 179.

Bonus Ideas for Communicating Vision to Congregation: On Labor Day Sunday, while all the children are at a special rally with a children's speaker or entertainer, I invite all the parents to a Children's Ministry Orientation. I share our philosophy, goals and important security procedures and answer questions. I hand out enrollment cards and brochures and do low-key recruitment. I also explain our promotion procedure. This helps promotion (which is held the following week) go more smoothly. *Dee Engel, Trinity United Presbyterian Church, Santa Ana, California*

Each month our church sends a newsletter to our congregation. We always include a brightly colored insert that highlights our children's ministry. As well as repeating our vision for ministry to children ("Committed to nurturing God's children with love, called to serving God's children with joy and connected together through the love of Jesus Christ"), the insert features kid and staff interviews and photos, helpful parenting articles and invitations to upcoming events. *Maureen Houtz and Kristy Weiss, Eastminster Presbyterian Church, Ventura, California*

The Value of Your Sunday School

Rate your church's progress toward each purpose and then list two or more actions you can take to reach each purpose.

PURPOSE 1: BIBLE LEARNING

Guide people in discovering and applying Bible truth.

1	2	3	4	5
Need to Start		Fair		Goal Achieved

Actions to Take:

PURPOSE 2: FELLOWSHIP

Provide positive interaction that provides encouragement and support.

1	2	3	4	5
Need to Start		Fair		Goal Achieved

Actions to Take:

PURPOSE 3: SERVICE

Promote opportunities to serve God and minister to others.

1	2	3	4	5
Need to Start		Fair		Goal Achieved

Actions to Take:

PURPOSE 4: OUTREACH

Equip and motivate teachers and students to reach people for Christ and incorporate them into the life of the church.

1	2	3	4	5
Need to Start		Fair		Goal Achieved

Actions to Take:

Chapter Three

Teach to Change Lives: Content and Curriculum

The key to a successful teaching ministry is having something significant to teach—something of lasting, eternal value that goes beyond the latest fads and gimmicks. The Bible is the proven textbook, offering God's perspective on all the affairs of human life.

What This Chapter Tells You

- The Sunday School needs to teach the Bible, encouraging students to want to know it better and put it into practice in their lives.
- Teaching should be done according to sound educational principles, helping people learn in ways appropriate to the lesson content and purpose.

What This Chapter Shows You

- How to choose curriculum resources that fit each age level;
- How to implement a consistent teaching plan that will produce growth for years to come;
- Tips for building positive attitudes and healthy relationships, taking students beyond information to real-life applications.

Where Do I Start?

> *"All Scripture is God-breathed and is useful for teaching, rebuking, correcting and training in righteousness."*
> Paul
> (2 Timothy 3:16)

> *"You must teach what is in accord with sound doctrine."*
> Paul
> (Titus 2:1)

> *"I will teach you the way that is good and right."*
> Samuel
> (1 Samuel 12:23)

Reflections

When a church entrusts the Sunday School with a major share of its teaching mission, that is no small thing. For a church to maintain its integrity as the people of Christ, there is really no place for approaching the ministry of teaching in ways reflected in these all-too-common remarks:

- "If you're willing to tackle that seventh grade class, you can choose any materials you want."
- "I know how busy you are, so I really don't expect you to spend time preparing. Thank goodness for VCRs."
- "Since you're teaching adults, all you'll need is a commentary or two. Don't worry about any teaching methods since the class just likes to sit and listen."
- "We really want to be current, so we ask our people what topics they're interested in and then we see what we can find on the Internet."

On Target

What is the aim of an effective Bible teaching ministry? Simply, teaching the Book the way it was intended to be used. That was where many of the Pharisees went wrong. They were totally committed to the idea of teaching the Scriptures, devoting themselves to rigorous study and discussion and application. But they missed the heart of what the book is all about. They got bogged down in minutia and in interpretations and rules. They missed the wonder and the power and the freedom of God's Word.

Look at Where You Are

Complete the "Bible Teaching" worksheet (p. 33) to take a closer look at the Bible teaching in your church

Bible Teaching

1. Rank the following reasons for making the Bible the textbook of your Sunday School (with 1 being the first reason):

    _____Jesus commanded His followers to teach His words. He told them to go and make disciples (literally, followers or learners), "teaching them to obey everything I have commanded you" (Matthew 28:20).

    _____Jesus said, "If you love me, you will obey what I command" (John 14:15). People cannot obey God's Word if they don't know God's Word.

    _____The New Testament Church actively taught the Scripture (Acts 2:42).

    _____Bible-based preaching and teaching complement one another (Acts 18:24-26).

    _____The study of Scripture equips people to discern what is really true (Acts 17:11).

    Write a sentence explaining why your top two choices are important.

2. Look at the curriculum being used in your Sunday School and answer the following questions:

    a. Is it Bible centered, using the Bible as the authoritative guide for life issues?
    ❑ Yes   ❑ No

    Comment:

    b. Does your curriculum provide a coordinated plan for studying both Bible content and life issues?   ❑ Yes   ❑ No

    Comment:

3. Are the selections of Bible content and the life application emphases appropriate to the age levels using the material?   ❑ Yes   ❑ No

    Comment:

Focus on the Goals

What About All Those Translations? Teachers of youth or adults sometimes cringe when someone in the group interrupts with, "That's not how my Bible says it!" And teachers of children tend to view such a declaration as a major threat to their teaching plan. However, in answer to the question "Which translation should a teacher use in class?" a good rule-of-thumb response is "Whichever one(s) the students have with them."

Most of the time, a different translation gives a fresh way of expressing essentially the same idea, often helping to clarify the point being made. While there are times that translators disagree on the meaning, those are relatively infrequent and should not discourage a teacher from encouraging group members to bring and use their own Bibles, regardless of translation.

GOAL 1: BIBLE-CENTERED TEACHING

The Bible is the Sunday School's textbook. It is studied according to a systematic plan and carefully selected portions are memorized.

In order to equip students to embrace and live the Christian life, the Bible is the essential guidebook for this process. Far from being outdated, the Bible is a timeless source of instructions, principles and examples, providing God's perspective on any area of human life. Leaders should hold a high respect for the Bible, seeking earnestly to understand and apply it in their own lives.

Unfortunately, some people approach Bible teaching as though the most important thing were to gain as much Bible information as possible. The Bible becomes little more than a resource of ancient facts and customs. The impact of a lesson is gauged by whether any new, original interpretation was presented, sending everyone home with a fact to impress people with arcane Bible knowledge.

Others focus so much on personal and societal issues that the Bible is merely given lip service, and a verse or two is read to support the position of some contemporary "authority."

Bible-centered teaching carefully walks a middle path between those two extremes. The teacher relies on Scripture as the ultimate statement of God's truth and always seeks to apply that truth to real life situations faced by students.

Over a period of months and years, it is vital that the Sunday School have an organized teaching plan. A hit-or-miss approach that jumps around leaves big holes in what people have learned. The plan of what to teach and when to teach it

Translation Tips

- Teachers of children and youth (especially) should make sure their students have access to Bibles that are easy for them to understand.

- Memorization (at all ages) is good to do in whatever translation is most widely used in your church. What does the pastor preach from? What version is most likely to be heard?

- Provide at least a few Bibles for every class so that students gain opportunities to open and read the Bible for themselves.

is a major feature to consider when selecting curriculum. Look for a balanced treatment of both Bible content and relevant life issues—and of course, an age-appropriate approach to both.

✔ Action Checklist

❑ Using the "Compare Your Curriculum Options" worksheet (pp. 37-38), evaluate the curriculum materials you now use and those you may be considering.

❑ Discuss this goal with your Sunday School teachers. Invite their comments on questions such as:

- What do our teachers and students say about the ways our present curriculum presents Bible content? What strengths have been noted? What areas of concern have been mentioned?

- What help is given to teachers to equip them to understand and communicate Bible content? What resources are available?

- How appropriate to the various age levels is the Bible content chosen by our curriculum materials? How effective is the curriculum in helping teachers present Bible content at the understanding levels of their students?

❑ Explore possible ways to make Bible teaching more interesting and more effective. A few areas to consider:

- Discuss whether to provide suitable Bibles in each class or to encourage people to bring their own Bibles to Sunday School. When Bibles are provided, most people can be reading from the same translation, and guests can participate easily with everyone else. This is very important in classes for children or youth, and in adult classes wanting to be accepting of new people. When people bring their own Bibles, they may be more likely to read from them during the week.

- Explore ways to display key Scripture portions being studied. Posters, overhead transparencies, slides and videos are excellent ways to emphasize or reinforce God's words.

- Vary the ways in which the Bible is read aloud, seeking to ensure that it is read with expression and understanding. Be cautious about unison and responsive readings which almost guarantee that the words will be read in a monotone with little attention to meaning. Asking readers in advance gives them the opportunity to practice and think about the message of what they will read.

A Bible-centered curriculum helps students learn what the Bible says instead of what people say about the Bible. Most Christian curriculum resources deal with the Bible, but approaches to the Bible often differ widely. While it can be very interesting and is often helpful to explore what an interpreter has written about the Bible, the ultimate impact of Bible teaching depends on allowing God's Word to speak directly to the student.

A good curriculum provides a balance of...
- Old and New Testament content;
- Doctrinal information and practical application;
- Themed principles and specific examples;
- Narrative stories and didactic instruction

...and all done in a manner appropriate to the age level being taught!

Does it make a difference if you use the same curriculum throughout the Sunday School? There was a time when curriculum was adopted by churches with the expectation that students would progress through a cohesive course of study. For a variety of reasons, it is very common today for churches to use an eclectic mix of materials from age level to age level and even within the same age group. A familiar statement on the subject goes something like, "Half the kids in our group weren't here last year. And most of the rest were absent most of the time, so why worry whether we repeat something?"

As a result, it is very common for students to get a steady diet of whatever seem to be the "popular" topics, not a balanced approach that addresses the full scope of what people need to be learning. Even in groups with high turnover, there is real value in taking a long-range look at what you will be teaching.

Using a jumble of curriculum and resources also makes training more difficult. While there may be more than one valid approach to learning, it is far more effective to train teachers to do one way well rather than to expect them to become proficient with varied materials that may be built on differing, even conflicting, educational and biblical principles.

 **One Youth Leader's Guide to Curriculum:** What do you do when you can't find a curriculum that seems to fit your class? Or when you feel like your teachers aren't really getting into the Word because they're depending on someone else's study?

Sometimes a published curriculum gives you a structure to adapt to meet the needs and interests of your class, and sometimes a published curriculum guides teachers in first studying the Word for themselves. But sometimes, it seems that you need to create your lesson plans.

Here's a way to do it:
1. Pray for God's guidance as you plan.
2. Read through the Scripture passage and brainstorm how this passage applies to your life.
3. Read through the passage again and brainstorm how this passage relates to the youth.
4. Read at least one commentary and then write helpful insights.
5. Choose one aspect of the passage that will be your main point for the lesson. Everything you plan for the lesson should support this main point.
6. Develop a lesson plan with the following: (a) an activity that introduces the passage; (b) an activity that requires reading the passage; (c) an activity that involves the class in thinking about the passage; (d) a main point to explicitly explain; (e); a conclusion and prayer.

Compare Your Curriculum Options

Curriculum _____ Age Level _____

Use the following rating scale and questions to rate your curriculum options:

5 = Superior   4 = Excellent   3 = Good   2 = Fair   1 = Poor

BIBLE CONTENT AND USAGE

_____ Is the curriculum designed to teach the Bible as God's inspired and authoritative Word?

_____ Is there balanced coverage of the Old and New Testaments?

_____ Does the overall plan of the curriculum point students to faith in Christ as Savior and Lord, and also nurture and guide them to "grow up in Christ"?

_____ Does the material present Bible truths in a manner appropriate to the abilities and development of the students' age levels?

_____ Are hands-on Bible usage and skill development encouraged at appropriate age levels?

TEACHER

_____ Does the curriculum challenge the teacher to prepare spiritually for the task of teaching?

_____ Is the material clearly arranged to show the teacher an understandable and logical lesson plan?

_____ Are the Bible-learning and life response aims specifically and clearly stated for each lesson?

_____ Does the material provide the teacher with a variety of Bible-learning approaches from which to choose?

_____ Are the materials clearly presented, enabling the teacher to be prepared with a reasonable amount of effort?

_____ Are there enough ideas and suggestions to adapt the material for longer or shorter sessions, larger or smaller groups, or limited equipment?

Use the following rating scale and questions to rate your curriculum options:

5 = Superior   4 = Excellent   3 = Good   2 = Fair   1 = Poor

STUDENT

_____ Is the vocabulary appropriate for the age and abilities of the students?

_____ Does the curriculum provide a variety of ways for students to participate actively in the learning process?

_____ Are the student materials attractive and do they encourage involvement?

_____ Do the teacher resources provide a variety of attractive aids to stimulate student interest and involvement?

_____ Are the Bible-learning approaches appropriate to the mental, spiritual, social and physical development of the students?

BEYOND THE CLASSROOM

_____ Does the material provide ideas for making and sustaining meaningful contact with both students and families outside the classroom?

_____ Does the take-home paper contain activities that assist the family in relating the student's learning to everyday life?

_____ Does the curriculum speak to issues relevant to the student's everyday life?

_____ Does the curriculum provide materials and suggestions for ways students may understand the responsibility and joy of sharing Christ?

_____ Does the curriculum encourage outreach and church growth?

GOAL 2:
OUTREACH AND EVANGELISM

All of your staff have been trained in, and regularly use, age-appropriate steps to reach new students and lead them toward a personal relationship with Christ.

No matter how skilled the teaching, no matter how true the content: if the church simply keeps teaching the same people year after year after year, the result will be stagnation. The effective Sunday School must make reaching new people a major priority. It is obvious that doing this is much harder than saying it, for Sunday Schools everywhere have gradually allowed themselves to become places for teaching the saints. Period.

The most common reason given for not reaching out to new people is that "People today aren't attracted to Sunday School." Rather than trying to find ways to make Sunday School attractive, churches have tended to continue holding classes in the same old ways for those who don't mind business as usual. (See chapter 10 for outreach ideas.)

In many churches, even people new to the church feel unwelcome in Sunday School. That's right: people who are already Christians and are interested in getting involved in the life of the church often report that the Sunday School classes they visited seemed closed off to new people. At the same time, people in those classes are disturbed about the lack of new people in their group. Only through a major commitment on the part of teachers and group members does a long-established group succeed in changing from an inward focus to an outreach focus.

The desire to see people develop a personal relationship with Christ is the single most important facet in building a Sunday School that welcomes and nurtures new people. A teacher who leads a student to Christ will be motivated to prepare, to be faithful, to reach others, to do the best job possible. Reports of students coming to Christ encourage all teachers in their ministry efforts. Even teachers of children not yet ready to make a personal commitment are rewarded by a child's open response to hearing about God's love.

An Ingrown Group: Seven signs that a Sunday School class or other group has lost its vision for outreach and become ingrown:
1. Most of the group have been together for at least three years.
2. Group members keep telling each other how friendly their group is.
3. Visitors are treated as outsiders, not as guests (a sometimes subtle distinction).
4. Topics and activities are chosen to fit those now in the group, not to draw others.
5. Group members automatically sit with friends.
6. Little or no planning is directed toward inviting and including new people.
7. Group members resist making changes that will appeal to others.

✓ Action Checklist

❑ Secure age-appropriate materials to use with each level in explaining how to become a Christian. Materials for children should limit the use of symbolism that creates confusion if interpreted literally. Many commonly used terms ("born again," "asking Jesus into your heart," etc.) often cause misunderstanding among children.

GOAL 3:
LIFE FOCUS

The purpose of your Bible teaching ministries is to help in meeting the basic life needs of students.

✔ **Action Checklist**

❑ At a meeting of teachers, give each person a copy of the "Focus on Life Needs" worksheet (pp. 42-43) to complete.

• After everyone has completed the page, instruct them to underline three items that need to be done more often.

• Ask each person to share one item he or she marked and tell why it is important.

• Lead a time of prayer for each other, asking God's help to improve in meeting the needs of students.

The effective Sunday School seeks to minister to the whole person, not just his or her mind or soul. Often it is difficult for a person to respond to spiritual truths when faced with pressing needs in other areas of life.

Physical Needs

A child who is restless or hungry will obviously not be able to learn efficiently. Neither is a senior citizen who is uncomfortable on a metal folding chair nor a teenager in a stuffy room. Some physical needs are temporary conditions caused by the very facility or schedule in which we desire to teach. Others are age related—two-year-olds need to move often. And others are faced by individuals with disabilities. In any case, teachers need to be guided in identifying and meeting these needs.

Social Needs

From infancy, people need positive, safe, friendly interaction with other people. Jesus made a point of linking love for God with love for neighbor, emphasizing the importance of relationships with other people. Jesus taught that the key mark that would identify His disciples was not doctrinal integrity nor moral purity, as important as they are. Instead, he said, "By this all men will know that you are my disciples, if you love one another" (John 13:35). Thus, teachers are not just lesson presenters, storytellers, activity directors, question askers and answerers. Teachers must seek to be friendship builders, getting to know individual students and aiding them in building relationships with others in the group.

Emotional Needs

Teachers in the nursery major in meeting these needs. When a baby is unhappy, the teacher seeks to comfort. When a toddler laughs, the teacher laughs along. But as students get older, more of their feelings are kept inside, and teachers often overlook the powerful ways in which emotions impact every other area of life. A reluctant teenager may sit quietly through a class, but negative feelings can color everything the young person hears. By the end of the session, reluctance may have turned to rejection. Effective teachers are sensitive to student feelings, accepting the student even when he or she displays an emotion other than positive, cheerful enthusiasm. When emotions are ragged, students need teachers who are willing to be flesh-and-blood illustrations of Jesus' love and care.

Intellectual Needs

People are inherently curious, wanting to understand their world. However, students do not automatically want to understand the lesson a teacher has prepared. The challenge that must be met every week with every group is to find ways to stimulate interest, to motivate students to seek answers in Scripture for the concerns of their life.

Spiritual Needs

Everybody needs a personal relationship with Christ. Everyone needs to experience forgiveness for sin. Everyone needs to grow in faith. So every teacher needs to prayerfully consider the spiritual condition of each student and seek to guide that student to encounter God's perfect provision.

Age-Level Needs

While people of all ages have needs in all the previously mentioned areas, each age level has specific needs that must be understood and planned for in a teaching ministry. The effective Sunday School does not assume that teachers will automatically understand the unique demands of people in that age group. Instead, teachers are provided with practical guidelines for meeting the needs of the age level they teach.

Individual Needs

Every person brings a unique configuration of needs based on personality, family history and life situations. Effective teachers learn to teach individual students, not just to present lessons.

Focus on Life Needs

Check the box that most closely answers the following questions:

1 = Always   2 = Often   3 = Sometimes   4 = Seldom   5 = Never

Teaching is too often focused only on what a teacher does, rather than on what a student does in response.

Physical **How often do you...**	1	2	3	4	5
Monitor the room's lighting, temperature and air flow to ensure students' comfort?					
Equip rooms with appropriate furniture arranged to encourage interaction?					
Provide access for those with physical limitations?					
Social **How often do you...**					
Encourage positive relationships, avoiding put-downs of others?					
Maintain group sizes and teacher ratios that make personal attention possible?					
Seek out ways to include people besides the regular attenders?					
Plan ways for group members to interact and work together?					
Emotional **How often do you...**					
Really listen when a student is talking?					
Actively seek to make your class an emotionally safe place?					
Show respect and acceptance for a student who is upset or bored or fearful?					
Honestly share your own feelings, including times when they have not been positive?					

Focus on Life Needs (Cont'd)

Intellectual How often do you...	1	2	3	4	5
Allow students the freedom to disagree without making them feel rejected?					
Guide students to discover Bible truth, not just listen to it being presented?					
Limit the use of questions that elicit one-word (yes, no, etc.) or straight factual answers?					
Encourage students to compare their opinions with what the Bible says?					
Give personal guidance to students who lack the Bible knowledge of others in the group?					
Spiritual **How often do you...**					
Actively seek to discover each student's spiritual condition and attitudes?					
Openly share your personal spiritual pilgrimage?					
Guide students to apply Bible truth in practical ways to life situations?					
Pray regularly for the needs of your students?					
Age Level **How often do you...**					
Consider the characteristics of the age group you teach when preparing your lessons?					
Plan ways to accommodate different skill levels of students in your group?					
Individual **How often do you...**					
Know the specific interests and needs that make each student unique in your group?					
Use varied teaching approaches to accommodate the different learning styles of students?					

GOAL 4: STUDENT INVOLVEMENT

Your teachers actively involve students in Bible study and positive application of Bible truth.

A Good Rule of Thumb

Every student will have a first-hand experience with the Bible every Sunday. A few examples:

1. Adult involvement may include group discussions where students explore a Bible passage to discover a biblical principle.

2. Teenagers need to be involved in finding, reading and answering questions from Scripture, and then responding to what God's Word says to them.

3. Children can be directly involved with Scripture through reading, memorizing and singing God's Word. They can express their understanding through art, drama and other creative approaches.

4. Preschool children spend a major portion of each session in activities (art, blocks, home living, nature, puzzles, music, etc.) with teachers who connect the children's play (a child's work) with the day's Bible story or verse.

Teaching is too often focused only on what a teacher does, rather than on what a student in response. The actions of the teacher can be a catalyst or a stimulus to learning, a resource that aids learning, even a guide to learning; but the teacher's actions by themselves do not produce learning. It is the action of the student that produces learning; therefore learning is controlled by the student.

Once a teacher understands this important distinction, his or her role focuses on guiding students to become actively involved. Passive observers may be entertained by an interesting story or lecture. They may even hear some information to which they nod assent. But very little real learning takes place in the mind, heart or life of a passive observer.

While this distinction has always been true, our multimedia society has conditioned people to briefly pay attention to remarkably diverse bits of knowledge without seriously evaluating, testing or applying what is heard or seen. People of all ages have become very skilled at casually changing the channel or signing off, moving on with little reflection even after having been confronted with the most significant startling facts.

The teacher who wants to present lessons that have an impact beyond the end of the session must employ approaches that actively involve students. This involvement may at times only be **mental** (listening, reading, thinking, etc.), but it is too easy for people in a group to look attentive when their minds are far away. (One of the nice things about teaching young children is that when their minds wander, their bodies go along with them, making it very obvious to the teacher when students are, or are not, paying attention.)

Most teachers include some approaches that seek to involve students **verbally** (responding to questions, sharing ideas, etc.). Even this involvement has limitations, as students of any age learn to give the "right" answers, the responses that they recognize the teacher desires or that others in the group will appreciate. Talking about the Christian life is too often a pale substitute for actually living it.

Therefore, just as Jesus often did—and master teachers down through the centuries have done—effective teachers must learn to involve students **physically and socially**.

Interaction, as opposed to simply sitting in chairs, will catch students' attention and stimulate curiosity. Various types of involvement can be useful in helping students discover meaning and develop understanding. Others may be used to apply content to life situations. Involvement that produces interaction among group members helps build relationships which, as we've already seen, is one of the main objectives for teaching in groups.

The Sunday School that seeks to present lessons with a lasting impact must *consistently* emphasize and demonstrate the values of student involvement by encouraging and equipping teachers to use approaches that produce involvement. Without the continued support of leaders, many teachers will revert to simply presenting material.

✔ Action Checklist

❑ If you are unfamiliar with the use of involvement learning procedures or if some or all of your teachers are emphasizing input over involvement, try the following approaches to make active learning more a part of your Sunday School:

- Consistently demonstrate involvement procedures in training sessions with teachers. Avoid the tendency to give a lecture on involving students.

- Emphasize that the goal of teaching is to make an impact on lives, not just transmit information.

- Arrange opportunities for teachers to observe someone using involvement approaches with students. Teaching videos are an effective option if you do not have easy access to teachers who can demonstrate these skills.

- Call attention to specific involvement ideas in the curriculum.

- Encourage teachers to try one new approach somewhere in every session to avoid getting into a rut and to keep students from getting too comfortable.

- Work together with teachers to help plan and use these approaches. Offer mutual encouragement and evaluation.

❑ If some of your classes are too large for everyone to readily participate, read chapters 5 and 7 to find practical help for organizing so that maximum learning can take place.

GOAL 5:
THE LEARNING PROCESS

Your teachers have received training in practical ways to guide students in the learning process.

We often think of learning as a result—something that is gained. We also need to examine learning as a process, a series of definable steps, although not always taken in neat, sequential order. Often, perhaps most commonly with young children, these steps may be taken in reverse order. While learning is not easily reducible to a formula, an effective Sunday School prepares its staff to mold their teaching efforts to conform with the God-given ways in which people learn. Consider the following five major steps in the process of learning and how each one interacts with the others.

Listen: Give Attention/Receive Information

Learning will not happen until the student becomes aware that *there is something to be learned*, something of interest or value. Most commonly in Christian education the ears are involved, as the teacher says something to secure the interest of the students. In no way, however, is this step limited to listening. The student's curiosity may be piqued by a poster at the front of the room or by a question written on the chalkboard or projected on the wall.

Any of the student's senses (hearing, sight, smell, touch, taste) can be used to gain initial interest. Hearing and sight are the avenues available to present information or instructions; however, far too many teachers approach the learning process as if this step were the whole journey. They feel they have succeeded if the class simply paid attention to what they had to say or show. But the student who has listened or looked has taken only the first step in the learning journey.

Explore: Examine Life and the Word

Having received the information, the next step in learning is to investigate further. Students need to *actively pursue new or expanded insights*. Guided by the teacher—both to avoid wasting time and to focus exploration in the direction of the current lesson—students need to examine life situations in the light of the Word of God.

Much exploration of life issues can be done by calling on the experiences and insights of class members. Sometimes activities need to be provided to stimulate awareness of a topic to be considered. With preschool children, for example, limited life experience requires various firsthand experiences

The student who has listened or looked has taken only the first step in the learning journey.

The wise teacher gets students actively involved in looking for answers to issues they care about.

(blocks, home living, art, puzzles, etc.) to build understanding of seemingly simple concepts (sharing, being kind, helping, giving thanks, etc.).

Exploring God's Word involves more than listening to or even reading it. Exploring entails actively looking for commands, examples, principles and answers that apply to the life situation being pursued. There is a big difference at any age level between approaching a passage cold and giving the students something specific to look for, between simply presenting God's Word to students and guiding them to explore. The wise teacher actively involves students in looking for answers to issues they care about; not only does this increase the student's understanding and retention of the passage being investigated, but it also works to develop the vital ability of using the Bible, instead of just listening to someone else report about it.

Nonreaders can be guided to begin exploring Bible truths by posing a question before presenting a Bible verse or story and asking students to listen for the answer to the question.

Discover: Find the Truth

Listening and exploring leads students to discover some answers, some insights, some understanding of what the Bible says. Discovering God's eternal truths in His Word is an exciting process; however, too often teachers are the only ones in their classes who enjoy this excitement. The teacher studies at home, reading, thinking and praying—eagerly wanting to tell the students about what has been discovered—then doesn't understand why the students don't share the same degree of excitement about these discoveries.

The wise teacher plans in every session for the class to make some discoveries themselves. There usually is not enough time for the class to explore everything the teacher has learned, but giving the opportunity to find the answers to a few questions can lead to the discovery of a portion of what the teacher has to share. The discoveries students make will be remembered longer and have more impact than insights simply handed down from the teacher.

The discoveries students make will be remembered longer and have more impact than insights simply handed down from the teacher.

Appropriate: Embrace the Truth

Somewhere in the learning process, the student needs to confront the personal implications of God's truth. The point is not that students will discover interesting bits of historical or theological information, but that students will recognize that the Bible is speaking directly to them. It is one thing to recognize that God is love; it is another to recognize that God loved the world; it is yet another to recognize that God loves them.

Taking Scripture personally does not happen automatically. Most people are adept at nodding assent and even

Taking Scripture personally does not happen automatically.

saying "Amen!" to truths while wishing all those other people would take it to heart. Through prayer, questions and guided activity, the teacher is used by the Holy Spirit to cause students to see themselves as a character in the story, a recipient of the epistle—the person to whom God is speaking.

Assume Responsibility: Apply the Truth

This step is the crown of the learning process, the point where God's truth actually makes changes in a person's heart, mind and actions. God's truth has been given to produce growth and change in us. Students must go beyond recognizing that God has spoken or even agreeing that what He said applies to each of us individually; they must take action and follow through on the insights gained.

Not every class session can end with a major life-changing experience for every student, but each class can include the opportunity to take another step toward personal spiritual maturity. Not every class session can end by carrying out a major new spiritual commitment, but each class can nudge students to look beyond the class time and think of ways to put God's Word into action in the coming week.

Nudge students to look beyond the class time and think of ways to put God's Word into action in the coming week.

✔ Action Checklist

❑ Schedule a training session for your teachers to explore and experience all five steps of the learning process. This can be done effectively by selecting a Scripture passage from your curriculum materials and guiding the teachers in its study.

❑ Encourage teachers to make sure they schedule time and plan activities to take students beyond discovery so that they have the opportunity to appropriate what they are learning and assume responsibility in some tangible manner. This may mean reducing the amount of information that is being considered, sharpening the focus of each session.

GOAL 6: THE TEACHER'S ROLE

Your teachers fulfill their roles as guides and motivators in the learning process, as models for (and friends to) their students.

The effective teacher is not just a dispenser of information or a presenter of truth; he or she is a guide, motivator, model and friend. The teacher's role is not merely to master the content and then transmit it to students; it is to plan and shepherd students through the steps of the learning process.

A Guide

To guide a class through the learning process, the teacher must take actions:

1. Select a meaningful and achievable aim for the session. This usually involves either accepting or adapting the aim(s) developed in the teacher's manual being used.
2. Based on the teacher's awareness of class members' needs, interests and abilities, prayerfully select (and adapt as needed) learning activities to help the students achieve the aim(s).
3. For each activity write down several questions to stimulate thought and encourage application of truth by students.

A Motivator

Teachers need to motivate students to explore God's Word and apply the truths discovered there by sharing his or her own enthusiasm for what is being studied and giving positive encouragement for growth. Affirming a student for taking a forward step is usually more effective at motivating continued growth than criticism for areas in which the student has fallen short.

Model and Friend

The most effective teachers are those who show interest and concern in their students' lives. A big part of this involves being open and honest about growth and struggles in their own lives. A teacher who can share specific ways that God has helped or examples of challenges that have been faced gives students a model to emulate. The teacher who becomes a personal friend to students becomes a model in three dimensions, allowing students to see a real person seeking to live for Christ, not a cardboard cutout with whom they cannot identify.

✔ Action Checklist

❑ Distribute copies of the "Evaluating and Improving Your Role as a Teacher" worksheet (p. 50) at a teachers' meeting. Allow five to seven minutes for everyone to complete the worksheet; then invite volunteers to share one or two items that they do most frequently and one or two items they realize they need to do more frequently. Guide a time of discussing ways to improve in several of the areas listed.

Look to the Future

Complete the "Teaching" worksheet (pp. 51-52) to determine how you can begin working to meet the goals stated in this chapter.

Evaluating and Improving
Your Role as a Teacher
Check each statement as it applies to you.

1 = Always   2 = Often   3 = Sometimes   4 = Seldom   5 = Never

	1	2	3	4	5
The Teacher Is One Who Guides					
I ask the Holy Spirit to help me guide my students.					
I study the Bible content and pray to apply it to my own life.					
I pay attention to the individual growth needs of each student.					
I set specific learning objectives for my class.					
I plan sessions that emphasize active learning experiences.					
I assist learning by creating a positive classroom environment.					
I plan and ask appropriate questions to guide learning.					
I am excited when students discover Bible truths for themselves.					
I evaluate each student's learning after each class session.					
I contact students outside of class to learn about their needs.					
The Teacher Is One Who Stimulates and Motivates					
I select activities that interest and challenge my class.					
I encourage students to explore and discover God's truth themselves.					
I invite students to honestly express ideas and feelings.					
I help students make plans to apply truths in life situations.					
I affirm students for evidence of positive changes.					
The Teacher Is One Who Models					
I practice specific ways for my class to put truth into action.					
I set a positive Christian example for students both in and out of class.					
I tell my students of both my victories and struggles in following Christ.					
I show students how I confess and repent when I fall short.					
The Teacher Is One Who Cares					
I know each student's name and family.					
I accept my students as they are, even when they are wrong.					
I show interest in each student by carefully listening.					
I clearly communicate the God-given value of each person.					
I pray for each of my students by name.					
I give time to each student outside of class.					
I provide practical help and friendship to my students.					
I foster a climate of positive discipline in my classroom.					
I contact absentees to show that I missed them.					

50

LOOK TO THE FUTURE

Teaching

Rate your church's progress toward each goal and then list two or more actions you can take to reach each goal.

GOAL 1: BIBLE-CENTERED TEACHING

The Bible is our Sunday School's textbook. It is studied according to a systematic plan, and carefully selected portions are memorized.

1	2	3	4	5
Need to Start		Fair		Goal Achieved

Actions to Take:

GOAL 2: OUTREACH AND EVANGELISM

All of our staff have been trained in, and regularly use, age-appropriate steps to reach new students and lead them toward a personal relationship with Christ.

1	2	3	4	5
Need to Start		Fair		Goal Achieved

Actions to Take:

GOAL 3: LIFE FOCUS

The purpose of our Bible teaching ministries is to help in meeting the basic life needs of students.

1	2	3	4	5
Need to Start		Fair		Goal Achieved

Actions to Take:

GOAL 4: STUDENT INVOLVEMENT

Our teachers actively involve students in Bible study and positive application of Bible truth.

1	2	3	4	5
Need to Start		Fair		Goal Achieved

Actions to Take:

GOAL 5: THE LEARNING PROCESS

Our teachers have received training in practical ways to guide students in the learning process.

1	2	3	4	5
Need to Start		Fair		Goal Achieved

Actions to Take:

GOAL 6: THE TEACHER'S ROLE

Our teachers fulfill their roles as guides and motivators in the learning process, as models for—and friends to—their students.

1	2	3	4	5
Need to Start		Fair		Goal Achieved

Actions to Take:

Chapter Four

Teaching Methods That Work

Workable schedules and learning activities that connect together and build on each other make it possible for effective teaching to take place.

What This Chapter Tells You

- Lesson aims help teachers know the purpose of each session.
- A cohesive session plan is crucial to learning and spiritual growth in your students.
- Creative learning activities help students connect Bible truths to their lives.
- Each session needs a balance of teacher input, student discovery and time for relationship building.

What This Chapter Shows You

- The value of lesson aims;
- How to plan a realistic session schedule for students;
- How to choose and use effective learning activities;
- What to do to build relationships among students and teachers;
- The value of small groups as part of a teaching plan.

Where Do I Start?

Planning schedules and activities isn't a question of "how many students can we handle?" Sunday School teachers aren't in the handling business. We're in the loving business, and what's going on in our classrooms needs to make it possible for us to communicate God's love and His Word in life-changing ways.

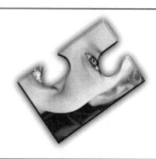

"The teacher is not just a quarterly [teacher's guide] wired for sound." Henrietta Mears, the author of this quote, knew that much more than Bible facts and Bible verses needs to be communicated between teacher and student.

Look at Where You Are

Complete the "Current Teaching Plan" worksheet (p. 55) to evaluate the session schedules and kinds of learning activities that make up the teaching plan in your church.

Putting the Pieces Together

Assembling the parts and pieces of a Sunday School or any ministry program often seems similar to the task of putting together a giant jigsaw puzzle. Sometimes we get so busy hunting for the pieces that we forget to look at the picture of the completed puzzle, overlooking that in order for all the planning and prayers to produce effective teaching, what's going on in the classroom must support our teaching philosophy (see chapter 3).

Get the Big Picture

Each Sunday School session must have a plan based on a schedule and activities that provide for effective sharing of God's Word with students.

The best approach to effective Bible teaching is four-part: Pay close attention to the lesson aims, use the session time wisely, creatively involve the students in the Bible learning process and plan ways for teachers and students to develop personal relationships. These four things cannot occur spontaneously—a carefully developed teaching plan is absolutely necessary. Here are the likely results of a thorough teaching plan:

- Students come to class with a sense of anticipation, knowing that the schedule and activities are planned with their needs and interests in mind;
- Learning aims or goals are more easily accomplished as all activities in a session are carefully chosen to build on one another;
- Activities and teacher/student ratios that make it possible for them to interact on a personal level allow teachers to experience one of the greatest rewards of their job—opportunities to share their faith with students.

LOOK AT WHERE YOU ARE

Current Teaching Plan

1. What is the schedule typically followed in the class(es) you are evaluating? How do new teachers learn about this schedule?

2. Are there specific lesson aims for the students' learning? Which parts of the schedule help to accomplish the aims?

3. How many different types of learning activities are provided for students?

4. What is the ratio of teachers to students? During a typical session, when do teachers and students talk together to build friendships and discuss spiritual truths?

Focus on the Goals

Lesson aims must be specific, dealing not only with biblical knowledge and attitude, but also with behavior.

Aims at a Glance

1. Cognitive learning is change in what or how much a person knows or understands about a particular subject.
2. Affective learning is a change in attitudes—the way a person feels or responds emotionally. Since feelings are hard to measure, however, aims for affective learning will state actions that will affect attitudes.
3. Psychomotor, or behavioral, learning is a change in what a person does with what he or she knows and feels.

Whenever possible, lessons should be grouped into units which focus on a central truth. The primary purpose for having a Sunday School (or any other related program) is to help students make positive changes in their lives as a result of learning God's Word. We want them to increase their Bible knowledge and understanding and to respond to the leading of the Holy Spirit. We want to see our students live according to the principles given in Scripture.

The greatest reason for not seeing dramatic changes in the lives of Sunday School students is that our teaching stops short of the third area of learning. Some students know and understand Scripture, and they even feel good about it, but they never *do* anything about it—so their lives are not changed by the truth that they learn. The world is not influenced by Christians whose actions and choices look just like those of unbelievers.

Since the ultimate goal is for students to change their behavior, effective aims are stated in terms of what the students will do to show that they have learned. Meaningful aims take into account three areas of learning: what you know, how you feel and what you are going to do about it. The more clearly you define what results you want, the more likely you are to do the right actions to achieve those results.

It is important to recognize that it will take time to guide students to make specific life changes as a result of their study of Scripture. To make the best use of teaching aims, therefore, you need both long-term and short-term goals. Group two to five lessons together around a central Bible truth to form a unit of study. This unit plan allows the teacher to use several lessons to build toward a specific student response. Most curriculum publishers group lessons in three to five units which make up a quarter (13 weeks) of study. A general aim for each unit is established, with supporting aims for each session within the unit. The session aims are specific and describe what the students may do to show the results of their studying particular Bible verses and/or stories.

In preparing to teach a lesson, the teacher first studies the Scripture passage and the aims listed in his or her curriculum. Learning aims prepared by curriculum writers cannot always be specific enough to exactly meet the needs of individual students; it's often helpful for a teacher to use the printed aims as a guide to restate the aims in terms of the particular needs of his or her own students.

At the end of each session, the teacher may evaluate what was taught and learned by using the lesson aims as a guide. Encourage teachers to ask themselves, *Which of these aims were accomplished this week? What activities worked well in meeting these aims? What evidence of behavior change did I see in students' words, attitudes and actions?*

✓ Action Checklist

❑ Give teachers copies of "Getting the Most Out of Your Lesson" (p. 58) to help them use lesson aims in preparing and evaluating their lessons.

❑ Carefully evaluate the curriculum used or written by your teachers to make sure aims are specific and measurable. (See chapter 3 for more information on choosing curriculum.)

Getting the Most Out of Your Lesson

GET READY TO TEACH

1. Read the lesson aims. What response(s) in the lives of students does this lesson aim to teach?

2. Read the Scripture passage on which the lesson is based. What examples of the life response are found in this Scripture?

3. Which of the learning activities suggested will best help your students meet the aims of the lesson? What changes might you need to make?

AFTER YOU TEACH

1. Which of the lesson aims were accomplished in your class?

2. Which learning activities worked well? What might you do differently next time?

3. What did students do or say that showed an understanding of the lesson aims?

GOAL 2:
TOTAL SESSION TEACHING

**Everything that occurs in a session must
work to accomplish the aim.**

It's not hard to find agreement among church leaders on the value of teaching God's Word. Sunday School, youth groups and adult Bible studies all place a high priority on communicating spiritual truths. However, all these programs face two similar obstacles: they only meet one to two hours a week and they often experience hit-or-miss attendance by students.

Despite the significant value of the time teachers and students spend together, churches tend to fit many activities into their education classes: announcements, special music, devotionals, taking attendance, birthdays, etc. Classes are often started late due to tardiness of students or because teachers are busy with last-minute preparations. Early arrivers are forced to wait until Sunday School "begins" when they could be involved in meaningful activity.

The end result is that the valuable time for the real purpose of the class—Bible study, learning activities, relationship building—is cut to a minimum. Class becomes, especially at the youth and adult levels, a "sit-and-listen" situation in which students do not have an opportunity to discover Bible truths for themselves or to interact with their teacher and with each other.

The most practical solution to these problems is a teaching plan in which the entire session is given to setting the stage for learning and teaching. All of the activities, songs, discussion times, study groups, etc. are avenues used to accomplish a single set of learning aims. To make the best use of the session:

1. Begin with activities that start the student thinking about the Bible truths to be studied. These activities allow for students to arrive at varying times and are used in ways so that latecomers can benefit from them as well.
2. Structure the session so that students are involved in studying God's Word for themselves to discover Bible truths, with a balance of teacher input and student interaction.
3. Challenge students to apply the Bible truths to their lives and take specific steps of action as a result of what God's Word teaches.

Bonus Ideas for Summer Outreach: The traditional Vacation Bible School our church led for years seemed to attract only our own church kids. So now we make up five-day kits. Parents take home the kits and lead VBS in their homes, backyards or nearby parks. The VBSs are held whenever it is convenient: Saturdays, weeknights, etc. With this plan, kids who don't know the Lord hear the good news. *Bonnie Aldrich, Pulpit Rock Church, Colorado Springs, Colorado*

Create a theme for what's happening during the summer and promote it everywhere in the community: Summer Splashdown, Summer Sundays, etc. *Hailey Armoogan, Waterloo Pentecostal Assembly in Waterloo, Ontario, Canada*

We provide daylong activities for our junior highers so that working parents don't have to worry about transportation in the middle of the day. *Yolanda Miller, First Presbyterian Church, Honolulu, Hawaii*

MAKING SUMMER A TIME FOR GROWTH

Many churches shut down their Sunday School in the summer, due to difficulty finding adequate staff. Others limp through a summer slump, trying to keep the doors open for the faithful few. But a great many churches consider summer to be one of the most productive times of year for meaningful ministry. Often, the focus is on special events that happen at times other than the Sunday School hour:

- Vacation Bible School and backyard clubs
- Camps and retreats
- Mission trips and projects
- Picnics, socials and other outings

The impact of these special events is directly connected to the effectiveness of the ongoing teaching ministries such as Sunday School. Detailed plans far in advance must be made to ensure that summer Sunday School does not run out of energy when the weather turns hot. There is great value in looking at the summer months as a unique time of year for fresh approaches, and following up on any special events on the schedule is an opportunity to draw people into your ministry. Why have VBS if no effort is made to draw those children into a continuing Bible learning ministry? Why send kids to camp if the relationships that are built do not continue in Sunday School in the weeks that follow?

Bonus Ideas for Summer Outreach: During the summer, instead of shutting down, we like to offer more programs than ever! We invite kids in the community to attend weeklong day camps with special emphases: soccer, music, cheerleading, puppets, drama, tri-sport. We staff the day camps with teachers who are out of school and pay them a salary for the week. We charge kids to attend and our camps are always popular! *David Arnold, Parkview Evangelical Free Church, Iowa City, Iowa*

We plan a "sharing hike" for our youth. Each hiker is paired with someone he or she doesn't know well. During the hike, they are asked to get to know each other better. At the end of the hike, each pair tells what they learned about each other and there's a prize for the pair that learned the most. *Henry Kim, Hana Presbyterian Church, Glendale, California*

 Bonus Ideas for Summer Curriculum Variation: We wanted a change of pace from the rest of the year for ten weeks in the summer with grades 1 to 5. We made each of our five department rooms a special site for a different lesson. We recruited two teachers for each room to work as a team to prepare a lesson and activities that they then repeated for five weeks. We also recruited two group teachers for each of the five department groups with the primary responsibility of building relationships with those children. Each week, the group teachers led their children to a new room and helped the site teachers with activities. After the five weeks, the cycle was repeated with the same teachers and five more lessons. Thus, the site teachers only had to prepare two lessons all summer, using each one for five weeks. We had no problem getting volunteers using this format. *Lisa Herman, First Presbyterian Church of Hollywood, Hollywood, California*

During July and August we put up a big parachute awning outside as the central location for first through fifth graders. We adapt our curriculum and rotate kids to different areas for a lesson and choice of activity. *Dee Engle, Trinity United Presbyterian Church, Santa Ana, California*

✔ Action Checklist

- ❏ Observe some classes to see what schedule is being followed (or ask teachers to give you a copy of their typical class schedules).
- ❏ At a training or planning meeting, lead a shortened session based on the appropriate schedule for teachers' classes.
  - See specific age-level suggestions in the age-level portion of this chapter: Early Childhood (pp. 66-73); Children (pp. 74-78); Youth (pp. 79-82); Adult (pp. 83-86).

Bonus Ideas for Summer Staffing: I enlist a summer staff team that leads all elementary-aged children in one group. The lesson is presented through drama, songs, puppets and funny skits. Children are included in the presentations as much as possible, so they don't become mere spectators. The lesson presentation is followed by small group circles of six to eight children where they complete a follow-up activity page from the curriculum or a creative art activity (group mural or collage, for example). Each circle is led by a parent who has been assigned a Sunday to be their child's group leader. A master summer calendar is sent to all regularly attending families in late spring. They are encouraged to trade with another family's date if needed, calling the office to keep the schedule accurate. A reminder postcard is sent the week before their assigned Sunday. We've had great response with very few "no-shows." *Karen Perkins, Walnut Creek Presbyterian Church, Walnut Creek, California*

This summer we changed to a VBS format with crafts, games, music, memory verse and Bible time. We asked each of our adult Sunday School classes to volunteer to staff one Sunday during the summer. Each adult was asked to staff one activity and the kids rotated between the different activities. I led training clinics throughout the summer. The response was great from the adults, and the kids are really enjoying this approach to summer. *Wayne Robey, Southern Gables Evangelical Free Church, Littleton, Colorado*

We hire summer interns (older teens and young adults interested in ministry opportunities) to help us provide quality summer programming when kids are most available. Among their assignments is to take Sunday School leadership, with our regular staff members signing up to assist for just three Sundays out of those two months. We also train high school students to work as teacher's assistants in early childhood classes, so the regular staff can have extra time off during the summer. These youth assistants quickly become familiar to the children, so they feel secure even when some of their regular teachers are away. *Dee Engel, Trinity United Presbyterian Church, Santa Ana, California*

Bonus Idea for Fall Kickoff: On Labor Day Sunday, we have a rally for first through fifth graders with a guest children's musician, speaker or entertainer. Any teachers who are present help in welcoming children, taking attendance and sitting with the children. But they have no preparation and we never have to secure substitutes for those who are away. At the same time, in one of our classrooms, I run a Children's Ministry Orientation class for parents. *Dee Engel, Trinity United Presbyterian Church, Santa Ana, California*

GOAL 3:
ACTIVITIES WITH PURPOSE

A variety of creative learning activities to help students discover Bible truths is a must for every class.

The third aspect of an effective teaching plan is to involve students in a variety of creative learning activities. Just as each student is different, so are the ways in which they learn—each needs to be motivated and challenged according to his or her unique abilities and interests. This can best be done by providing a variety of learning experiences and offering choices whenever possible.

How many learning activities can you think of right now? There are *hundreds*! Yet some teachers stick to their old favorites (usually the way in which they were taught) like lecture, discussion and question and answer. Because different activities teach different things, teachers can make Bible study intriguing by using a variety of creative activities based on the following:

1. The learning aim desired;
2. The length of time available;
3. The materials, equipment and facilities available;
4. The needs and interests of the students;
5. The age of the students;
6. The teacher's ability and enjoyment of a particular activity.

Encourage teachers to practice beforehand any activities with which they are not familiar or to invite a friend with experience in a particular activity to be a guest teacher, rather than skipping what might be an effective learning tool.

> **Note:** See sample questionnaires and lists of learning activities in the age-level portion of this chapter: Early Childhood (pp. 66-73); Children (pp. 74-78); Youth (pp. 79-82); Adult (pp. 83-86).

Keeping Up with Learning: It seems that a new analysis of how people learn becomes popular every few years. "Right brain versus left brain," "learning styles" (how many styles there are depends on who you talk to) and "multiple intelligences" are all phrases that have been used recently to describe the way in which we learn. And it's true! Each of us has God-given strengths in which we learn best (our style) for certain types of intelligence.

It may seem like guesswork to determine which intelligence your students demonstrate (verbal, visual, musical, logical, bodily, interpersonal or intrapersonal) or which learning style (visual, kinesthetic or auditory) they have. But the basic idea is simple: people learn in different ways, and teachers who sincerely want to help students of all ages learn, plan lessons and activities that take advantage of the different ways of learning represented in their classes.

As you consider the students you teach, here are some questions to help you identify the different ways in which they learn:

Do your students like activities...

- With words?
- With questions?
- With pictures?
- With music?
- With movement?
- With others?
- By themselves?

Answer these questions for each student (typically more than one area will apply to each student) and keep a tally of your responses. At the end, you should have a better understanding of the kinds of activities that will be most effective in teaching your class.

✔ Action Checklist

❑ Encourage teachers to become familiar with their students by using a brief questionnaire to determine students' interests. This will enable teachers to better plan learning activities that will benefit their students the most.

❑ Demonstrate one or more learning activities and the way they are taught at a teachers' planning meeting, encouraging the use of similar techniques in teachers' own classes.

❑ Highlight a specific teacher's use of a learning activity in a brief article for a church newsletter or display on a bulletin board a few photos of the class in action.

❑ Set and publicize goals for how many different learning activities are used on a particular Sunday or within a specific department.

❑ Arrange for teachers who are skilled in the use of specific activities to demonstrate how those activities are used.

❑ Distribute copies of the "Learning Activities" charts to teachers at a training or planning meeting. The charts show examples of a variety of learning activities—teachers' curriculum will provide the instructions for these and other activities. Use the charts in one of the following ways:

- Choose a Bible story, memory verse and life application from an upcoming lesson. Ask teachers to form pairs or small groups and plan a learning activity to help teach or reinforce the lesson. Pairs or groups briefly share their ideas with each other.
- Ask teachers to put a check mark by any activity they have used in the last three to four months; put a star by four activities they would like to use in the next three to four months; circle four activities their students enjoy. Invite several volunteers to share their responses.

GOAL 4: TEACHER AND STUDENT INTERACTION

A balance of teacher input and student discovery strengthened by opportunities for teacher and student interaction is crucial.

Two elements are necessary to make learning happen: *time* for teachers to guide learning in a direct fashion (leading a Bible study, telling a Bible story, guiding a discussion) and *initiative* by students to discover and apply Bible truths (reading and commenting on a Scripture passage, participating in a Bible learning game, drawing a picture in response). A key factor in a workable teaching plan is to discover the right balance between the two.

Small Groups

Grouping students in small groups of five to eight students will encourage personal discovery and application of Bible truth. Consider the benefits of small group interaction.

1. Teachers and students relate on an individual basis, using questions and comments to connect Bible truths to the specific needs of each student.
2. Teachers can share brief personal stories that demonstrate the way they have applied a Bible truth.
3. Teachers can monitor and clarify the understanding of concepts and ideas.
4. More students are able to take part in discussions and answer questions.
5. Students who are not comfortable speaking in large groups or whose contributions are often overshadowed by more verbal students are more likely to respond and become involved.
6. Students are more likely to share concerns, anxieties and needs.
7. Each group can discuss a separate question or discover information in different ways and then share their findings and observations with the large group later on.

Look to the Future

Complete the "Teaching Plan Goals" worksheet (p. 87) to determine how you can begin working to meet the goals stated in this chapter.

Complete the "Teaching Plan Goals" worksheet (p. 87)

Bonus Idea for Building Relationships: Give each teacher a notebook with blank information forms for each student in the class. Provide teachers with basic name, address, phone and birthday information to enter on forms. Include questions about interests, family and concerns. Encourage teachers to plan one-on-one time with each student (before, during or after class; over a soda or a cup of coffee, etc.) to get better acquainted. Teachers then use the notebook as a reference in praying for the students. *Ron Richardson, Hillsong Church, Chapel Hill, North Carolina*

✔ Action Checklist

❑ Encourage teachers to look at the activities they currently provide in their sessions and to ask themselves which activities would be more productive and allow more student involvement if used in small groups.

❑ Invite teachers to share any reluctance to use small groups in their sessions. Short of staff? Not enough space? Brainstorm with teachers possible solutions to these problems.

❑ Demonstrate the use of small groups in training meetings.

Early Childhood Questionnaire

(NURSERY THROUGH KINDERGARTEN)

Ask children the following questions to familiarize yourself with their interests and to help you plan effective learning activities:

Name _____ Date _____

1. What's your favorite toy or game at your house?

2. What do you like to do outside?

3. What do you like to do at Sunday School?

Early Childhood Session Schedules

NURSERY

Bible study is often viewed as a somewhat scholarly activity, one that involves reading, comparing, analyzing and other high-level processes. What do any of them have to do with tickling a baby's toes, singing a lullaby or changing a diaper? Far too often the answer is "Not much." Bible study doesn't really come to life until the truths of God's Word begin to penetrate our actions, our feelings and our character, yet those are things that actually have a great deal to do with caring for little ones in the nursery!

Not just anyone can show God's patient love to a fussy baby, a terrified toddler or a roomful of both and more! But a person whose heart has hidden away God's truths is the kind of person whose life radiates that love—love that is a worthwhile topic of study by observant little eyes, sensitive little ears and curious little hands; love that has been taken from a sacred page and written in a smile, a caress, a gentle voice.

The message of God's love can be shared with babies and toddlers as teachers provide loving care and attention. And as their children are safely and lovingly cared for, outreach to parents and other family members takes place.

The best session for babies and toddlers is one in which children freely play in a safe and interesting environment. Teachers interact with children, participating in a variety of activities (singing, playing with toys, reading books, telling a simple Bible story) and caring for physical needs. Young children are not developmentally ready for structured group activities, so while two or more children may gather to do the same activity at the same time, don't expect toddlers to participate in a group learning time. Babies and toddlers learn best when the activity is one they have initiated or when they express obvious enjoyment and interest in a teacher-initiated activity.

This sample one-hour schedule provides a consistent routine while remaining flexible to meet a variety of demands. Adapt this schedule to fit your situation. Be sure that each child individually receives both the needed physical care and several opportunities to interact with a teacher.

Before the Session

Teachers and helpers arrive 5 to 10 minutes early in order to prepare the nursery facility or to make the transition between staff orderly.

Schedule at a Glance:
Step 1: Arrival
10 to 15 minutes
   Purpose: To welcome children and parents and complete all necessary check-in procedures.
Step 2: Learning Activities
30 to 45 minutes
   Purpose: To provide children with loving care meeting their physical and emotional needs and a variety of learning activities in which to participate.
Step 3: Dismissal
5 to 15 minutes
   Purpose: To give parents a brief update on the children's morning as they pick up their children and complete checkout procedures.

During the Session

Children arrive during the first 10 to 15 minutes of the session. A teacher or helper welcomes families at the door and supervises check-in procedures (labeling of all diaper bags and bottles, signing in, doing health checks, etc.).

Teachers play and care for babies and toddlers, providing a mix of quiet and active experiences. Teachers may follow curriculum suggestions for guided play experiences, storytelling, songs and conversation about a monthly theme. All toddlers need not participate. A prayer and snack may be provided for toddlers. Teachers and helpers refer to sign-in sheet for care suggestions.

At the End of the Session

Parents arrive to pick up their children. Teachers and helpers briefly communicate with parents about their children and the activities they enjoyed.

After the Session

Teachers and helpers clean up the nursery, making sure all toys and equipment are free of bacteria, or work with incoming teaching staff to allow the start of a new program or class with a minimum of disruption.

AGES 2½ THROUGH KINDERGARTEN

Teachers of young children are helping to launch these little ones toward new understandings, new experiences and new relationships. How important it is for us to prepare a young child to become God's person in a rapidly changing society!

In the first five years of life a child falls far short of adult understandings, skill and responsibilities; however, the young child is still equipped with an amazing array of capabilities that make thoughtful, loving ministry to them a necessity. A church must share Jesus' deep respect for children, sensing the great value God places on each one.

An effective session for young children provides them with choices of learning activities, a group time for singing, prayer and storytelling and a time to explore how the Bible truth connects to their lives.

This sample schedule will help you teach young children so that the needs of the whole child are met, including the involvement of children from the minute they arrive—few children are ready to sit quietly when they get to Sunday School!

Before the Session

Teachers and helpers arrive 5 to 10 minutes early in order to prepare the classroom or to make a smooth transition between staff.

During the Session

Children arrive during the first 10 minutes of the session. A teacher or helper welcomes children at the door and supervises check-in procedures. As children enter the room, they choose from two or more Bible-learning activities. Allowing children to choose what to do captures their interest; they are more likely to enjoy participation, and it prevents discipline problems. As the children interact with teachers during the Bible-learning activities, Bible truths are shared by means of guided conversation: the teacher asks questions and makes comments that help accomplish the learning aims.

The second major time segment is a large group time. Everyone gathers for worship experiences such as singing, prayer, Bible verse activity and other group activities that continue to emphasize the learning aims. Most often, children and teachers are comfortably seated on a rug. If the group is small (6 to 12 children), some churches find it best to end this large group time with telling the Bible story.

The last part of the session is focused on the Bible story and verse. The objective for telling Bible stories and repeating and discussing Bible verses is not just for the children to remember the details but also to allow Bible truths to speak to them about the everyday business of living. The Bible story is told near the end of the session so that children will have already experienced and talked about the main truth to be taught. As a result, the story has more meaning to the child than if it were told before the activities.

At the End of the Session

Parents arrive to pick up their children. Teachers and helpers briefly communicate with parents about their children and the activities they enjoyed.

After the Session

Teachers and helpers clean up the classroom or work with incoming teaching staff to allow the start of a new program or class with a minimum of disruption.

Schedule at a Glance:
Step 1: Learning Activities
30 to 45 minutes
  Purpose: To help children talk about and practice Bible truths while participating in one or more learning activities.
Step 2: Large Group Time
10 to 15 minutes
  Purpose: To provide children with informal worship opportunities and group activities. May include the Bible story time.
Step 3: Application
10 to 15 minutes
  Purpose: To help children hear and respond to the Bible story and Bible verse.
Note: Each time segment includes the time necessary for moving from one part of the schedule to the next.

Bonus Idea for Multiple Sessions: To get better use of our facilities, we have three worship services at 8:30, 9:45 and 11:00 A.M. with Sunday School running at all three sessions. We encourage people to register to attend a particular Sunday School session. We have children's and adult classes at all three sessions, but our youth classes only meet at 9:45 A.M. The adult classes are not duplicated at each hour, but similar topics are offered with classes focused to specific groups. For example, we offer groups for parents of elementary-age children, parents of teenagers, single adults, newlyweds, etc. *David Arnold, Parkview Evangelical Free Church, Iowa City, Iowa*

Additional Sunday Morning Programs

Depending on your church's Sunday morning schedule, some children may be present for more than one hour. Instead of sitting through an adult worship service or simply being cared for in a baby-sitting program, young children will benefit from an additional program that provides time for learning activities, a Bible story, snack, outdoor play (when possible) and large group activities. When this session teaches and enriches the same set of learning aims that are emphasized during Sunday School, the child's learning is strengthened. Even better, the young child is not confused by trying to remember the details of different Bible stories and verses.

The staff of additional Sunday morning programs should be aware of the Sunday School lesson aims so that they can plan appropriate activities. An effective schedule follows the same pattern as for Sunday School.

Learning Activities for the Nursery

MUSIC

- Listen to music (teacher singing, cassette, CD).
- Clap hands, wave scarves or move in time to music.
- Play child-safe rhythm instruments (bells, shakers).
- Sing a few words of familiar songs.

TOYS

- Stack cardboard blocks.
- Play with toy cars, people, animals and houses.
- Solve three- or four-piece wooden puzzles.
- Experiment with skill-building toys (nesting toys, pop-up toys, etc.).

PRETEND PLAY

- Care for dolls.
- Set table with dishes and cups.
- Talk on telephone.

BOOKS AND PICTURES

- Listen to a teacher talk about a book or picture.
- Point to objects pictured.
- Turn pages of a book for teacher to read.

ACTIVE PLAY

- Roll ball.
- Toss beanbags.
- Play outdoors on climbing structure.

NATURE ITEMS WITH TEACHER SUPERVISION

- Touch a leaf, flower or seasonal items (pumpkin, Indian corn, pinecone, etc.).
- Watch and touch soap bubbles.
- Observe self in unbreakable mirror.
- Feel a variety of textured materials.
- Taste foods (cracker, banana).

Learning Activities for Ages 2½ Through Kindergarten

HOME LIVING

- Set table with play dishes and food.
- Care for dolls.
- Wear dress-up clothes.
- Act out real-life situations (family life, grocery shopping, getting ready for church, etc.).
- Prepare, serve and eat food.

GOD'S WONDERS

- Use tools (magnifying glasses, measuring devices, cassette recorders, etc.).
- Conduct simple experiments.
- Observe and touch animals.
- Plant and care for growing things.

BLOCKS

- Play with toy cars, trucks and people.
- Build houses, towers and roads.
- Build structures and act out Bible stories.

ART

- Experiment with and form objects with play dough or clay.
- Draw Bible story scenes for murals.
- Cut and glue pictures for collages.
- Draw and color pictures.
- Cut and color patterns.
- Make greeting cards.
- Construct items (pasta necklaces, paper-plate tambourines, etc.).
- Fingerpaint or sponge paint.
- Make Bible-story-related objects (scrolls, Bible-times houses, etc.).

Learning Activities for Ages 2¹/₂ Through Kindergarten (Cont'd.)

MUSIC

- Play rhythm instruments.
- Do rhythmic motions for words of songs (clapping, stomping, etc.).
- Suggest new words for songs.

BOOKS

- Look at books.
- Listen to teacher read and talk about books.
- Answer questions about pictures.

TOYS

- Complete puzzles.
- Develop skills in building and construction (wooden blocks, interlocking blocks, etc.).

GAMES

- Toss beanbags.
- Find hidden objects.
- Practice physical skills (jumping, hopping, etc.).

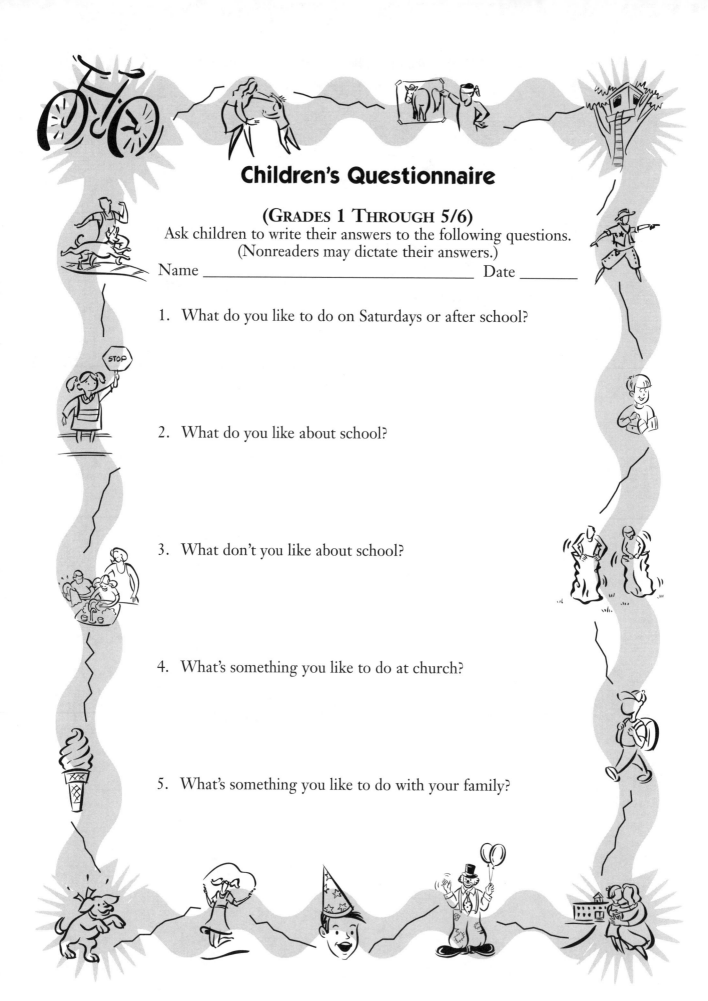

Children's Questionnaire

(GRADES 1 THROUGH 5/6)

Ask children to write their answers to the following questions.
(Nonreaders may dictate their answers.)

Name _____ Date _____

1. What do you like to do on Saturdays or after school?

2. What do you like about school?

3. What don't you like about school?

4. What's something you like to do at church?

5. What's something you like to do with your family?

Elementary Session Schedule

The teacher of children in the elementary grades has the awesome responsibility of effectively communicating God's Word to children whose life circumstances are not only quite different from the teacher's, but also may be quite different from other children's. A session schedule that allows for significant interaction among teachers and students as well as multiple opportunities to read and understand the Bible is key to helping children begin and grow in their relationship to Jesus Christ.

The following schedule allows teachers to teach children through meaningful learning experiences, each experience contributing to the session's learning aims.

BEFORE THE SESSION

Teachers and helpers arrive 5 to 10 minutes early in order to prepare the classroom or to make a smooth transition between staff.

DURING THE SESSION

Children arrive during the first 10 minutes of the session. A teacher or helper welcomes children at the door and supervises check-in procedures. As children enter the room, they are immediately involved in a discovery activity that introduces the life focus or memory verse for the lesson. Discover activities accommodate varying arrival times and can be led by teachers with a small group of students or with all students together. Depending on the type of activity, ratio of students to teachers and the space and materials available, more than one activity may be offered.

These fun, brief activities at the beginning of the session help the child begin thinking about the concepts that will be developed during the session. When possible, offering a choice of activities not only helps the teacher meet the varied needs of students, but it also allows each child involved to accept personal responsibility for participating and learning as well.

The second major time segment is Bible study. Students can be grouped in small groups or in one large group, depending on the number of teachers and students. To provide the most learning and interaction among students, it's best to group no more than 12 to 14 students for Bible study. During this time the teacher introduces the Bible story, weaving in opportunities for students to find, read and discuss Bible verses. This segment becomes much more than listening to a story as children become active participants. Even beginning readers can find the books in the Bible or locate names of Bible characters.

Schedule at a Glance:
Step 1: Discover
5 to 15 minutes
   Purpose: To help build relationships among students and start them thinking about the life focus and/or memory verse of the lesson.
Step 2: Bible Study
20 to 30 minutes
   Purpose: To guide students to read, study and discuss the Bible for themselves.
Step 3: Apply
20 to 30 minutes
   Purpose: To help students explore the relationship between the Bible truth they have been studying and their day-to-day experiences.

During the last part of the session, the teacher guides children in discovering the relationship between the lesson's Bible truth and their day-to-day experiences by using a creative learning activity that encourages students to identify and discuss specific ways their behavior can be affected by the day's lesson. Over a period of weeks, a variety of learning activities are provided so that each child's interests and needs are met. This time segment wraps up with one or more brief worship activities (song, prayer, group activity).

An alternative session schedule moves worship activities to the middle of the session after Bible Study. After worship, students complete an application activity, sometimes choosing between two or more activities, each of which is led by a different teacher.

AT THE END OF THE SESSION

Depending on your church's safety policies (see p. 108 ff.), students are dismissed or parents arrive to pick up their children, and teachers briefly communicate with parents about their children and the activities they enjoyed.

AFTER THE SESSION

Teachers and helpers clean up the classroom or work with incoming teaching staff to allow the start of a new program or class with a minimum of disruption.

ADDITIONAL SUNDAY MORNING PROGRAMS

In many churches some or all of the grade-school children may participate in an additional program that takes place either before or after the Sunday School session.

Unlike the younger children, elementary-aged children need a change of pace to vary the program from Sunday School. The additional program needs to include new topics, different activities, a wide variety of learning approaches and a varied time schedule, all used to accomplish the learning aim chosen for the session.

Tip: Any group of children may include a mix of those who are present for two or more sessions and those who are present for only one session. Thus, teachers need to view each session as a complete learning experience.

Learning Activities for Grades 1 Through 5/6

ART

- Draw Bible story scenes for murals or time lines.
- Draw sidewalk chalk pictures.
- Draw cartoons of situations.
- Create mobiles with words and/or pictures.
- Make greeting cards.
- Make Bible-story-related objects (scrolls, Bible-times houses, etc.).
- Construct tabletop scenes.
- Make banners, posters or collages.

MUSIC

- Create rhythmic motions for words of songs.
- Illustrate words of songs.
- Write new words for songs.
- Learn sign language for words of songs.

ORAL

- Complete sentence starters.
- Write and/or answer questions.
- Brainstorm ideas.

GAMES

- Play ball, beanbag or balloon toss.
- Have relay races.
- Guess words.
- Find hidden objects.
- Unscramble words or sentences.
- Play familiar children's games such as Hot Potato, Pictionary or Musical Chairs.
- Build obstacle courses.

Learning Activities for
Grades 1 Through 5/6 (Cont'd.)

RESEARCH

- Construct Bible-times objects (instruments, clothing, etc.).
- Find information in Bible dictionaries and/or encyclopedias.
- Interview others.
- Find locations on Bible maps.

WRITTEN

- Rewrite a psalm.
- Write contemporary stories.
- Compose prayers for a journal.
- Write diary of Bible-times character.
- Write ads.

DRAMA

- Write and act out scripts.
- Pantomime stories.
- Participate in role play.
- Pose scenes.
- Videotape skits.
- Make and use puppets.

SERVICE PROJECTS

- Help younger class (prepare games, make snack, etc.).
- Sort supplies or clean furniture.
- Make greeting cards or baskets.
- Advertise for and collect donations.
- Adopt a missionary child or family.
- Make welcome packets for new families.

Youth Questionnaire

(Grades 6 Through 12)

Name _____ Date _____

1. What's your favorite thing to do every day after school?

2. What do you and your friends like to do on weekends?

3. What's your favorite music group?

4. What advice would you give to the teacher of this youth group?

5. What's a book of the Bible you'd like to know more about?

Schedule at a Glance:
Step 1: Introduction
10 to 20 minutes
   Purpose: To help build relationships among students and start them thinking about the topic of the lesson.
Step 2: Bible Study
20 to 30 minutes
   Purpose: To guide students to read, study and discuss the Bible for themselves.
Step 3: Conclusion
10 to 20 minutes
   Purpose: To help students explore the relationship between the Bible truth they have been studying and their day-to-day experiences.

Note: A brief time of worship might be included as part of any of these steps. When worship leaders are aware of the session learning aims, they are able to be most effective in connecting songs and prayer topics to the lesson topic rather than merely leading a miscellaneous collection of songs and prayers.

Youth Session Schedule

Students in middle school or junior high school and high school need a variety of learning activities and varied session schedules to keep their interest. Significant opportunities for relationship building are key components of any effective session schedule.

At the youth level, more so than at any other age, teachers tend to develop their own lesson plans. Inexperienced teachers would be wise to follow the basic plan of a written curriculum plan, adapting it as needed. New and veteran teachers alike, however, recognize that there are generally three parts to a well-planned youth Bible study, whether it occurs in Sunday School or at another time on Sunday or during the week.

> **Note for College Age:** While college-age students are considered adults by most standards, leadership for teaching this age group is commonly provided from a church's youth ministry. The schedule and activities that work best with this age group are usually some combination of those suggested for both youth and adult. College students look for some noticeable difference from their high school group. Even so, they are still highly energetic and enthusiastic, needing a variety of approaches to maintain interest and challenge continued growth.

BEFORE THE SESSION
Teachers and helpers arrive 5 to 10 minutes early in order to prepare the room.

DURING THE SESSION
Students arrive during the first 10 minutes of the session. As students arrive, focus their attention on the topic or theme of the Bible study for the day. Brief involvement methods (brainstorming, sentence completions, questions and answers, etc.) can be used. It's helpful if whatever method is used encourages students and teachers to talk together. These introductory activities can be completed in small or large groups.

The second major time segment is Bible study. When their interest has been caught, students are ready to explore and discover God's point of view in the Scriptures and to examine the possibilities for applying the biblical principles to contemporary living. At least some of the learning activities are most effective when done in small groups of four to eight students.

- Middle school/junior high students require an adult leader in each group to make the time productive. These students tend to see many activities (games, skits, art, etc.) as simply fun things to do. An adult is needed, not just to guide the activity, but to ask questions and make comments to ensure that the students process the purpose of the activity.
- High school students can sometimes work in groups without an adult leader if mature students have been prepared to provide leadership. Some of the activities listed may initially seem to be juvenile to older students, especially in a group with freshmen and sophomores. Teachers may need to experiment with a mix of activities that strikes a balance between what are viewed as "lighter" and more "serious" approaches.

During the last part of the session, the teacher leads the students in activities that give them opportunities to decide how they will act on the knowledge they have discovered.

AT THE END OF THE SESSION
Students are dismissed.

AFTER THE SESSION
Teachers and/or students clean up the room.

ADDITIONAL SUNDAY MORNING SESSIONS
Even if there are multiple Sunday School sessions, in most churches the youth classes usually only meet during one of them. (Often, the middle school group may meet during one session and the high school group will meet during another one.) This pattern reflects the high emphasis on group identity. Teens want to be with their friends, and youth leaders want the whole group to be together.

Learning Activities for Grades 6/7
Through 12.

DRAMA
- Write and act out scripts.
- Pantomime stories.
- Participate in role play.
- Pose scenes.
- Videotape skits.

MUSIC
- Illustrate words of songs.
- Write new words for songs.

GAMES
- Have a ball or coin toss.
- Guess words.
- Find hidden objects.
- Unscramble words or sentences.
- Solve clues or riddles.

ART
- Draw cartoons.
- Create mobiles.
- Make banners, posters or collages.

SERVICE PROJECTS
- Advertise for and collect donations.
- Adopt a missionary child or family.
- Paint buildings.

RESEARCH
- Find information in Bible dictionaries and/or encyclopedias.
- Interview others.
- Watch videos to discover information.

ORAL
- Complete sentence starters.
- Write and/or answer questions.
- Brainstorm ideas.
- Complete agree/disagree statements.
- Interview.

WRITTEN
- Rewrite a psalm.
- Write contemporary stories.
- Compose prayers for a journal.

Adult Questionnaire

Name _____ Date _____

1. How do you like to spend your free time?

2. What do you enjoy about coming to church?

3. What topics are you interested in learning about?

Session at a Glance:

Step 1: Approach
10 to 20 minutes
    Purpose: To help students focus attention on the Bible study topic.

Step 2: Bible Study
20 to 30 minutes
    Purpose: To guide students to explore and discover God's point of view in the Scriptures and to examine possibilities for life application.

Step 3: Conclusion
10 to 20 minutes
    Purpose: To help students decide how to use what they have discovered in their own lives.

Note: A brief time of worship might be included as part of any of these steps. When worship leaders are aware of the session learning aims, they are able to be most effective in connecting songs and prayer topics to the lesson topic.

Adult Session Schedule

The best learning for adults takes place when the amount of teacher input is balanced with student discovery.

Discovering biblical principles is an opportunity for adults to evaluate ways in which they may put into practice what they have learned and become better acquainted with fellow students. An effective session schedule for adults takes into consideration all these components.

BEFORE THE SESSION

Teachers arrive 5 to 10 minutes early in order to prepare the classroom.

DURING THE SESSION

As adults arrive, their attention is focused on the topic or theme of the Bible study for the day. Brief involvement methods (brainstorming, sentence completions, questions and answers, etc.) can be used. It's helpful if whatever method is used encourages students and teachers to talk together, asking and answering questions in a caring and nonthreatening way. These lesson approach activities can be completed in small or large groups.

In Bible study time students are directly involved in the study of God's Word through a variety of creative learning activities such as listing, comparing, analyzing, researching, prioritizing, paraphrasing or other interaction with Scripture.

In the third time segment, students are given an opportunity to make decisions about personally following through on the Scripture they have studied and assuming responsibility for making the needed change in their lives.

AT THE END OF THE SESSION

Students are dismissed. You can safely assume it's within church policy to release them without their parents' permission!

AFTER THE SESSION

Teachers and students clean up the classroom.

ADDITIONAL SUNDAY MORNING SESSIONS

Churches with more than one Sunday School session usually have to do some creative scheduling to attract adult participation. Among the issues that need to be considered:

- Parents are most likely to participate in adult groups that meet at the same time as groups for their children. Since most churches provide programs for children during every session, this scheduling factor usually applies only to parents of teens.

- Classes for young adults are typically best attended when not held too early. Like all generalities, this one does not fit every group.

- Are there enough adults in specific age groups or interested in certain topics to warrant offering the same classes (usually with different teachers) at multiple hours?

- Are there any classes that are large enough that moving them to a different session would significantly impact worship attendance? Sometimes overcrowding in one session can be resolved by switching the time a popular class meets.

Learning Activities for Adults

ART
- Draw cartoons.
- Create mobiles.
- Make banners, posters or collages.
- Draw symbols or words or concepts.

GAMES
- Guess words.
- Find hidden objects.
- Unscramble words or sentences.
- Play Charades.

RESEARCH
- Find information in Bible dictionaries and/or encyclopedias.
- Interview others.
- Watch videos to discover information.

DRAMA
- Write and act out scripts.
- Pantomime stories.
- Participate in role play.
- Videotape skits.

ORAL
- Complete sentence starters.
- Write and/or answer questions.
- Brainstorm ideas.

WRITTEN
- Rewrite a psalm.
- Write contemporary stories.
- Compose prayers for a journal.
- Complete graphs.

SERVICE PROJECTS
- Assist a class of younger students by serving as helpers.
- Collect money or donated items for church or community aid organizations.
- Plan to help someone in need.

MUSIC
- Illustrate words of songs.
- Write new words for songs.

Teaching Plan Goals

Rate your church's progress toward each goal and then list two or more actions you can take to reach each goal.

1   2   3   4   5
Need to Start   Fair   Goal Achieved

Actions to Take:

GOAL 1: AIMS THAT TEACH

Lesson aims are specific and deal not only with biblical knowledge and attitude but also behavior. Whenever possible, lessons are grouped into units that focus on a central truth.

1   2   3   4   5
Need to Start   Fair   Goal Achieved

Actions to Take:

GOAL 2: TOTAL SESSION TEACHING

Everything that happens in a session helps accomplish the lesson aim.

1   2   3   4   5
Need to Start   Fair   Goal Achieved

Actions to Take:

GOAL 3: ACTIVITIES WITH PURPOSE

Every class provides students with a variety of creative learning activities to help students discover Bible truths.

1	2	3	4	5
Need to Start		Fair		Goal Achieved

Actions to Take:

GOAL 4: TEACHER AND STUDENT INTERACTION

Every class provides a balance of teacher input and student discovery strengthened by opportunities for teacher and student interaction, most often in small groups.

1	2	3	4	5
Need to Start		Fair		Goal Achieved

Actions to Take:

Chapter Five

Organize for Effective Learning

A Sunday School's overall plan for the organization of students and teachers and the implementation of a safety policy is the foundation of a Sunday School that impacts lives.

What This Chapter Tells You

- Grouping students of similar ages and with an appropriate number of teachers directly affects the quality of learning and relationships in Sunday School and other programs.
- Leaders are best able to encourage teachers and helpers if they are responsible for supervising and assisting no more than five to eight people.
- A Sunday School experiencing rapid growth or whose attendance patterns significantly change during the summer or other seasonal times may need to adapt the way in which students are grouped.
- As churches organize their Sunday School and other programs, they need to develop and put into practice safety guidelines.

What This Chapter Shows You

- How to organize your teachers and students so that effective learning takes place;
- Record-keeping plans;
- Recommended teacher/student ratios;
- Sample ways to organize teachers for easy supervision;
- Suggestions for adapting organizational plans to meet temporary needs while continuing to maximize the opportunities for student learning;
- How to write and present a church safety policy.

Where Do I Start?

Get the Big Picture

To ensure that the safety policy can be followed, a Sunday School needs to be organized in such a way that students are grouped according to their age level and teachers must have a realistic number of people to supervise.

While few teachers give much thought to their Sunday School's organization, success or failure is largely determined by the manner in which the Sunday School is structured. A Sunday School that values involvement learning (see chapter 4) but groups students of many ages together every week will find it difficult to accomplish its teaching goals. However, a Sunday School in which the organization is well planned will experience the following benefits:

- Long-term growth toward a consistent teaching plan;
- Spiritual growth in the lives of the students that will encourage teachers;
- A positive, proactive handling of liability issues.

ONE BUILDING BLOCK AT A TIME

No matter which age level you may be leading, you may find yourself caught between two positions: Keeping the same organizational plan year after year no matter how things change because that's the way it's always been done, and changing the plan because you've heard about a new idea or because it's summer and the regular teachers are on vacation or just because something different sounds appealing. Either position can help or hurt your Sunday School—the difference is whether or not consideration is given to the ultimate goal of your ministry and if your organizational plan provides a solid foundation for that goal to be accomplished.

"I sincerely believe that the Sunday School, properly organized and functioning, is the best way to accomplish the Great Commission in the ministry of the local church."
Thomas J. Cook

Look at Where You Are

Complete the "Organization" worksheet (p. 92) to describe the organizational plan of your Sunday School.

Mr. Smith realized that the church's safety policy is serious business.

PERSPECTIVE

If you find yourself occasionally overwhelmed by the constant effort of persuading teachers to follow the guidelines of your church's safety policy, you're not alone! It helps to keep everyone focused on the ultimate goal: Teachers are free to give 100 percent of their attention to their ministry when the basic details of a well-thought-out safety policy are followed.

Organization

1. How are the students in your Sunday School or in the area you supervise grouped?

2. How many teachers are in each group?

3. Identify ways you feel the grouping of students is not working well. Why do you think these groupings aren't working?

4. Does your church have a safety policy for children and youth? How are teachers introduced to the policy and trained in its use?

Focus on the Goals

GOAL 1:
REALISTIC TEACHER SUPERVISION

An organized Sunday School where each supervisor is responsible for no more than five to eight teachers and helpers is essential.

A leading supervisor's primary responsibility is to help teachers be successful and feel a sense of satisfaction from their jobs. This kind of support can best happen when the number of people supervised is limited to no more than eight, allowing supervisors to focus on discipling the small group of staff members he or she is directly responsible for. When the number is greater than eight, supervisors should recruit and train assistants and divide the responsibilities.

Sunday Schools are usually organized according to one of three basic plans. The plan you choose will depend on the size of your church. Look closely at the following description of each basic plan and identify which one (or combination of plans) best fits your church:

Basic Plan 1

In this plan, there are no departments; rather, classes are led by teachers who report directly to one person: the Christian Education Director or Sunday School Coordinator (titles vary from church to church). The director or coordinator may be a paid or volunteer position. Smaller churches usually follow Basic Plan 1 because they do not have enough classes in any one age group to make up a department (two to four classes of similar size that meet together for large group activities).

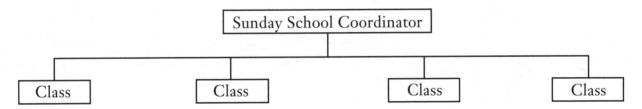

Basic Plan 2

Classes in this plan are grouped into age-level departments (for example, multiple classes of four-year-olds). A department may have two or more classes where class teachers report to department leaders who in turn report to the Sunday School Coordinator or Christian Education Director.

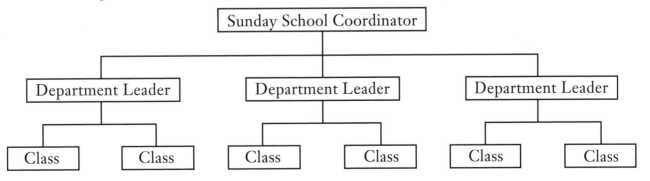

Basic Plan 3

Some churches are large enough to group departments by age level. Each age level has a coordinator who supervises the department leaders and reports to the Sunday School Coordinator or the Christian Education Director. A variation of this plan is to have a separate director, coordinator or pastor for each age division.

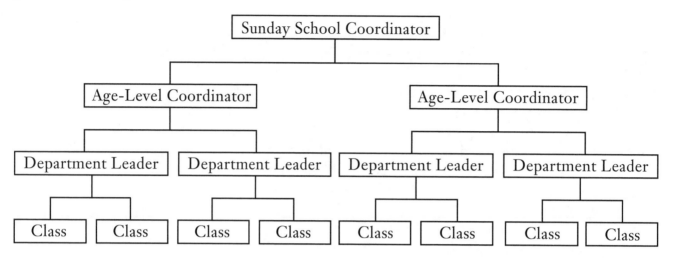

Often a church will develop an organizational plan that combines elements from each of the basic plans. For example:

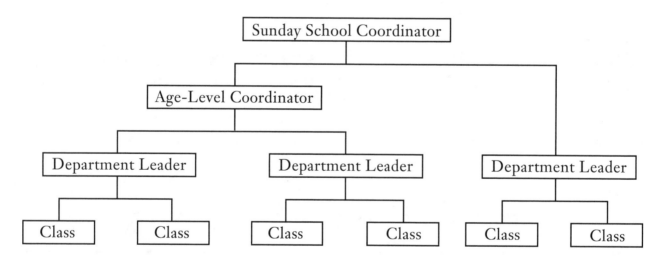

Sample Combination 1

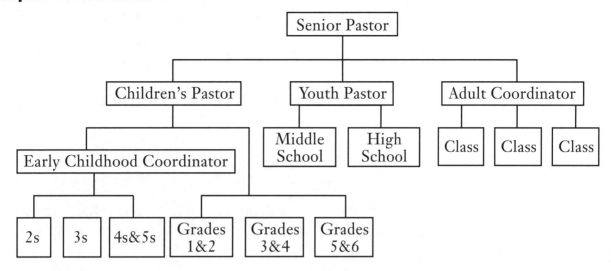

Sample Combination 2

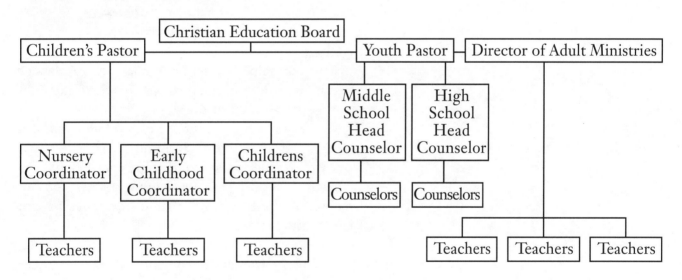

✓ Action Checklist

Determine which of the plans described in this chapter your church follows (or should follow) and identify which of your supervising leaders (if any) supervise more than five to eight other staff members. Take steps to lighten that leader's workload:

❑ Create new positions as needed, recruiting and training additional teachers.

❑ Split some assignments. For example, if you have a children's minister who supervises 10 teachers, designate one of the teachers to also serve as an age-level coordinator who will supervise three or four teachers in the same age level.

The reason for organizing into these four broad divisions is that within each division the same basic teaching plan (see chapter 4) can be followed with similar kinds of learning activities due to the basically similar needs and characteristics within each age group.

The leader's task in supervising and training is simplified when the division organizational plan is followed:

- All of the staff in each division can be trained together;
- A teacher or helper from one Sunday School class or program in a division can move easily to another class or program within that division;
- The leader of each division needs to be skilled in just one basic teaching plan and can more effectively work with all the teachers and helpers in the division;
- A strong class or department within the division can be observed by new teachers and helpers as part of their training process;
- Students are involved in a consistent Bible learning approach as they move from one class to another within a division.

Specific Age-Level Ideas

Kindergarten Questions

The early childhood division has traditionally included all children prior to starting first grade. However, many educators, parents and church leaders now feel that kindergarten children fit better with younger elementary children than with older preschoolers.

Much of the reason for this view is that most children by this age have already had extensive classroom experience in day care and/or preschool before beginning kindergarten. No longer is this the age when most young children encounter their first group learning situation, and many kindergarten children already possess some of the cognitive skills (beginning reading, writing, math, etc.) previously introduced in first grade.

There are valid reasons to be cautious about attempting to merge kindergartners with elementary-aged children, however. Kindergartners still need the informal, physically active session plan that is the hallmark of early childhood. Attempts to accelerate them into groups, activities, materials and schedules designed for older children run great developmental risks. In most cases, the emotional, social, physical and mental needs of kindergartners are better met by providing them with one more year of early childhood, guided by teachers who are aware of the great learning strides being made in this exciting year of life.

Solving the Middle School Puzzle

Many churches find that schools in their areas have changed the way in which students are grouped at the junior high or middle school level. Some churches have even found that the grouping is not consistent within the school districts from which their students come. So what is a church to do?

- Follow the same plan as the majority of schools in your area to minimize the confusion of students and parents.
- If sixth graders are attending middle school in your community, you may wish to create a separate sixth grade class or department that is part of either the children or youth division. This option is best when the middle school group is primarily made up of eighth graders.

Bringing Teens into the Church Family

Many churches feel caught on a two-edged sword. First, they feel compelled to provide a variety of youth activities to attract young people. Then they find the young people prefer those activities to anything involving the other age groups in the church, especially their parents' age group! Here are a few tips for helping young people feel good about belonging to the larger church family:

- **Evaluate church events from the perspective of the young people.** What efforts are being made to help teens feel included? For example:

    Worship Services: Do those who speak to the congregation give thought to the presence of teenagers, planning ways to help teens feel the words are directed to them? Are teens included in any planning, evaluation, leadership or serving roles? Are issues of concern to teens addressed in sermons?

    Service Projects/Work Days: Are teens given opportunity to work alongside adults, or are they assigned the most menial tasks?

Ministry Roles: Are teens actively asked to serve (music, teaching, committees, etc.) and are they given training to equip them to succeed?

- **Recruit youth leadership that will commit to long-term involvement so that strong relationships are built with adult leaders.** For example, many churches ask youth Sunday School teachers to also participate in at least one other youth activity each week. Also, some churches have found very positive results in promoting at least some youth staff along with the young people each year, building continuity from grade to grade.
- **Take time in youth groups to talk about things going on in the rest of the church.** For example, in youth Sunday School classes, introduce the morning's sermon topic or a hymn. Have teachers share what they find meaningful in their church involvement.

Building a College/Career Ministry

The years after leaving high school are among the most significant in a young person's life. Increased independence and responsibility and new circles of friends play a big role in setting lifelong values and beliefs. An effective teaching/support ministry for young adults is vital. During this time young people who have been part of the life of the church reevaluate their faith, often seeing it deepen, but many times choosing to move away from it. Sadly, many churches—even those with strong ministries to middle school and high school students—find the challenges of this ministry too great to maintain it.

Because young people in this age group are often in transition (going away to school, serving in the military, moving out of their parents' homes, moving back home, working irregular hours, etc.), it can be difficult to sustain consistent attendance. The following important actions result in a ministry that makes a significant impact on the lives of young adults:

- **A Committed Leadership Team:** Recruit several people with a heart for young adults and who will work together to build relationships and provide meaningful teaching. Both male and female staff members are needed.
- **Flexible Scheduling:** If there is any Sunday School group that may be better off not meeting when the rest of the school meets, this could be the one. Young adults with new freedom to stay out late at night are often reluctant to get up for a Sunday morning group. An evening early in the week is often the best time to get consistent attendance. And meeting

somewhere other than at church (a home, an apartment, a restaurant) can be effective, too.

- **Tailor Approaches to Size and Personality of Group:** College/career groups can fluctuate dramatically in their size. A group that suddenly gets bigger can seem impersonal. A group that suddenly gets smaller can seem depressing. Teachers need to quickly adapt their goals and styles of interaction, perhaps emphasizing discipleship when the group is small and then shifting to a more inclusive outreach method when it is larger.

Helping Older Students Keep Learning

Just because people pass the age of retirement does not mean they have passed the time of learning and growing. Scripture presents many examples of people who made remarkable contributions late in life:

- Abraham and Sarah believed God and became parents long after normal childbearing years.
- Moses was 80 years old when God called him to lead Israel out of Egypt.
- Joshua and Caleb led the conquest of Israel well into their 80s, after all their peers had died.
- Simeon and Anna were the only people in the Temple who noticed the infant Jesus.
- Apostle John wrote the Book of Revelation when he was aged.

Classes that involve senior citizens need to make provision for their physical, social, emotional and spiritual needs:

- **Physical:** Transportation is often necessary for those no longer able to drive, seating needs to be comfortable, printed materials should use large type and consideration must be given to those with hearing loss. It is equally important to remember that many seniors need to be active, rather than sitting and listening for a full session.
- **Social/Emotional:** People who have outlived friends and loved ones have a great need for new friendships to fill those gaps. Similarly, if children and grandchildren live far away, loneliness can be very debilitating. Thus, teachers of the elderly must be kind, gentle and caring. At the same time, many seniors need the stimulation of new, interesting challenges and to be encouraged to reach out to others. A class for seniors that keeps getting smaller by attrition is very depressing; a class that continually seeks out and welcomes new people is truly exciting. For the latter to happen, adequate leadership must be enlisted, not just to

teach lessons, but to guide a variety of ministry activities. While much of this leadership may be available from the seniors themselves, usually there is a need to enlist a somewhat younger team who will commit to sharing the responsibility.

- **Spiritual:** Just because a person has been a Christian for many years does not mean all his or her spiritual battles are in the past. Those who came late to faith also require nurturing in their pilgrimage. Teachers sometimes become focused on temporal matters facing the elderly and assume that spiritual issues are fine. On the contrary, prayer, active Bible study and sharing the faith always need to be given priority attention.

A balanced ministry to senior adults should include opportunities for outreach, service and fellowship in addition to times of learning and spiritual growth. A few activities to consider are:

- **Homebound Ministry:** Provide Bible study, prayer and fellowship for individuals and couples who are shut in.
- **Senior Living Ministry:** Offer worship services, Bible study groups, and fellowship times at nursing homes and/or senior housing complexes.
- **Outings, Recreation and Travel:** Many seniors have time and resources for a wide variety of activities and trips. Such events are excellent means for current members to reach out to friends and neighbors.
- **Service Projects:** Many seniors groups take on one or more community or missions projects (literacy tutoring, Meals on Wheels, handyman services, etc.).

Teaching Those with Special Needs

For several decades building codes have required new and remodeled church buildings to provide physical access to people with limitations. Typically, churches tend to confront this issue when a person with a disability begins attending the church. Relatively few churches have actively sought to provide ministry access to people with special needs.

Ministry to persons with disabilities also begins when an individual or group feels drawn to reach out into the community and share Christ's love with those who are disabled and their families. A church that develops a heart for people with special needs will discover great opportunities to make a positive difference in the lives of people—those to whom they minister as well as those seeking to *be* ministers.

When creating a program to minister to those with special needs, consider the answers to these essential questions:

1. **Should a special class or classes be provided or should students be mainstreamed into existing groups?**

   In general, it is highly desirable to seek ways to include people with disabilities along with everyone else. There is great benefit for the members of a group when they adapt to welcome a student with special needs.

   Students with a physical impairment (blind, deaf, wheelchair-bound, etc.) usually need only a very focused type of help (a Braille Bible, a signing interpreter, a ramp, etc.) in order to participate fully in a class. A student with multiple impairments may require specialized one-on-one assistance.

   Students with a learning disability (e.g., dyslexia) usually need only a caring, sensitive teacher who will plan ways the student can succeed without putting the student on the spot (e.g., not having him or her read aloud).

   Students with mental or emotional disabilities can often participate in regular groups, depending on the severity of the impairment. Even when it is determined that a special class is the best option for such students, regular opportunities should be provided for interaction with those in other groups.

2. **What qualifications are required by those who teach special needs students?**

   Look first for people with caring hearts, whose lives display the love of Christ. Then provide them with some basic information about the disabilities of the students being taught and give them guidance for appropriate ways to assist students in learning.

3. **What curriculum and other resources are available for this ministry?**

   Many denominations and some independent curriculum publishers provide information on special needs ministries, often with current listings for additional resources.

   Ministries that focus on people with special needs are excellent sources for useful materials. Contact Joni Eareckson Tada's ministry: JAF (Joni And Friends) Ministries, P. O. Box 3333, Agoura Hills, CA 91301 or jafministries.com.

   Ask your local Christian bookstore for resources on ministry to people with disabilities.

   The National Organization on Disabilities can also provide resources on a wide variety of disability-related issues, including very complete information on religion and disabilities. Contact NOD, 901 16th Street, NW, Suite 600, Washington, DC 20006.

Here is an example of a purpose statement for a disability ministry: "To make disciples within the disabled community by demonstrating Christ's love, and to equip the congregation to minister to the special needs of the disabled so that all might fellowship, worship, and serve." (*from Golden Hills Community Church, Brentwood, California*)

4. **What other activities can enhance a ministry to those with special needs?**

> Parent support groups and training workshops
> Transportation ministry
> Clearinghouse of information regarding specific disabilities
> Family assistance (i.e., regularly scheduled relief for family members needing time alone, for errands, etc.)
> Camping experiences or other special events

Teaching in a Bilingual Setting

Sunday Schools face varied situations when seeking to minister to people who speak different languages. In some cases the church may share facilities with one or more congregations of a different ethnic or language background, or a church may simply find two or more languages being spoken by the people to whom it ministers. Leaders or teachers seeking to guide learning for students with different languages will find the following guidelines useful:

1. Enlist at least one bilingual teacher or aide for each group. Sometimes a parent, child or sibling is a helpful interpreter during a class session.
2. Provide Bibles in each language spoken. Students of all ages need to hear God's Word in their own language. An English-speaking teacher can assist a student in locating a passage in a non-English Bible.
3. Provide teachers with a bilingual phrase list so that they can communicate some friendly greetings and essential concepts in the students' language. Add to this list over time to help teachers build their own language skills.
4. Before each class session, have teachers prepare posters with key points, Bible verses and directions in each language. Student worksheets may need to be at least partially translated also.
5. Most people understand more of another language than they are able to speak themselves.
   Consideration should be given to the necessity of interpreting entire lessons or only when asking questions or guiding activities. If it is necessary to interpret the whole lesson, less content can be covered because of the time it takes for ideas to be presented twice. Simultaneous translation (where the speaker does not wait for the translator) of a Bible story presentation or class lecture requires greater skill than most bilingual people possess.

> **Three-legged, Yellow-eyed Trombone Players:** This group of people definitely needs to be kept to themselves, preferably in a room far removed from everybody else.

GOAL 3:
APPROPRIATE TEACHER/STUDENT RATIOS

The number of students and teachers that each class or department has makes discovery learning and the development of relationships among students and teachers possible.

The benefits of small group involvement are many—the teacher is more apt to build relationships with individual students, follow up on absentees and visitors, extend outreach to families of class members and remember special occasions such as birthdays. Teachers with too many students often don't attempt follow-up and outreach because the task appears overwhelming, and these teachers may also feel that there are already more students than they can teach (or have room for) on Sunday morning.

If your church is large enough to have more than one class at each age level, group classes into departments, limiting each department to three to five classes who all meet in one room for large group activities. In departments larger than this, the large group activities become difficult to carry out and require a skilled teacher to lead. When a department approaches the recommended maximum number of students, it is best to create a new department.

You may feel that the teacher/student ratios recommended are not achievable. Remember that students need the *personal* guidance of a teacher if they are to truly participate in learning. If classes and departments get too large before they are divided, teachers are less likely to function as guides even if they have the desire and skill; their role becomes that of crowd control. Since a primary role of teachers is to care for and support their students, a small ratio is even more essential.

In determining the grouping of students, also consider the amount of space available. Overcrowded conditions at any age level severely limit the quality of teaching. If you are temporarily forced to choose which classes meet in the largest rooms, give priority to the classes of young children because of their need for movement.

If you are unable to build or rent additional rooms because you are meeting in a community center, school facility or warehouse space, consider these options for additional classroom space: outdoor classrooms when climate permits, the living room of an adjacent church member's home, portable dividers in large rooms, staggered class meeting times, beginning duplicate sessions or moving some or all Sunday classes to another time (i.e., weekdays). (See chapter 9 for more information about facilities.)

Bonus Idea for Encouraging Attendance: Invite the youth class to a special evening at the youth leader's home. Let kids choose the menu. Focus the evening on encouragement! *Scott Grabendike, First Presbyterian Church, Palmdale, California*

Within an age-level division, the grouping of students is also affected by the number of students per age. In some cases, the number of students may not be balanced. For example, in the adult division you may have a large group of college students but very few senior adults; or in the early childhood division, you may have many three-year-olds but very few kindergartners. Regularly evaluate the number of students in classes to determine if you need to move classes to different rooms or combine two or more classes with few students. It's best to complete this evaluation process at the start of every school year.

It is often helpful in evaluating the need for additional classes or the creation of a department if class attendance records have been kept. Provide forms on which teachers record the attendance in their classes. In a department, one teacher might record the attendance for all the classes within the department. Attendance sheets could be collected on a weekly, monthly or quarterly basis (see Attendance Sheets 1 and 2 on pages 105-106). Attendance sheets preprinted with names of regular attenders make it convenient for teachers to record attendance.

Sample

Attendance Sheet 1

Weekly Attendance

Class: Parenting Elective
Teacher(s): John Smith and Sue Jones
Date: *October 15, 2000*

❑ Marcia Adams
❑ Dick Adams
❑ Lewis Francis
❑ Margaret Grafton
❑ Joe Harper
❑ James Riley

Visitors:
David Nelson

Jane Nelson

Sample

Attendance Sheet 2

Quarterly Attendance

Class: Fifth and Sixth Grade

Teacher/Helper(s): Julie Johnson and Alison Stephens

	10/1	10/8	10/15	10/22	10/29
Sarah Alexandre	✓		✓		
Emily Callahan	✓		✓		
Lori Hanson	✓	✓	✓		
Nick Thomas	✓	✓			
Joey Harper	✓	✓			
Jamie Riley	✓	✓	✓		

VISITORS					
Steven Nelson	✓		✓		
Mason Williams	✓				
Jessica Patterson		✓	✓		

WHEN CLASSES BECOME TOO LARGE

When a class has grown so large that it needs to be divided, create a smooth transition in the following manner:

- Have the new teachers sit in the class with the current teachers to observe and become better acquainted with the students;
- Ask the new teachers to assume some of the teaching responsibilities;
- After several weeks, when teachers and students are well acquainted, create two classes with two teachers leading each class.

Sometimes people play down the importance of keeping and using attendance records. "It's not numbers that are important—it's people!" they say. But numbers *are* people. And you can do a much more effective job of ministering to people if you keep records and use them to help you reach out to people. Accurate enrollment and attendance records are an invaluable source for statistics which will help you:

- Evaluate the effectiveness of your Sunday School;
- Predict future growth;
- Discover problem areas that need attention;
- Determine areas where more consistent follow-up is needed.

Use records to determine reasons for attendance or a lack of it. In some cases you may need to talk with individual teachers to see what clues they may give you about the reasons for certain attendance patterns. Attendance patterns over several years may also be affected by economic or social changes in your community, an increase (or decrease) in the number of church programs that affect the church's appeal to various groups of people, changes in church leadership that influence the effectiveness of church programs in reaching people. (For more information on how to develop an outreach program in your Sunday School, read chapter 10.)

✓ Action Checklist

❑ List the numbers of teachers and students in each Sunday School class. Compare these ratios to the recommended ratios. See specific age-level suggestions for teacher/student ratios in the age-level portion of this chapter: Early Childhood (p. 121); Children (p. 122); Youth (p. 123); Adult (pp. 124-126).

❑ Evaluate the record-keeping methods in your Sunday School, making changes as needed in order to begin or improve your attendance records.

❑ Answer the following questions, based on your attendance record keeping:

- Which classes have consistently high or low attendance?
- Which classes have the highest or lowest number of visitors?
- Which classes have the highest or lowest number of dropouts?
- Which classes have shown steady growth or decline in enrollment?
- What percentage of your church enrollment is in attendance?

GOAL 4: DEVELOP A SAFETY POLICY FOR EARLY CHILDHOOD, CHILDREN AND YOUTH

All leaders and teachers must be provided with a written child and youth safety policy and its guidelines must be strictly followed to ensure child and youth safety and to protect church workers.

✔ **Action Checklist**

❑ Evaluate and update the safety policies and forms in your church. Make a plan for distributing forms as needed and training the teachers in your Sunday School and other programs.

❑ Invite the local fire department to walk through the church facilities with you and make recommendations for safety improvement.

❑ Post or update current emergency phone numbers (doctor, nurse, electrician, plumber, etc.) in each building, as well as evacuation and emergency exit plans. Some churches schedule medical personnel to be available on a rotating basis.

❑ Ask your insurance provider for an update on liability laws (attractive nuisances, etc.).

Developing safety procedures for preventing and reporting child abuse and endangerment is an important process for your church. While never expecting to have a problem, it is wise to take necessary precautions by developing a written safety policy. A safety policy should include:

- Guidelines for teacher selection (including some or all of the following: application forms, personal interviews, follow-up of references, fingerprinting and criminal history checks);
- Policies to be followed in the classroom and on any church-sponsored outings (number of adults required, name tags, check-in and checkout procedures, etc.);
- Reporting obligations on the part of teachers;
- Step-by-step plans for response to an allegation.

In addition, a child release form should be signed by all parents whose children are participating in church events. All applications and reference checks are required to be kept confidential.

A safety policy should be approved by church leaders, and all staff should be familiarized with the policy on an annual basis. It is also recommended that a lawyer evaluate your policy to be sure it conforms to your state's laws regarding the reporting of child abuse.

It is always best to present the safety policy with an introduction explaining the purpose of such a policy: to make your church the best place it can be for the children and youth in your community and to protect teachers should allegations of abuse or child endangerment be made.

Use the sample Volunteer Application Form, Medical Release and Liability Form, Infectious Disease/AIDS and HBV (Hepatitis B Virus) Policy, Church Office Notification Injury Report, Child and Youth Safety Policy, and Introductory Letter on the following pages as a guide in developing your own procedures. Always have a lawyer evaluate your forms and procedures based on the laws in your state. Also check with your state's social services department to determine licensing laws that apply to church programs such as day camps, summer programs, tutoring centers, recreational camps and any other ministries you might have.

Volunteer Application Form

IMPORTANT: *This is a sample form, not intended to be reproduced.*
Adapt to your specific needs.

First Church has a child/youth safety policy founded on respect and love for the children and youth of our church and community. This safety policy gives children, youth, parents and all Sunday School staff a sense of confidence and peace. We ask your cooperation in completing and returning this application.

Personal Information

Name_____

Address_____

Phone_____

Best time to call: Morning _____ Afternoon _____ Evening _____

Day and month of birth_____

Occupation_____

Where employed_____

Phone_____

Can you receive calls at work? ❑ Yes ❑ No

Do you have a current driver's license? ❑ Yes ❑ No

License number _____

Children ❑ Yes ❑ No

Name(s) and age(s)_____

Spouse ❑ Yes ❑ No

Name_____

Are you currently a member of First Church? ❑ Yes ❑ No

If yes, how long? _____

Please list other churches and locations where you have regularly attended over the past five years. _____

Are you currently under a charge or have you ever been convicted of or pled guilty to child abuse or a crime involving actual or attempted sexual misconduct or sexual molestation of a minor? ❑ Yes ❑ No

If yes, please explain_____

_____

Are you currently under a charge or have you ever been convicted guilty of or pled guilty to possession/sale of controlled substances or of driving under the influence of alcohol?
❑ Yes ❑ No

If yes, please explain_____

_____

Is there any other information that we should know?_____

_____

_____

_____

Church Activity

1. Please write a brief statement of how you became a Christian.

   _____
   _____
   _____

2. In what activities/ministries of our church are you presently involved?

   _____

3. Experience:
   a. What volunteer or career experiences with children/youth have you had in the church or the community?

   _____

   b. List any gifts, calling, training, education or other factors that have prepared you for ministry to children/youth.

   _____

4. Preferences: In what capacity and with what age group would you like to minister? Explain your choice.

   _____
   _____

5. Concerns: What causes the greatest feelings of apprehension as you contemplate this ministry?

   _____

Personal References

(Not a former employer or relative)

Name _____ Phone _____

Address _____

Name _____ Phone _____

Address _____

Applicant's Statement

The information contained in this application is true and correct to the best of my knowledge. I authorize any of the above references or churches to give you any information that they may have regarding my character and fitness to work with youth or children.

I hereby certify that I have read and that I understand the attached provisions of (insert title of your state's penal code regarding the reporting of child abuse and neglect).

Signature _____ Date _____

Medical and Liability Release Form

IMPORTANT: *This is a sample form, not intended to be reproduced.*
Ask a lawer who is familiar with your states's church liability laws to evaluate this form.

Parent Permission/Release Form

(Church Name)
(Address)
(Phone Number)

Child's Name _____

Birthdate _____ Grade _____

Address _____

City _____ Zip _____

Phone _____

Date(s) of Activity _____

Authorization of Consent for Treatment of Minor

I, the undersigned parent or guardian of _____, a minor, do hereby authorize any duly authorized employee, volunteer or other representative of the (church name), as agent(s) for the undersigned, to consent to any x-ray examination, anesthetic, medical or surgical diagnosis or treatment, and hospital care which is deemed advisable by, and is to be rendered under the general or specific supervision of, any licensed physician and surgeon, whether such diagnosis or treatment is rendered at the office of said physician and surgeon or at a clinic, hospital or other medical facility.

It is understood that this authorization is given in advance of any specific diagnosis, treatment or hospital care being required, but is given to provide authority and power on the part of our aforesaid agent(s) to give specific consent to any and all such diagnosis treatment or hospital care which the aforementioned physician in the exercise of his or her best judgment may deem advisable.

This authorization shall remain effective from_____to _____ .

I, the undersigned, on behalf of myself and _____ (child's name), shall indemnify, hold free and harmless, assume liability for and defend the (church name), its agents, servants, employees, officers and directors from any and all costs and expenses, including but not limited to attorneys' fees, reasonable investigative and discovery costs, court costs and all other sums, which the (church name), its agents, servants, employees, officers and directors may pay or become obligated to pay on account of any, all and every demand for, claim or assertion or liability, or any claim or action founded therein, arising or alleged to have arisen out of _____ (child's name)'s use of real or personal property belonging to the (church name), its agents, servants, employees, officers and directors, or by reason of _____ (child's name)'s participation in any (church name) activity(ies).

Parent or Legal Guardian Signature _____ Date _____

Home Phone _____ Work Phone _____

Other Emergency Contact _____ Phone _____

Family Doctor _____ Phone _____

Insurance Company _____ Policy Number _____

Medication/Allergies _____

Last Tetanus Immunization _____

Will you allow blood transfusions? _____

Any special needs? _____

_____

Infectious Disease/AIDS
and HBV Policy[1]

IMPORTANT: *This is a sample form, not intended to be reproduced.*
Adapt to your specific needs.

STATEMENT OF PURPOSE

We commit ourselves to being knowledgeable and informed about infectious diseases/AIDS (Acquired Immunodeficiency Syndrome) and HBV (Hepatitis B Virus), and to be a support network that is nonjudgmental, compassionate and Christ-centered, capable of providing spiritual and emotional support to those infected as well as affected family members and friends. While we do not condone the behaviors that sometimes result in AIDS, we know Jesus loves every individual and desires for all to come to Him in repentance. We believe we are assisting God's work in the person's life when we extend compassionate care to infected people. It could well be that our loving ministry to an HIV (Human Immunodeficiency Virus)-infected person is what will successfully communicate God's love to him or her.

MEDICAL FACTS ABOUT AIDS

Acquired Immunodeficiency Syndrome (AIDS) is a serious, life-threatening condition. The best scientific evidence indicates that AIDS is caused by a virus known as HIV (Human Immunodeficiency Virus), which is transmitted through exposure to infected blood or semen through sexual contact, injury, sharing of contaminated needles, or from an infected mother to child before or around the time of birth. Not every infant who tests positive is actually HIV infected. One-half to two-thirds will be completely free from evidence of infection by 18 months, after antibodies from the mother have dissipated from the infant's blood.

OUR RESPONSE

Any individual who has been diagnosed with any infectious disease and/or is HIV positive or has AIDS should be treated similarly to any other individual attending our church. In general, we will not reject or ostracize anyone who has an infectious disease, is HIV positive or has AIDS as long as that individual presents no real threat to the safety of others in the congregation (for example, open sores or inability to control bodily functions). Confidentiality regarding individuals who have infectious diseases or are HIV positive or have AIDS will be respected.

United States Public Health Service guidelines for infectious diseases will be followed for all individuals including infants and children in the nursery, Sunday School and day/after-school care. Nursery and children's workers and other appropriate groups will be trained accordingly, using universal precautions.

"Universal precautions" refers to the handling of body fluids from all students and not just those known to be infected with a blood-borne pathogen.

Universal precautions require the use of protective barriers such as gloves, protective eye-wear, gowns and masks. Precautions beyond the use of gloves would only be required in unusual circumstances in the school setting. Gloves do not, however, prevent possible exposure due to penetrating injuries from needles or sharp instruments.

The AIDS Committee

A standing AIDS Committee will be established to help anyone in our congregation who is HIV positive. The committee will assess how the church can be most supportive of the person/family and will administer the guidelines of this policy to ensure that the patient's church experience is as good as the experience of any other church attender.

The specific duties of the committee include the following:
1. When a person identifies him- or herself or his or her child as HIV positive to anyone in the congregation, the person should be told about the AIDS Committee and encouraged to contact the chairman. The chairman will arrange for one or more committee members to visit with the person or family and assess the needs and desires of the patient.
2. One member, preferably a health-care professional, will volunteer to receive calls from anyone in the congregation who has a question or concern about AIDS. The person's phone number will be published in appropriate church publications.
3. The committee will meet on a case-by-case basis to talk to and help any family bringing an infected child to church. The committee or its representative will convey the goals of the church and initiate the procedures adopted for infected children.

Each case will be examined individually and flexibility will be maintained. The child's physician, parents or guardian, and the AIDS Committee will decide how to bring such a child to church.

While these decisions are being made, an adult will be assigned to personally minister to and monitor the HIV-infected child.

Toddlers and infants with HIV infection will be integrated slowly into the classroom. The child will begin in a playpen and an assigned monitor will stay with the child at all times. This monitor might initially be a doctor or nurse who would care for the child, keep the child's toys away from others and change diapers. Later the monitor could be any responsible adult. (The close observation is not necessary to prevent transfer of HIV disease but to alleviate the anxieties of other parents.) Play outside the playpen and full integration into the class will depend on the child's behavior and the sentiment of the parents of the other children.

Infants through sixth graders who are infected will be identified to the parents of the other children in the Sunday School class and to the Sunday School teachers. The AIDS Committee will be in charge of a concentrated communication and education effort with the desired effect of reducing anxieties and providing a quality church environment for the HIV-infected child. If the anxiety of the other parents and children is so high that the infected child is in danger of being ostracized, the committee will find at least two people who can play with the infected child, teach the Sunday School lesson and serve him or her in every need.

EDUCATION FOR THE CONGREGATION

According to the most recent research data from the Centers for Disease Control, "No documented cases of HIV infection have been traced to casual contact." Since knowledge can dispel fear and set the groundwork for compassionate understanding, we shall commit to educating the church regarding infectious diseases and HIV-related issues.

Protective Measures

The best way to prevent the spread of blood-transmitted infections such as HIV is to utilize universal precautions, which means the blood of everyone is considered potentially infectious. Since the vast majority of people who have HIV are unaware of their infection, the greatest danger is exposure to the blood of an infected child or adult who is assumed to be uninfected. Therefore, all blood spills will be handled with caution.

Latex examination gloves will be worn when contact is anticipated with blood, open sores, cuts or the inside of a person's mouth. Gloves will also be used when handling objects that are contaminated with blood. Children's workers with open sores on the hand will wear gloves. Open sores elsewhere on the body will be covered with an adequately sized bandage.

Gloves will be readily available throughout the church. They will be stored in the nursery, in children's Sunday School rooms, in the kitchen and on the playground.

Since HIV is destroyed by household bleach, a solution of one part bleach to 10 parts water will be kept in the first-aid cabinet. The bleach solution will be stored at room temperature in closed, opaque plastic containers and made fresh at the beginning of each session. Small blood spills will be cleaned while wearing gloves, using disposable paper towels moistened with the bleach solution. If a large spill of blood occurs, the area will be cleaned with disposable paper towels or linens while wearing gloves. The bleach solution will then be poured over the area and the area cleaned again.

PARENTAL RELEASE FORM FOR HIV-POSITIVE CHILD

As a parent of _____,
I do give my consent for a bona fide need-to-know person to be informed that my child is HIV positive so that he or she can be attended to in case of emergency.

_____

Signed

Note
1. Adapted from Sheryl Haystead, ed., *Nursery Smart Pages* (Ventura, CA: Gospel Light, 1997), pp. 45-47.

Church Office Notification Injury Report

Name, age and gender of child who was injured:

_____

Address _____

City _____

Zip _____

Name of Parents _____

Phone _____ Date and Time of Accident _____

Describe in detail how the child was injured, including location, names and actions of all children and adults involved.

_____

_____

_____

Describe the child's injuries and what action was taken to treat the injuries.

_____

_____

How and when was the parent notified?

_____

List names and phone numbers of witnesses to the accident.

1. _____

2. _____

3. _____

Additional Comments _____

_____

_____

_____

_____

Your Name, Address and Phone Number

_____

_____

Note:
Adapted from Sheryl Haystead, ed., *Nursery Smart Pages* (Ventura, CA: Gospel Light, 1997), p. 50.

Child and Youth Safety Policy

IMPORTANT: *This is a sample form, not intended to be reproduced.*
Adapt to your specific needs.

We desire to protect and support those who work with our youth and children. These policies to prevent child abuse, neglect or any unfounded allegations against workers or teachers address three major areas:

1. Worker selection
2. Worker practices
3. Reporting obligation

SELECTING YOUTH AND CHILDREN'S WORKERS

- All paid employees, full or part-time, including clergy, and all volunteer children and youth workers should complete a "Volunteer Application Form."
- A personal interview will be included as part of the selection process.
- Where circumstances merit, personal references listed in the application will be checked to further determine the suitability and character of the applicant. The reference check shall be documented.
- All workers with youth or children should normally be members of First Church or have been attending First Church for a minimum of six months.

SAFETY POLICIES FOR YOUTH MINISTRIES

- Volunteers and other workers are encouraged to be in public areas where both the youth and teacher are visible to other people.
- All drivers transporting youth on out-of-town activities shall be a minimum age of 25 and maximum age of 65 and shall complete and have approved a "Driver Form."
- The desirable minimum age for all drivers for in-town activities is 25. No one under age 18 will be permitted to drive for any church-sponsored activity.
- Youth workers should not provide transportation to and from church on a regular basis.
- For overnight outings and camps, whenever both genders are present as participants, both genders need to be present in leadership.
- For outdoor activities, participants are to be in groups of at least three.
- Counseling of youth is to be by a leader of the same gender and is to be done in public areas where both the youth and leader are visible to other people.

SAFETY POLICIES FOR CHILDREN'S MINISTRIES

- Each group of children should have at least two workers who are not related to each other, at least one being an adult, present at all times.
- For children, infant through kindergarten age, the desirable ratio is one worker for every five children. For grades one through five, the desirable ratio is one worker for each eight children.
- Window blinds and doors are to be kept open (or doors should have windows). A supervisor or designated adult representative will circulate where children's activities are occurring.
- When taking children to the rest room, workers should supervise children of the same gender. The worker should stay out of the rest room at the open door until the child is finished in the stall. Workers enter to assist only when necessary.
- All drivers transporting children on out-of-town activities shall be a minimum age of 25 and maximum age of 65 and shall complete and have approved a "Driver Form."
- In the nursery, diapers are to be changed only in designated areas and in the presence of other caregivers.

REPORTING OBLIGATION AND PROCEDURE

1. All caregivers are to be familiar with the definitions of child abuse (see below).
2. If a caregiver suspects that a child in the nursery has been abused, the following steps are to be followed:
   - Report the suspected abuse to your supervisor.
   - Do not interview the child regarding the suspected abuse. The interview process will be handled by trained personnel.
   - Do not discuss the suspected abuse. It is important that all information about the suspected child abuse (victim and abuser) be kept confidential.
3. Caregivers reporting suspected child abuse will be asked to complete the Suspected Child Abuse Report (available from your state's Department of Social Services). Confidentiality will be maintained where possible. This report must be completed within 24 hours.
4. Once a suspected child abuse case has been reported by a caregiver to a supervisor, it will be reported to the designated reporting agency.

DEFINITIONS OF CHILD ABUSE

Defined by The National Committee for Prevention of Child Abuse

Physical Abuse

Nonaccidental injury, which may include beatings, violent shaking, human bites, strangulation, suffocation, poisoning, or burns. The results may be bruises and welts, broken bones, scars, permanent disfigurement, long-lasting psychological damage, serious internal injuries, brain damage, or death.

Neglect

The failure to provide a child with basic needs, including food, clothing, education, shelter, and medical care; also abandonment and inadequate supervision.

Sexual Abuse

The sexual exploitation of a child by an older person, as in rape, incest, fondling of the genitals, exhibitionism, or pornography. It may be done for the sexual gratification of the older person, out of a need for power, or for economic reasons.

Note
Adapted from Sheryl Haystead, ed., *Nursery Smart Pages* (Ventura, CA: Gospel Light, 1997), p. 52.

Safety Policy Introductory Letter

IMPORTANT: *This is a sample form, not intended to be reproduced.*
Adapt to your specific needs.

(Date)
(Church Name)
(Address)
(Phone Number)

Dear _____ (name) _____ ,

Here at First Church we believe that having a well-thought-out Child and Youth Safety Policy is part of the wisdom to which Christ calls us. We are aware that even with such a policy in place, we remain dependent on Christ and His ultimate protection. However, this policy will give us confidence that our children and youth will have a safe environment in which to learn and grow in their Christian faith.

We are asking that anyone in the children's and youth ministries complete the required forms and attend a training session about the Child and Youth Safety Policy. The next training session is scheduled on (date). We thank you for your help and cooperation in advance.

Our efforts in this area are a bit like a CPR class. You never expect to have a problem, yet you take all the precautions you possibly can. You train in order to know how to respond if there is a situation calling for action, believing and praying that it will not be needed.

Thank you for caring about children and youth and helping them grow in the nurture and admonition of the Lord.

Sincerely,

_____

(name)

_____

Pastor

Teacher to Student Ratios for Early Childhood

Use the following chart as a guide to the number of teachers and helpers to provide in the early childhood division. Limiting the maximum number of students in each room is especially important. Classes or departments that are too large require multiple learning activities, and children can be overwhelmed by the number of choices and by the other children. Recent studies have shown that stress levels increase when more than the recommended numbers of children are present in one room. (If your rooms are large enough for more than the recommended number of students, use portable dividers to create smaller spaces.)

Some churches find themselves temporarily unable to

Ages	Teacher to student ratio	Maximum number of students per room*
Birth to 1 year	1 to 2 or 3	10 to 12
1 to 2 1/2 years	1 to 3 or 4	12 to 15
2 1/2 to 3 years	1 to 5	16 to 20
4 to 5 years	1 to 6	20 to 24
Kindergarten	1 to 6	20 to 24

*See chapter 9 for suggested room sizes.

achieve the recommended ratios. While continually striving to recruit teachers as needed, here are some tips for making the best of a less than ideal situation:

- Keep doors between classrooms and doors to hallways open (blocked by a child safety gate or Dutch door if needed) so that teachers can rely on teachers of nearby classrooms should an emergency occur. Open doors (or doors with windows) are always a good idea so that teachers may be observed at all times and thus prevent false accusations of improper teacher behavior;
- Ask parents to take turns serving as helpers in their children's classrooms;
- Ask members of an adult Sunday School class to take turns assisting the regular teacher in a class;
- Recruit one person who will rove between two or three classrooms, assisting as needed.

Resist the temptation to recruit teenagers to teach or help on a regular basis in Sunday School. It is best for students of this age to participate in and benefit from the teaching provided at their own age level. Often, however, teens are a great source of help for second-hour or weekday programs. Offer training classes for teen helpers.

What's the best way to move preschool children from one class to the next? In order to accommodate the rapidly changing skills and abilities of preschool children, one class or department in your church needs to be designated as a "holding" class or department, where children are received from a younger group more than once a year but are promoted up to the next older group at one time. As a general rule of thumb, a two-year-old class or department works best as the holding level, since the nature of twos requires very flexible procedures and schedule. The holding department requires a very adaptable staff since this group may be very small at the start of the year; then it may potentially grow dramatically as children continue to be promoted into this class or department throughout the year. It is best not to promote children to the holding class or department on their birthdays, but to have periodic promotion days when all those who have reached a designated age (or developmental milestone such as crawling, walking, etc.) are moved to the next class or department as a group.

What's the best way to move (or promote) children from one class to the next?
Students move from one class to the next as a group at the start of the school year (or another time of year designated by your church policy).

Designate a specific Sunday as "Promotion" or "Graduation Sunday." On that Sunday, students begin class with their current teachers and at an announced time are escorted to their new classes for a get-acquainted time with their new teachers. Another option is for students to simply attend their new classes on Promotion Sunday. Whichever option you choose, be sure to send information ahead of time to parents and children specifying the date of Promotion Sunday and the teachers' names and locations of all classes.

Occasionally, parents will request that their children be moved ahead to an older class before Promotion Sunday. While occasionally a very small church may be able to accommodate the parents' request, it is usually best to keep students in their appropriate grade-level class. Discuss with the parents and teachers how the student's needs and interests can be met in the classroom.

Teacher to Student Ratios for Children

Use the following chart as a guide to the number of teachers and helpers to provide in the children's division. One- or two-grade groups are easiest for the average teacher to guide; mixing three or more grades together calls for highly skilled teachers. It is generally not necessary to have separate classes for boys and girls, especially in the younger grades.

Limiting the maximum number of students in each room is especially important. In classes or departments that are too large, children are distracted by too many children to interact with, and teachers find their time is focused more on giving directions rather than the teaching. (If your rooms are large enough for more than the recommended number of students, use portable dividers to create smaller spaces.)

Some churches find themselves temporarily unable to

Grades	Teacher to student ratio	Maximum number of students per room*
1 to 5 or 6	1 to 6 or 8	24 to 30

*See chapter 9 for suggested room sizes.

achieve the recommended ratios. While continually striving to recruit teachers as needed, here are some tips for making the best of a less than ideal situation:

- Keep doors between classrooms and doors to hallways open so that teachers can rely on teachers of nearby classrooms should an emergency occur. Open doors are always a good idea so that teachers may be observed at all times and thus prevent false accusations of improper teacher behavior;
- Ask parents to take turns serving as helpers in their children's classrooms;
- Ask members of an adult Sunday School class to take turns assisting the regular teacher in a class;
- Recruit one person who will rove between two or three classrooms, assisting as needed.

Resist the temptation to recruit teenagers to teach or help on a regular basis in Sunday School. It is best for students of this age to participate in and benefit from the teaching provided at their own age level. Often, however, teens are a great source of help for second-hour or weekday programs. Offer training classes for teen helpers.

Teacher to Student Ratios for Youth

Use the following chart as a guide to the number of teachers and helpers to provide in the youth division:

Grades	Teacher to student ratio	Maximum number of students per room*
7 to 12	1 to 8	30 to 40

*See chapter 9 for suggested room sizes.

The vast difference between seventh and twelfth graders mentally, socially and emotionally makes two groups advisable in the youth division. Depending on the size of your church, you may want to group students in a variety of ways. Here are some options:

YOUTH GROUPING OPTIONS

Option A	Option B	Option C	Option D	Option E
Grades 7-9	Grades 7-8	Grades 7-8	Grades 7-8	Grade 7
				Grade 8
	Grades 9-10	Grade 9	Grade 9	Grade 9
Grades 10-12		Grade 10-12	Grade 10	Grade 10
	Grades 11-12		Grades 11-12	Grade 11
				Grade 12

Keep in mind the division of grades in your school system as you form groups and classes. It is best to follow the age-level divisions of the majority of schools in your community. Remember, though, that teens enjoy meeting others and feeling a part of a larger group, so even if you have Sunday School classes formed by grade, you should provide activities for all of your junior highers and senior highers to come together and develop a sense of identity as part of the larger group.

Should We Ever Form All-Male or All-Female Classes?

Educators wrestle with the pros and cons of grouping students into single-gender or coed groups. Most youth teachers agree, however, that while time for learning and discussing spiritual concepts in single-gender groups is essential for spiritual growth to take place, teens need opportunities for both kinds of interaction if they are to build wholesome Christian social relationships. A good youth program will provide these opportunities regularly.

Teacher to Student Ratios for Adults

Use the following chart as a guide to the number of classes to provide in the adult division. The optimum size for an adult class is no more than 30 to 40 in attendance with up to five small groups in each class.

Ages	Teacher to student ratio	Maximum number of students per room*
18+	1 to 8	30 to 40

(**Note:** See chapter 9 for suggested room sizes.)
*Number indicates suggested ratio for small groups formed within an adult class.

AGE GROUPINGS

Age-grouped classes should be formed with a generally recognized age range, rather than specific age limits.

There are two basic plans for grouping adults: by age or by interest. Both plans have a variety of pros and cons.

Pros	Cons
Adults of the same general age have similar needs and lifestyles.	Small churches may have limited numbers of adults in a certain age range.
Teaching is more effective and social interaction is easier.	Participants do not gain the benefit of hearing about the experiences of adults in other age groups.
Age grouping helps build stability of relationships.	Class members are not able to choose from several topics of study (except in a very large church where there is more than one class for each age level).
Age grouping is easily understood by the participants—everyone has an age and visitors can therefore immediately determine what class to visit and join. (A married couple of different individual ages can choose which of the two groups they would rather be in.) Inactive adults can be more easily guided into a group.	
Age grouping makes it easy to develop and administer an adult division because new classes are not being formed on a regular basis. Follow-up is easier to coordinate.	

Participants do not usually "graduate" between groups, but rather a group matures together. New classes are formed as class size increases—subdividing a class into two new classes. Because **college-age adults** (ages 18 to 25) have unique characteristics and needs, it is advantageous to have a separate class for them. While students and nonstudents often work well in a "college/career" class, when seeking to reach college students living away from home, it is usually best to have a group that focuses on students and another for nonstudents. **Single adults** are often helped by having a class specifically for them.

If you have never formed groups based on age, the easiest way to determine the class groups needed is to take an anonymous age poll. Give the adults in your congregation 3x5-inch cards on which to record their age and marital status. Collect the cards and use the information to determine what age groupings will give you the correct size classes.

If classes are formed by ages, consider the following divisions:

Young Adults	18 to 35 years
Middle-aged Adults	36 to 59 years
Older Adults	60+

INTEREST GROUPINGS/ELECTIVES

Form classes based on topics of study.

Pros	Cons
Some adults are more likely to attend a class in which the topic is one they are interested in and have chosen to learn about.	Long-term relationships among class participants are difficult to build and maintain because the class structure is always changing.
Participants benefit from interaction with adults of all ages.	Follow-up of inactive adults takes additional work and participants may get "lost in the shuffle" between electives.
Beginning a class on a new topic creates interest and may motivate inactive adults to begin attending a class.	Administration is time consuming and often confusing because electives may vary in length and size according to the nature of the topic.

Look to the Future

Duplicate and complete the "Organization" worksheet (p. 127) to determine how you can begin working to meet the goals stated in this chapter.

A combination of age level and elective classes provides the opportunity to gain the benefits of both structures while minimizing the weaknesses of each. In this case, electives should usually be offered to fill recognized needs not being met by the ongoing classes.

Care Groups

Whatever structure you choose, offer opportunities for all adults to participate in small "care" groups. Care groups may be organized within each adult Sunday School class or as a part of the overall adult ministry offered in your church. Care groups (often called by other names such as home Bible study groups, covenant groups, family, discipleship, cell or shepherding groups) are small groups of people meeting together for support and encouragement as they explore what it means to love God and follow scriptural principles in everyday life. Meaningful relationships can best be built in small groups with six to eight participants, or five to six couples with one individual or couple serving as a teacher.

A strong care group ministry in your church provides the following benefits:

- Care groups are excellent ways of integrating new believers into the church;
- Care groups help participants be discipled and benefit the congregation as a whole;
- Care groups provide a practical way in which scriptural commands about meeting each other's needs can be met (see Romans 12:10,13,15; Galatians 6:2; James 5:16).

Some church teachers are so convinced of the value of these small groups that they encourage their development in place of adult Sunday School classes. However, a balanced adult ministry takes a "both" approach instead of an "either/or." Small groups that are linked to adult classes have greater opportunity to expand participants' circle of contacts. The larger class also provides a ready pool of potential small-group teachers and a built-in structure for nurturing growth.

Organization

Rate your church's progress toward each goal and then list two or more actions you can take to reach each goal.

GOAL 1: REALISTIC TEACHER SUPERVISION

Your Sunday School is organized so that each teacher is responsible for supervising no more than five to eight teachers and helpers.

1	2	3	4	5
Need to Start		Fair		Goal Achieved

Actions to Take:

GOAL 2: FORM AGE-LEVEL DIVISIONS

In order to efficiently recruit, train and supervise teachers, your Sunday School is divided into the following age-level divisions: Early Childhood (birth to kindergarten); Children (grades 1 to 5/6); Youth (grades 6/7 to 12); Adult (18 years and up).

1	2	3	4	5
Need to Start		Fair		Goal Achieved

Actions to Take:

GOAL 3: APPROPRIATE TEACHER/STUDENT RATIOS

Each class or department has a number of students and teachers that makes discovery learning and the development of relationships among students and teachers possible.

1	2	3	4	5
Need to Start		Fair		Goal Achieved

Actions to Take:

GOAL 4: DEVELOP A SAFETY POLICY

A written child and youth safety policy is provided to all teachers and its guidelines are followed to ensure child and youth safety and to protect church workers.

1	2	3	4	5
Need to Start		Fair		Goal Achieved

Actions to Take:

Chapter Six

Job Descriptions Do Make a Difference

Staff members who have clear job descriptions to follow and who feel encouraged by their fellow staff members will develop a love for their jobs.

What This Chapter Tells You

- Written up-to-date job descriptions not only help you make sure the jobs are getting done but also make your teaching ministries run smoothly.
- Creating a sense of community among staff members helps them enjoy their jobs as they serve together.

What This Chapter Shows You

- How to write and evaluate job descriptions;
- Sample job descriptions you can adapt;
- Practical ideas for building teaching teams who care about and support each other.

Where Do I Start?

A Word from the Wise

"Two are better than one, because they have a good return for their work: If one falls down, his friend can help him up. But pity the man who falls and has no one to help him up!"
King Solomon,
Ecclesiastes 4:9,10

Look at Where You Are

Duplicate and complete the "Job Descriptions and Teamwork" worksheet (p. 131) to take a closer look at how the teaching teams in your church function.

Wake-Up Call

A new Christian education director once confessed that after several months in her job, she noticed that people were starting to avoid her—not only at church but even in the grocery store! It was then she realized that something had to be done. Teaching Sunday School had become such a drudgery for the teachers in her church that only the most dedicated teachers wanted to be part of the team.

The solution includes better recruiting and training (see chapter 7); improved understanding of what teaching is all about (see chapter 4); and a vision that will help teachers clearly understand what's expected of them and encourage them to connect with each other in meaningful ways (that's what this chapter is about, so keep reading).

Get the Big Picture

Each teacher or helper must understand his or her responsibilities as part of a teaching team that serves together and grows together as fellow believers. As in any organization, the Sunday School staff must learn to work together as a smoothly functioning team. When team members don't know what their jobs are or are confused about what they are doing, teachers and students alike often find participation in the program disheartening.

Developing this sense of teamwork can make all the difference in your Sunday School. When the right people are doing the right jobs with the right attitudes toward each other, the goals and purposes of your Sunday School are more likely to be met. Here's what can happen:

- Clearly written job descriptions help everyone know who's doing what and allow the Sunday School to run more smoothly;
- Students (of all ages!) benefit from being taught by teachers who are well prepared and work as a team to support one another;
- Leaders, teachers and helpers look forward to fulfilling their assignments and feel a sense of accomplishment from their work.

Job Descriptions and Teamwork

1. Are there written job descriptions for each leader, teacher and helper? If not, which job descriptions are missing?

2. When was the last time all job descriptions were updated? How are the descriptions communicated to each leader, teacher or helper?

3. How would you rate the level of satisfaction among your team members?

4. How do team members show support for one another?

Focus on the Goals

✔ Action Checklist

- ❑ If no job descriptions are available, ask current staff members (leaders, teachers and helpers) to give you a list of what they do: in a letter, E-mail or even through a quick telephone interview.
- ❑ If job descriptions have not been updated recently, ask staff members to make written notes about suggested changes on the description.
- ❑ Give job descriptions to prospective staff members that outline exactly what a particular job involves and describe the support they will receive.
- ❑ Distribute job descriptions at the beginning of each person's teaching term as a way of making sure job expectations are understood.
- ❑ Ask staff members to read job descriptions at the end of their terms and to note areas in which they feel more training and/or support is needed.
- ❑ If you have a rotating staff, post the job descriptions in the classrooms.
- ❑ Make sure substitutes receive copies of the appropriate job descriptions.

See specific job descriptions in the age-level portion of this chapter: Early Childhood (pp. 136-141); Children (pp. 142-147); Youth (pp. 148-152); Adult (pp. 153-154).

GOAL 1: A PERSON FOR EVERY JOB AND A JOB DESCRIPTION FOR EVERY PERSON

Everyone on the Sunday School staff must be provided with a current, written job description.

Management experts agree that in order for people to be accountable for assignments, a supervisor must explain exactly what is expected in a job and the time frame in which the job is to be completed.

Most people are motivated by a desire to achieve and will respond favorably to clear and reasonable job expectations; Sunday School leaders, teachers and helpers are no exception. How will your teaching team know what is expected of them unless you communicate this information to them? In addition to being a good personnel practice, putting your expectations in writing:

- Saves you from repeating yourself when sharing with new staff members;
- Allows both you and staff members to refer back to a written standard as needed;
- Guarantees that the same standards are applied to all similar positions;
- Helps you discover possible conflicts among jobs (for example, two people responsible for the same job or a job for which no one is responsible).

A detailed job description increases the likelihood that a new volunteer will have a positive experience in his or her job. Each job description should follow the same basic format: job title; length of service (usually no more than a year at a time); name of supervisor; general description of the job (one to three sentences); specific responsibilities of the job (include times, locations, etc.); and the date the job description was revised. To be truly helpful, a job description will list the specific tasks expected and describe what a person needs to believe, know about and be able to do in order to be successful at the job. If time and money commitments are expected, these should also be included in the job description.

Many churches have found that a job description can also be a tool for encouraging a staff member when it specifies what support the staff member will receive (including a description of curriculum and materials provided, training opportunities, etc.).

GOAL 2:
CREATE A FEELING OF TEAMWORK

It's important to build teaching teams that not only enjoy serving together but give support and encouragement to each other as well.

The teaching team that truly enjoys being together and counts each other as supportive friends is a team that will experience a sense of accomplishment in their ministry. These team members are also likely to continue their terms of service! (Read chapter 7 for more on recruiting.) Some churches encourage teaching teams to function as a small group which meets together not only to prepare for teaching but also for worship and prayer.

While there is no way to know in advance how staff members will work together on a teaching team, it is a good idea to give some thought to whom you ask to serve together. For example, when you are recruiting staff members, look for people who already know each other and who enjoy each other's company. Prospective teachers often will respond positively to the idea of serving with a friend, and you have some measure of assurance that they will find it easy to work together.

Larger churches that have several teachers in one class or program may find it easier to assign people to a team; smaller churches may need to prepare teaching assignments a bit more carefully.

In either small or large churches, however, Sunday School coordinators or Christian education directors can find ways to build relationships among their teachers, helping them to feel they are gaining as well as receiving from their teaching ministry.

Look to the Future

Duplicate and complete the "Job Descriptions and Teamwork" worksheet (p. 155) to determine how you can begin working to meet the goals stated in this chapter.

Bonus Ideas for Building Teamwork: At a department teachers' meeting, each person writes his or her name and a prayer request or two on a slip of paper. We put the papers in a basket. Each person chooses a paper and promises to pray for the person for the next month until our next meeting. At the next meeting, we invite everyone to tell about their answers to prayer. *Elsa Barber, Central Church, Memphis, Tennessee*

Regularly send handwritten notes to staff members highlighting a specific way in which they have contributed to the Sunday School. Keep a record of these highlights and once a quarter or so write an article for a church newsletter thanking these staff members for their good work. *Hailey Armoogan, Waterloo Pentecostal Assembly, Waterloo, Ontario, Canada*

We took our staff on a high ropes course/adventure retreat at which teamwork and dependency upon each other was stressed. This kind of event built incredibly good relationships by placing the staff outside their normal daily activity. *Henry Kim, Hana Presbyterian Church, Glendale, California*

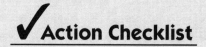

✔ Action Checklist

❏ When you introduce a new team of teachers to each other, identify occupations, hobbies or family situations they may have in common (for example, teachers who have preschool children or who enjoy gardening).

❏ Invite one or two members of a teaching team who may not be well acquainted to join with you for a cup of coffee or a dessert before they begin teaching together.

❏ Encourage team members to get together once a month or once a quarter "just for fun." Teachers with family members can meet at the park for a picnic or join together in a potluck spaghetti dinner. In a small church, get-togethers such as these can be planned for all teachers together. In larger churches, department leaders can coordinate department get-togethers.

❏ Encourage teachers to exchange prayer requests. Give teachers prayer request forms to exchange with each other; consider displaying a white board in your teacher supply room on which they can write prayer requests; include prayer requests in a monthly teacher newsletter.

❏ At planning or training meetings, lead your staff in one or more activities which are designed to build relationships among the staff: pair up staff members and see how many words they can make from the letters in their combined names within three minutes; invite each person to write "two truths and a tale" about themselves, and then have them read aloud for others to guess who is being described and what's true and what's not.

❏ Look for opportunities to mention specific ways in which you see workers functioning together as a supportive team. Compliment them publicly!

❏ At the end of a leader's or teacher's term, don't assume they will wish to continue on the same teaching team. Give each team member the opportunity to change age levels, classes, jobs, etc. ("Jean, you and Lois have made a great teaching team this year. I'm hoping you'll continue together next year, but if you'd like a change or a new opportunity, please let me know.")

Bonus Ideas for Building Teamwork: We build teamwork among our Sunday School teachers and other youth program leaders in several ways. Once or twice a year we schedule an all-day retreat to which leaders and teachers of all programs are invited. We also try to encourage everyone to meet together once a week to pray. One of the best ways to build teamwork is to ask three teachers to work together on an assignment for a Sunday School lesson or a youth group activity. *Tom Stephen, Eastminster Presbyterian Church, Ventura, California*

Each year we hold a teambuilder event for our teachers, usually early in the fall. We divide the group into teams based on the age group they teach. Then we challenge each team to build a capsule that will protect an egg when dropped from a height of about 20 feet. They must use the following materials: one sheet of cardstock, a balloon, six feet of yarn, one three-foot strip of cellophane tape, one spool of thread, four paper clips and one sheet of newspaper. The teams have 20 minutes to design and build their capsules, and everyone must contribute an idea to the project. After the project, we discuss how they worked as teams, how the eggs represent the students we impact and how our goal is to build tools around the students to help them withstand the hard knocks of life. *Wayne Robey, Southern Gables Evangelical Free Church, Littleton, Colorado*

Sunday School Coordinator/Director

> **Note:** A church with one or more age-level coordinators may assign some of these responsibilities to those leaders. This leadership role then becomes more one of coordination, encouragement and support.

Task: To guide planning and development of a program of Bible learning for all age levels

Term: One year, beginning in September

Supervisor _____ (name)

RESPONSIBILITIES

- Recruit leaders, teachers and helpers for all Sunday School departments.
- Plan and coordinate a regular program of training for all Sunday School staff.
- Observe, evaluate and affirm leaders, teachers and helpers in order to note strengths to encourage and areas where improvement is possible.
- Pray regularly for Sunday School staff.
- Coordinate regular planning meetings for team members that include training and opportunities for spiritual growth.
- Oversee the purchase, distribution and use of all equipment and supplies (curriculum, snacks, art supplies, etc.).
- Communicate the church's approved safety policy to all Sunday School staff, regularly evaluate its use and take necessary steps to put the policy into practice.
- Lead in planning a Sunday School staff get-together at least twice a year in order to build a sense of teamwork among all teachers.
- Express appreciation to the Sunday School staff, including an end-of-the-year event.
- Communicate with church leaders and the congregation regarding the purpose, value and procedures of Sunday School.
- Communicate regularly with leaders of related programs (weekday preschool, second-hour coordinator, etc.).

Note: This position may be held by a volunteer or paid staff person. In a small church, one or more of these tasks may be the responsibility of the pastor, Christian education committee member, children's ministries elder, etc. (See chapter 10 for the job description for the Sunday School Outreach Coordinator.)

Nursery Staff

COORDINATOR

Task: To recruit and schedule caregivers, overseeing their training and the nursery environment

Term: One year, beginning September 1

Supervisor _____ (name)

Responsibilities

- Recruit the following positions:
  Caregivers (use the screening procedures established by our church)
  Supply Coordinator
  Snack Coordinator
  Greeters
- Post and distribute caregiving schedules.
- Distribute parent and staff newsletters each month.
- Plan at least one training event for teachers.
- Develop a budget for one year.
- Update and distribute *Nursery Handbook*.
- Communicate regularly with supervisor.

CAREGIVER/TEACHER

Task: To lovingly care for babies and toddlers

Term: Six months, September through February or March through August

Supervisor _____ (name)

Responsibilities

- Be present in the nursery from 10:45 A.M. until 12:15 P.M. each Sunday morning.
- Upon arriving, quickly scan the room for safety hazards and remove any potential problem items (broken toys, coffee cups, etc.).
- Provide physical and emotional care for children.
- Engage children in the learning activities suggested in the newsletter.
- Follow guidelines for diapering, feeding and caring for children as described in the *Nursery Handbook*.
- Attend at least one training event prior to term of service.
- Communicate regularly with supervisor.

Nursery Staff

SUPPLY COORDINATOR

Task: To purchase and distribute nursery supplies
Term: One year, beginning September 1
Supervisor _____ (name) _____

Responsibilities

- Inventory and purchase needed supplies (obtain approval from Nursery Coordinator for purchases over $25).
- Turn in receipts to church for reimbursement.
- Keep records of all purchases.
- Help determine nursery budget.
- **Supply List**
  - Snacks: crackers and juice (label with date of purchase and store on nursery shelves)
  - Diapering: baby wipes, disposable gloves, hand soap, diapers, changing-table covers
  - Cleaning: trash-can liners, bleach, sponges, paper towels
  - Miscellaneous items: crib sheets, blankets, toys

GREETER

Task: To greet families and check in children as they arrive in the nursery
Term: Six months, September through February or March through August
Supervisor _____ (name) _____

Responsibilities

- Be present in the nursery from 9:30 A.M. until 10:00 A.M. each Sunday morning.
- Put out a new check-in form each Sunday. Place previous check-in form into the Attendance Form box in the reception office.
- Assist parent(s) as needed to check in (following the procedures described in our *Nursery Handbook*).
- Offer a friendly greeting to each family.
- Be alert for symptoms of illness. Do not admit babies with signs of illness, such as a cold or fever.
- Encourage parents and older children to stay outside of nursery area.
- Pay special attention to visitors, giving them *Nursery Handbook* and name tags, and providing directions to adult programs.
- Communicate regularly with supervisor.

Early Childhood
(Ages 2¹/₂ to Kindergarten)

SUNDAY SCHOOL COORDINATOR

Task: To plan and develop a program of Bible learning through loving adult care, Bible stories and Bible learning activities for preschool children each Sunday morning

Term: One year, beginning September 1

Supervisor _____ (name)

Responsibilities

- Recruit leaders, teachers and helpers for all Sunday School classes.
- Plan and lead a regular program of training for all Sunday School staff.
- Observe, evaluate and affirm teachers in order to note strengths to encourage and areas where improvement is possible.
- Pray regularly for Sunday School leaders, teachers and helpers.
- Lead regular planning meetings for teachers and helpers that include training and opportunities for spiritual growth.
- Oversee the purchase, distribution and use of all equipment and supplies (curriculum, snacks, art supplies, etc.).
- Communicate the church's approved safety policy to all Sunday School staff, regularly evaluate its use and take necessary steps to put the policy into practice.
- Plan a Sunday School staff get-together at least twice a year in order to build a sense of teamwork among all teachers.
- Express appreciation to the Sunday School staff, including an end-of-the-year event.
- Communicate with parents regarding the purpose, value and procedures of Sunday School.
- Communicate regularly with supervisor and teachers of related programs (weekday preschool, second-hour coordinator, etc.).

Note: This position may be held by a volunteer or paid staff person. In a small church, one or more of these tasks may be the responsibility of the supervisor (Christian education committee member, children's ministries elder, etc.).

Early Childhood

DEPARTMENT LEADER

Task: To prayerfully build relationships with both teachers and children in order to ensure effective Bible learning

Term: One year, beginning September 1

Supervisor _____ (name) _____

Responsibilities

* Coordinate teacher tasks, including use of supplies and room setup.
* Greet children as they arrive and guide them to an activity.
* Assist teachers as needed (discipline, activity completion, etc.), maintaining the time schedule for the session.
* Observe, evaluate and affirm teachers, noting strengths to be encouraged and areas to be improved.
* Lead the large-group learning time, involving other teachers as appropriate.
* Pray regularly for others on the teaching team.
* Work with your supervisor to identify and enlist qualified people to join your teaching team.
* Lead regular session planning meetings, including training and opportunities for spiritual growth.
* Plan a team get-together in order to build friendships among the team once a quarter.
* Communicate regularly with supervisor.

Note: In a class with just two teachers, the teacher responsibilities may be informally shared. When three or more people are on the team, one person should be designated as department leader.

Early Childhood

TEACHER

Task: To prayerfully build relationships with children in order to guide them in life-changing Bible learning

Term: One year, beginning September 1

Supervisor _____ (name)

Individual Responsibilities

- Maintain a personal relationship with Jesus Christ.
- Desire to grow in faith and commitment to God and participate in personal Bible study and prayer.
- Worship regularly with the church family.

Team Responsibilities

- Pray regularly for each child and others in your teaching team.
- Participate in scheduled teachers' meetings.
- Participate in at least one training event during the year to improve teaching skills.
- Express needs as a teacher to department leader or Sunday School coordinator.

Sunday Morning Responsibilities

- Arrange materials and room to create an effective learning environment.
- Greet each child upon arrival and involve him or her in conversation and meaningful activity.
- Model the love of Christ by getting to know children and sharing their concerns, needs and joys.
- Guide Bible learning by
  1. Being well prepared to use Bible stories, verses/passages, questions and comments appropriate to the age level in order to accomplish the lesson aims;
  2. Selecting a variety of Bible learning activities and encouraging each student to actively participate in each lesson;
  3. Participating with children in learning activities and in large-group times.

Student Follow-Up Responsibilities

- Follow up on visitors and absentees with mailings, phone calls and/or personal visits.
- Care for each class member with prayer, telephone calls, birthday cards, etc.
- Communicate individual student needs to parents.

Early Childhood

GREETER

Task: To greet families and check in children as they arrive for Sunday School

Term: Six months, September through February or March through August

Supervisor _____ (name)

Responsibilities

- Be present in the classroom from 9:30 A.M. until 10:00 A.M. each Sunday morning.
- Put out a new check-in form each Sunday. Place previous check-in form in the Attendance Form box in the reception office.
- Assist parent(s) as needed to check in.
- Offer a friendly greeting to each family, alerting families to any special announcements or procedural changes.
- Pay special attention to visitors. Get names and addresses, give name tags, direct children and parents to appropriate rooms, etc.
- Communicate regularly with supervisor.

FOOD COORDINATOR

Task: To oversee the provision of food (snacks, meals) when needed at Sunday School and related early childhood programs

Term: One year, beginning September 1

Supervisor _____ (name)

Responsibilities

- Determine the food needs for all early childhood programs, working with early childhood ministry leaders.
- Provide food through purchases and donations of money or food. If parents are asked to provide food, set up and oversee a schedule of donations.

Children's Ministry

SUNDAY SCHOOL COORDINATOR

Task: To plan and develop a program of Bible learning through loving adult care, Bible stories and learning activities for preschool children each Sunday morning

Term: One year, beginning September 1

Supervisor _____ (name) _____

Responsibilities

- Recruit leaders, teachers and helpers for all Sunday School classes.
- Plan and lead a regular program of training for all Sunday School staff.
- Observe, evaluate and affirm teachers in order to note strengths to encourage and areas where improvement is possible.
- Pray regularly for Sunday School leaders, teachers and helpers.
- Lead regular planning meetings for teachers that include training and opportunities for spiritual growth.
- Oversee the purchase, distribution and use of all equipment and supplies (curriculum, snacks, art supplies, etc.).
- Communicate the church's approved safety policy to all Sunday School staff, regularly evaluate its use and take necessary steps to put the policy into practice.
- Plan a Sunday School staff get-together at least twice a year in order to build a sense of teamwork among all teachers.
- Express appreciation to the Sunday School staff, including an end-of-the-year event.
- Communicate with parents regarding the purpose, value and procedures of Sunday School.
- Communicate regularly with supervisor and leaders of related programs (weekday preschool, second-hour coordinator, etc.).

Note: This position may be held by a volunteer or paid staff person. In a small church, one or more of these tasks may be the responsibility of the supervisor (Christian education committee member, children's ministries elder, etc.).

Children's Ministry

DEPARTMENT LEADER

Task: To prayerfully support and build relationships with both teachers and children in order to ensure effective Bible learning

Term: One year, beginning September 1

Supervisor _____ (name) _____

Responsibilities

- Coordinate teacher tasks, including use of supplies and room setup.
- Greet children as they arrive and guide them to an activity.
- Assist teachers as needed (discipline, activity completion, etc.), maintaining the time schedule for the session.
- Observe, evaluate and affirm teachers in order to note strengths to encourage and areas where improvement is possible.
- Lead the large group time (Bible study and/or worship), involving other teachers as appropriate.
- Pray regularly for others on the teaching team.
- Work with your supervisor to identify and enlist qualified people to join your teaching team.
- Lead regular session planning meetings, including training and opportunities for spiritual growth.
- Plan a team get-together in order to build friendships among the team once a quarter.
- Communicate regularly with supervisor.

Note: In a class with just two teachers, the leader responsibilities may be informally shared. When three or more people are on the team, one person should be designated as the Department Leader.

Children's Ministry

TEACHER

Task: To prayerfully build relationships with children and guide them in life-changing Bible learning

Term: One year, beginning September 1

Supervisor _____ (name) _____

Individual Responsibilities

- Maintain a personal relationship with Jesus Christ.
- Desire to grow in faith and commitment to God and participate in personal Bible study and prayer.
- Worship regularly with the church family.

Team Responsibilities

- Pray regularly for each child and others on your teaching team.
- Participate in scheduled teachers' meetings.
- Participate in at least one training event during the year to improve teaching skills.
- Express needs as a teacher to your supervisor.

Sunday Morning Responsibilities

- Arrange materials and room to create an effective learning environment.
- Greet each child upon arrival and involve him or her in conversation and meaningful activity.
- Model the love of Christ by getting to know children and sharing their concerns, needs and joys.
- Guide Bible learning by
  1. Being well prepared to use Bible stories, verses/passages, questions and comments appropriate to the age level in order to accomplish the lesson aims;
  2. Selecting a variety of Bible learning activities and encouraging each student to actively participate in each lesson;
  3. Participating with children in learning activities and in large-group times.

Student Follow-Up Responsibilities

- Follow up on visitors and absentees with mailings, phone calls and/or personal visits.
- Care for each class member with prayer, telephone calls, birthday cards, etc.
- Communicate individual student needs to parents.

Children's Ministry

GREETER

Task: To greet families and check in children as they arrive for Sunday School
Term: Six months, September through February or March through August
Supervisor _____ (name)

Responsibilities

- Be present in the classroom from 9:30 A.M. until 10:00 A.M. each Sunday morning.
- Put out a new check-in form each Sunday. Place previous check-in form into the Attendance Form box in the reception office.
- Assist parent(s) as needed to check in.
- Offer a friendly greeting to each family, alerting families to any special announcements or procedural changes.
- Pay special attention to visitors. Get names and addresses, give name tags, direct children and parents to appropriate rooms, etc.
- Communicate regularly with supervisor.

SUPPLY ROOM ORGANIZER

Task: To keep the supply room organized and ready for teacher use
Term: Six months, September through February or March through August
Supervisor _____ (name)

Responsibilities

- Once a week, check the supply room to clean up and sort donated materials and pick up supply requests from teachers.
- Purchase supplies as needed. Consult with Sunday School coordinator as needed. Turn in receipts to (name).
- Place supply requests for donated items in newsletter and/or bulletin as needed.
- Keep a current copy of appropriate supply and equipment catalogs.
- Update supply list twice a year, post list in supply room and distribute to teachers.
- At least twice a year, thoroughly clean and reorganize the supply room.
- Communicate regularly with supervisor.

Children's Ministry

PUBLICITY COORDINATOR

Task: To communicate the Sunday School and related children's programs and events

Term: One year, beginning September 1

Supervisor _____ (name) _____

Responsibilities

- Determine the ongoing publicity needs for children's programs, including mailed publicity, displays at church, bulletin and/or newsletter inserts.
- Oversee the production and distribution of all children and parent letters, flyers, posters, etc., working with others as needed (office staff, children's leaders, etc.).

FOOD COORDINATOR

Task: To oversee the provision of food—snacks or meals—as needed at Sunday School and related children's programs

Term: One year, beginning September 1

Supervisor _____ (name) _____

Responsibilities

- Determine the food needs for all children's programs, working with children's ministry teachers.
- Provide food through purchases and donations of money or food. If parents are asked to provide food, set up and oversee a schedule of donations.

Children's Ministry

CAMP COORDINATOR

Task: To plan and reserve summer and/or winter camp reservations, publicize the camp program and oversee all details (counselors, registration, transportation, etc.)

Responsibilities

- In coordination with supervisor, reserve date and number of campers at (name of camp). Coordinate camp dates with school schedules.
- Request and display camp brochures in the appropriate Sunday School rooms and in other well-traveled areas of the church facility.
- Write bulletin notices for camps and send publicity materials with parent letters well in advance of registration due dates.
- Set up and oversee procedures for accepting registrations and fees.
- Mail all checks and registration to the camp registrar.
- Plan and coordinate scholarships and fund-raisers as needed.
- Two weeks prior to camp, send an information letter to each camper. Include information about final payment of all camp fees, transportation arrangements, luggage, address at camp, medical release forms, etc.
- After camp, ask several campers to write an article for church newsletter and/or arrange for several campers to be interviewed in church service.
- Communicate regularly with supervisor.

Youth Ministry

SUNDAY SCHOOL COORDINATOR

Task: To plan and develop a program of Bible learning through Scripture study and interaction with adults and peers for youth each Sunday morning

Term: One year, beginning September 1

Supervisor _____ (name) _____

Responsibilities

- Recruit teachers for all Sunday School classes.
- Plan and lead a regular program of training for all Sunday School staff.
- Observe, evaluate and affirm teachers in order to note strengths to encourage and areas where improvement is possible.
- Pray regularly for Sunday School teachers.
- Lead regular planning meetings for teachers that include training and opportunities for spiritual growth.
- Oversee the purchase, distribution and use of all equipment and supplies (curriculum, snacks, art supplies, etc.).
- Communicate the church's approved safety policy to all Sunday School staff, regularly evaluate its use and take necessary steps to put the policy into practice.
- Plan a Sunday School staff get-together at least twice a year in order to build a sense of teamwork among all teachers.
- Express appreciation to the Sunday School staff, including an end-of-the-year event.
- Communicate with parents regarding the purpose, value and procedures of Sunday School.
- Communicate regularly with supervisor and teachers of related programs (weeknight youth group, small group Bible studies, etc.).

Note: This position may be held by a volunteer or paid staff person. In a small church, one or more of these tasks may be the responsibility of the supervisor (Christian education committee member, youth ministries elder, etc.).

Youth Ministry

DEPARTMENT LEADER

Task: To prayerfully support and build relationships with both teachers and youth in order to ensure effective Bible learning

Term: One year, beginning September 1

Supervisor _____ (name)

Responsibilities

- Coordinate teacher tasks, including use of supplies and room setup.
- Greet youth as they arrive.
- Assist teachers as needed (activity completion, supply distribution, etc.), maintaining the time schedule for the session.
- Observe, evaluate and affirm teachers in order to note strengths to encourage and areas where improvement is possible.
- Lead the large-group Bible study and/or worship time, involving other teachers as appropriate.
- Pray regularly for others on the teaching team.
- Work with your supervisor to identify and enlist qualified people to join your teaching team.
- Lead regular session planning meetings, including training and opportunities for spiritual growth.
- Plan a team get-together once a quarter in order to build friendships among the team.
- Communicate regularly with supervisor.

Note: In a class with just two teachers, the leader responsibilities may be informally shared. When three or more people are on the team, one person should be designated as the department leader.

Youth Ministry

TEACHER

Task: To prayerfully build relationships with youth and guide them in life-changing Bible learning

Term: One year, beginning September 1

Supervisor _____ (name)

Individual Responsibilities

- Maintain a personal relationship with Jesus Christ.
- Desire to grow in faith and commitment to God and participate in personal Bible study and prayer.
- Worship regularly with the church family.

Team Responsibilities

- Pray regularly for each youth and others on your teaching team.
- Participate in scheduled teachers' meetings.
- Participate in at least one training event during the year to improve teaching skills.
- Express needs as a teacher to your supervisor.

Sunday Morning Responsibilities

- Arrange materials and room to create an effective learning environment.
- Greet each youth upon arrival and involve him or her in conversation.
- Model the love of Christ by getting to know youth and sharing their concerns, needs and joys.
- Guide Bible learning by
  1. Being well prepared to use Bible stories, verses/passages, questions and comments appropriate to the age level in order to accomplish the lesson aims;
  2. Selecting a variety of Bible learning activities and encouraging each student to actively participate in each lesson;
  3. Participating with youth in learning activities and in large-group times.

Student Follow-Up Responsibilities

- Follow up on visitors and absentees with mailings, phone calls and/or personal visits.
- Care for each class member with prayer, telephone calls, birthday cards, etc.
- Communicate individual student needs to parents.

Youth Ministry

PUBLICITY COORDINATOR

Task: To communicate the events of Sunday School and related youth programs
Term: One year, beginning September 1
Supervisor _____ (name) _____

Responsibilities

- Determine the ongoing publicity needs for youth programs, including mailed publicity, displays at church, bulletin and/or newsletter inserts.
- Oversee the production and distribution of all youth and parent letters, flyers, posters, etc., working with others as needed (office staff, youth leaders, etc.).

FOOD COORDINATOR

Task: To oversee the provision of food (snacks, meals) when needed at Sunday School and related youth programs
Term: One year, beginning September 1
Supervisor _____ (name) _____

Responsibilities

- Determine the food needs for all youth programs, working with youth leaders.
- Provide food through purchases and donations of money or food. If parents are asked to provide food, set up and oversee a schedule of donations.

SUPPLY ROOM ORGANIZER

Task: To keep the supply room organized and ready for teacher use
Term: Six months, September through February or March through August
Supervisor _____ (name) _____

Responsibilities

- Once a week, check the supply room to clean up and sort donated materials and pick up supply requests from teachers.
- Purchase supplies as needed. Consult with Sunday School coordinator as needed. Turn in receipts to (name).
- Place supply requests for donated items in newsletter and/or bulletin as needed.
- Keep a current copy of appropriate supply and equipment catalogs.
- Update supply list twice a year, post list in supply room and distribute to teachers.
- At least twice a year, thoroughly clean and reorganize the supply room.
- Communicate regularly with supervisor.

Youth Ministry

CAMP COORDINATOR

Task: To plan and reserve summer and/or winter camp reservations, publicize the camp program and oversee all details (counselors, registration, transportation, etc.)

Responsibilities

- In coordination with supervisor, reserve date and number of campers at (name of camp). Coordinate camp dates with school schedules.
- Request and display camp brochures in the appropriate Sunday School rooms and in other well-traveled areas of the church facility.
- Write bulletin notices for camps and send publicity materials with parent letters well in advance of registration due dates.
- Set up and oversee procedures for accepting registrations and fees.
- Mail all checks and registration to the camp registrar.
- Plan and coordinate scholarships and fund-raisers as needed.
- Two weeks prior to camp, send an information letter to each camper. Include information about final payment of all camp fees, transportation arrangements, luggage, address at camp, medical release forms, etc.
- After camp, ask several campers to write an article for church newsletter and/or arrange for several campers to be interviewed in church service.
- Communicate regularly with supervisor.

Adult Ministry

MINISTRY COORDINATOR

Task: To plan a variety of Bible learning classes for adults
Term: One year, beginning September 1
Supervisor _____ (name) _____

Responsibilities

- Work with supervisor to plan a balanced offering of Bible learning classes. Get input from others involved in the program as necessary.
- Work with supervisor to identify and enlist qualified people to teach classes.
- Assist teachers as needed (room setup, supplies, etc.).
- Observe, evaluate and affirm teachers in order to note strengths to encourage and areas where improvement is possible.
- Pray regularly for the teaching team.
- Lead regular planning meetings, including training and opportunities for spiritual growth.
- Plan a team get-together in order to build friendships among the team once a quarter.
- Participate regularly in planning and/or training events in order to improve the effectiveness of the Sunday School program.
- Communicate regularly with supervisor.

TEACHER

Task: To lead adults in Bible learning that results in life change
Term: One year, beginning September 1
Supervisor _____ (name) _____

Responsibilities

- Arrange materials and room to create an effective learning environment.
- Model the love of Christ by getting to know participants and sharing their concerns, needs and joys.
- Guide Bible learning by
  1. Being well prepared to lead adults in study of the Bible and related topics;
  2. Selecting a variety of Bible learning activities.
- Pray regularly for each participant and others on your teaching team.
- Follow up on visitors and absentees.
- Participate regularly in planning and/or training events in order to improve the effectiveness of your teaching.
- Communicate regularly with supervisor.

Adult Ministry

GREETER

Task: To greet participants as they arrive
Term: One year, beginning September 1
Supervisor _____ (name)

Responsibilities

- Be present in classroom by 9:30 A.M. each Sunday morning.
- Each Sunday mark attendance on the Weekly Attendance form. After class, place completed form in the reception office and get a new form for the next Sunday.
- Offer a friendly greeting to each participant.
- Pay special attention to visitors, recording their names, addresses and phone numbers and introducing them to others in the class.
- Communicate regularly with supervisor.

PUBLICITY COORDINATOR

Task: To communicate the events of Sunday School and related adult programs
Term: One year, beginning September 1
Supervisor _____ (name)

Responsibilities

- Determine the ongoing publicity needs for adult programs, including mailed publicity, displays at church, bulletin and/or newsletter inserts.
- Oversee the production and distribution of all letters, flyers, posters, etc., working with others (office staff, adult ministry leaders, etc.) as needed.

FOOD COORDINATOR

Task: To oversee the provision of food (snacks, meals) when needed at Sunday School and related adult programs
Term: One year, beginning September 1
Supervisor _____ (name)

Responsibilities

- Determine the food needs for all adult programs, working with adult ministry leaders.
- Provide food through purchases and donations of money or food. If participants are asked to provide food, set up and oversee a schedule of donations.

Job Descriptions and Teamwork

Rate your church's progress toward each goal and then list two or more actions you can take to reach each goal.

GOAL 1: A PERSON FOR EVERY JOB AND A JOB DESCRIPTION FOR EVERY PERSON

Everyone on the Sunday School staff has a current, written job description.

1	2	3	4	5
Need to Start		Fair		Goal Achieved

Actions to Take:

GOAL 2: CREATE A FEELING OF TEAMWORK

Build teaching teams that not only enjoy serving together but that also give support and encouragement to one another.

1	2	3	4	5
Need to Start		Fair		Goal Achieved

Actions to Take:

Chapter Seven

Getting and Keeping Volunteers

Developing a well-thought-out, step-by-step plan for recruiting and valuing teachers is the backbone of an effective Sunday School.

What This Chapter Tells You
- It's important to develop a long-term view of recruiting.
- Successful recruiting is not only preparation but also follow-up.

What This Chapter Shows You
- How to identify, contact and follow up prospective teachers and other staff;
- Guidelines for a complete volunteer survey of your congregation;
- Tips for publicizing the staffing needs of your Sunday School;
- Steps to follow to train a new staff member.

Where Do I Start?

> *Recruiting is simply talking to one person at a time.*

> *There must be some reason almost 50 percent of the adults in the United States volunteer their time to worthy causes.[1]*

Look at Where You Are

Duplicate and complete the "Recruiting" worksheet (p. 159) to take a closer look at how the important job of recruiting has been accomplished in your church.

Attitude Adjustment

If you ask a director of Christian education—paid or volunteer—what the hardest part of his or her job is, chances are you'll hear the answer "Recruiting!" Keeping the numerous and varied positions of a well-run Sunday School staffed is a challenge—but one that offers many rewards! After all, what other job in the Christian education ministry offers the opportunity to not only help people discover their God-given gifts but also encourage them in developing these gifts?

THE FLIP SIDE

Remember that recruiting and training are two sides of the same coin—they need to be considered as part of the same process. Check out chapter 8 for training tips!

Get the Big Picture

A workable, continuing plan for recruiting qualified personnel to serve in your Sunday School is a must. In today's world, people can make frequent job changes and face constant demands on their time; as a result, you will always be looking for new teachers and other workers in your Sunday School. And as your Sunday School grows and your programs expand into new ministries, the need for additional staff will increase.

The task is daunting, but the rewards are great! Consider the benefits that will result from an effective recruiting program:

- The teacher/student ratios in your Sunday School will improve, resulting in more opportunities for building friendships and followers of Jesus;
- Better group sizes result in fewer discipline problems for teachers of children and youth and a feeling among teachers of all ages that the time they spend in ministry is productive and enjoyable—satisfied teachers keep coming back for more;
- You will experience the satisfaction of helping others find places of meaningful service for the Lord.

LOOK AT WHERE YOU ARE

Recruiting

1. Who is responsible for recruiting teachers and other staff?

2. How do people in the congregation find out about Sunday School?

   What actions have you or your staff used within the last 12 months to publicize your Sunday School program to the congregation (especially to people other than parents)?

3. Do all staff positions have written, up-to-date job descriptions?

4. How do you get the names of people who might be interested in teaching or helping in your Sunday School?

5. What are your church's policies for volunteers?

   Who approves and screens volunteers?

6. How are new staff members trained?

Focus on the Goals

GOAL 1:
MAKE RECRUITING EVERYBODY'S BUSINESS

Everyone on the Sunday School staff should know about and pray for recruitment needs.

If recruiting is the responsibility of only two or three people, those people often become overworked and discouraged—and recruitment prospects are limited to the friends and acquaintances of these few people.

The total Sunday School staff needs to accept part of the concern for recruitment. The pastor, Christian education board or council members, Sunday School coordinators, teachers and helpers must support, encourage and, above all, pray that potential teachers will accept an invitation to ministry.

This involvement does not mean everyone is trying to sign up new teachers. That would only invite chaos! Rather, everyone on the staff must be informed of recruiting needs, pray regularly that the needs will be met, and be willing to help where appropriate in the recruiting process. In addition, particularly in a larger church, it is often helpful to have a committee that is responsible for the various steps to effective recruiting. Form a new committee at least once a year. Invite people to be on the committee who have skills in a variety of areas: publicity, teacher appreciation, new teacher orientation, personal contact, etc.

✔ Action Checklist

❑ Keep your staff informed of personnel needs. Consider listing staff needs in a monthly staff memo or newsletter, E-mail, or mini-posters displayed in a coffee room.

❑ Encourage the staff to remember these needs in prayer. Remember also to list answers to prayer as needs are met and to thank God for the answers.

❑ Invite three to five people to be on a recruiting committee with you, meeting monthly to plan for effective recruiting.

 Bonus Idea for Prayer and Recruiting: I ask our entire children's ministry team and our prayer ministry team to commit to a 30-day prayer covenant. I give them a booklet with 30 different areas of our kid's ministry and 30 related Scriptures on which to focus each day. *Vikki Randall, Arcadia Presbyterian Church, Arcadia, California*

GOAL 2:
PLAN POSITIVE PUBLICITY

Creating a churchwide campaign will let people know the good things happening in your Sunday School.

Crucial to a successful recruitment program is churchwide awareness of ways God is using your Sunday School to make a difference in people's lives. People don't want to make a deep commitment to an organization or program they know little about. And they can't get excited about becoming part of a group that is constantly making desperate pleas for somebody—anybody—to *please help!*

Present your Sunday School or other program in a positive light:

- What is God accomplishing through this ministry?
- How are people's lives being helped?
- What are some benefits, challenges and rewards to those who become involved in this exciting and fruitful ministry?
- What opportunities are open to those who want to have a part in the work of the Sunday School?

Effective publicity involves not only public presentations but also individual and small-group sharing by teachers who are excited about their ministry.

✓ Action Checklist

❏ Display pictures of class activities and/or students' work on strategically located bulletin boards. Occasionally set up displays on portable bulletin boards which can be moved to a fellowship area or to adult classrooms. Show pictures of students, as well as pictures of teachers, and include descriptions of open job positions.

❏ Include prayer requests related to the Sunday School in pastoral prayers, prayer lists and church newsletters highlighting the entire church's commitment to the importance of the teaching ministry.

❏ Write brief features about Sunday School activities for your church newsletter or bulletins.

❏ Include a "Featured Teacher" column in the church newsletter.

✓ Action Checklist

❏ Conduct interviews of teachers in church services—it's great if the senior pastor will do the interview—or ask an adult class teacher to interview members of their class or other adults who are teaching elsewhere in the Sunday School. Good questions to ask are "What's something you enjoy about teaching?" and "How have you benefited from being a teacher?"

❏ Create a video or slide presentation featuring a specific age level or class in action. Show the presentation in a worship service, in an adult class, in a coffee or fellowship area after worship or for an open house.

❏ Encourage teachers to share answers to prayer, prayer concerns, how God is working in their lives and through them in the lives of their students.

❏ Invite parents to observe your teaching and learning philosophy at work by sitting in on a session.

❏ Serve coffee and donuts during a time when your Sunday School is not in session (right after worship service ends, etc.) and invite the congregation to tour the facilities. Sunday School teachers can display photos of their classes and recent class projects.

❏ Arrange for a church committee or board to tour several Sunday School classrooms as part of its meeting. Select as your tour guide an enthusiastic teacher who can explain how God's Word is being taught.

GOAL 3: HELP PEOPLE KNOW THEIR JOBS

Each Sunday School staff position should have a current, written job description.

✔ **Action Checklist**

❏ Write job descriptions for every position on your Sunday School staff. (Read chapter 6 for information on how to write job descriptions that actually motivate people to volunteer!)

❏ Several months after distributing job descriptions, ask each teacher to write a letter to him- or herself briefly describing one or two ways in which he or she would like to better fulfill the job description. Keep the sealed letters for several months, and then mail them to teachers as a self-check on their progress.

In order to recruit a person to do a job, you need to be able to clearly describe the job and what is required of the person who accepts that responsibility. No one is going to get excited about taking a position that is vaguely defined. People want to know what they're getting into and how much time, effort and ability the job will require. Providing job descriptions will give you a head start on your recruiting.

Looking for Relationships: Much of what we desire of a person in ministry has to do with relationships. Most everything else in ministry—how to lead a small group, how to tell a Bible story, how to guide students in an art activity—can be taught. But relationships deal with more intangible things. So first, we want our leaders and teachers to be people whose relationship with God is foremost in their lives. That relationship is the foundation upon which all other parts of ministry is built. But we also are looking for people who are able to build relationships with the students they teach or lead. Especially in youth ministry, there is a high expectation for significant relationship building—and a realization that building relationships takes time. Be certain that your job descriptions for teachers and leaders highlight this key part of ministry.

GOAL 4:
FIND THE RIGHT PERSON FOR THE RIGHT JOB

List prospects for your staff with the goal of helping individuals find fulfilling places of ministry and growth.

Too often Sunday School administrators find themselves spending most of their time frantically trying to fill vacant positions on their staff. But no sooner is one position filled than two more positions become vacant! The emphasis on recruiting then becomes one of filling vacancies rather than helping individuals find fulfilling places of ministry and growth.

A very important part of an effective recruitment program is a consistent and continuing effort to identify people who might enjoy a place of ministry on the Sunday School staff. Consider the benefits of a well-planned, year-round program of identifying and evaluating prospects.

- People will not feel they have to fill a vacancy because no one else is available.
- There can be a planned emphasis on helping individuals find places of ministry through which they will grow spiritually, find fulfillment and purpose in their own Christian life, use their spiritual gifts and benefit others as a result of their ministry.
- There can be ample time for observation, training and finding the most satisfying spot for ministry.
- There is opportunity to match interests and skills with specific needs, rather than positions. For example, someone with music ability who is not interested in a regular teaching position might be recruited to help with a children's choir program, worship time or a youth singing group.

 Bonus Ideas for Recruiting Themes: One year our recruiting theme was "Leave a footprint in the life of a child." So one Sunday all our teachers came to church barefoot, and the pastor (barefooted and in a suit) preached on the topic: Helping Kids Walk with Jesus. We recruited 70 people that Sunday. *Bonnie Aldrich, Pulpit Rock Church, Colorado Springs, Colorado*

On a spring Sunday, all the Sunday School children, infants through youth (including their teachers), parade through the sanctuary. Play lively contemporary music while they march down one aisle and up the other. Make cardboard placards mounted on sticks for children to carry to advertise your message: "We Love Sunday School!" "Sunday School Teachers Are the Best!" After the parade, invite those interested in Sunday School to stop by the information table after the worship service. *Karen Perkins, Walnut Creek Presbyterian Church, Walnut Creek California*

A Qualified Sunday School Teacher: Do Sunday School teachers and helpers need to be church members? If so, for how long?

If not, for how long does the prospective volunteer need to have attended our church?

Is there a minimum age for Sunday School teachers and helpers?

How well is the volunteer known by other church members?

What personal qualities are needed in Sunday School staff?

How would the volunteer work with other staff members?

What is the volunteer's past Sunday School experience in our church or another church?

What types of ministry would seem to be appropriate for the prospect?

Note: Written policies of this kind are essential to protect the liability of your church and its staff, whether paid or volunteer. Ask an experienced church liability lawyer in your state to regularly evaluate your policies.

✓ **Action Checklist**

❑ As you search for volunteers, consider all areas of the congregation. Use the church membership list, adult class lists, suggestions from adult teachers or adult class leaders, new members' classes, lists of previous staff and survey forms on which a prospect can show previous experience or willingness to serve. Often the best leads are suggestions by current teachers and other staff.

❑ Talk with other church leaders and staff about ways they can help you find possible teachers and helpers. Emphasize your desire to help people find places of ministry and growth that are best suited to their interests and gifts.

❑ Survey the people in your congregation, asking them to briefly list their talents and interests (see "Volunteer Survey" on page 166). Present the survey in an adult Sunday School class or as part of a worship service which emphasizes opportunities for ministry. (**Note:** You'll receive more of the surveys if people complete them and turn them in before leaving rather than taking them home to fill out.) Make a card file of prospects based on the information in the survey.

❑ Meet informally with adult-class leaders and teachers to review names of class members and identify those who might be capable to teach or help in the Sunday School.

❑ Plan a brief (four- to eight-week) course for all adults who are interested in finding out more about their spiritual gifts and how their talents and abilities can be used in the church's ministries. An "Identifying and Using Your Gifts" workshop can review the biblical passages dealing with gifts: the purposes of gifts in the church, how to determine our gifts and the need to use our gifts.

❑ Consider establishing a clearinghouse that can help even out the workloads of those who may be asked to take so many jobs that they become overloaded. This group could also determine who will contact each prospect, eliminating the problems caused when four or five people all descend upon a prospect at the same time!

The members of the group should represent a broad range of ages and interests within the church and should be familiar with the written policies of your church for volunteer screening and approval.

Bonus Ideas for Contacting Potential Volunteers: To keep your contact list of potential volunteers growing, regularly set aside one or two hours every week in which to call or meet with people who you think might be interested in teaching in your Sunday School (or calling people who can give you possible names). Then, when a position needs to be filled, you will have a backlog of already-identified possibilities. *Children's Christian Ministries Association, Ventura, California Chapter*

For recruiting early childhood and children's teachers, I visit each of the adult Sunday School classes in my church. I always leave each person in the class with a little gift that would remind them of children's ministry: helium-filled balloons, teddy bear pins or Post-it Notes imprinted with our children's ministry theme. I also handed out cards for people to fill out to indicate their interest in children's ministry. *Ivy Beckwith, Ventura, California*

Bonus Idea for Recruiting Male Teachers: We have a large number of women teachers but very few men. We set a goal of recruiting at least one man to work in each of our children's classrooms. To meet this goal, we offered a free men's lunch one Sunday after church. We served lots of "guy food"—deli sandwiches, chips, etc.—and showed a humorous sports blooper video. Then a male member of our pastoral staff shared how men had been an important part of his spiritual development. We passed out brochures describing our ministry and asked the men to brainstorm their own ideas of how they would like to be involved. They were enthusiastic, and nearly everyone signed up for some area of ministry. *Vikki Randall, Arcadia Presbyterian Church, Arcadia, California*

SAMPLE VOLUNTEER CARD

Name _____

Address _____

Phone _____ Date _____

❑ Church Member ❑ Nonmember

Age level of interest (if known) _____

Circle positions of previous service and <u>underline positions of possible interest</u>:

Department Leader	Teacher
Helper	Substitute Teacher
Secretary	Bulletin Board Decorator
Music (guitar or piano)	Snack Coordinator
Supply Coordinator	Transportation Coordinator

Comments _____

_____

Volunteer Survey

Date:_____   _____ Male _____ Female

Name:_____ Phone:_____

Adddress:_____

City:_____ Zip:_____

Occupation:_____

Check the appropriate columns:
EXP = Experience (note length) INT = Interested

EXP	INT		EXP	INT	
		Officers/Boards/Committees			Soloist
		Deacon/Deaconess/Elder			Special group singing
		Trustee			Piano/Organ
		Facilities			Guitar
		Christian education			Keyboard
		Evangelism			Other instrument
		Membership			Orchestra
		Missions			Children's choir director
		Finance			Music teacher
		Communications/Media			Songleader (age group_____)
		Illustration			**Christian Education Positions**
		Graphic design			Division coordinator
		Photography (still/video)			Department leader
		Bulletin boards			Teacher
		Lettering			Greeter
		Posters			Helper/Aide/Substitute
		Projectionist			Secretary
		Librarian			Pianist
		Cassette duplication			Recreation leader
		Equipment maintenance			**Christian Education Programs**
		P. A. system			Sunday School
		Prepare teaching aids			Churchtime
		Recommend books/tapes			Sunday evening
		Music			Weekday club
		Choir member			VBS

Volunteer Survey (Cont'd)

EXP	INT		EXP	INT	
		Special Education			Provide meals
		Camp			Provide child care
		Christian Education Age Level			Entertain visitors at home
		Baby/Toddler			**Property Maintenance**
		Ages 2 to 5			Carpentry
		Grades 1 to 5/6			Landscaping/Gardening
		Grades 5/6 to 8			Painting
		Grades 9 to 12			Electrical
		College			Cement work
		Adults			Plumbing
		Seniors			Custodial
		Outreach			Mechanical
		Home visits/calling			**Helpers, Various**
		Discipleship			Bus driver (license class)
		Sick/Shut-in ministry			Kitchen cook
		Men's/Women's ministries			Kitchen help
		Counseling			Dinners (plan/serve/clean-up)
		Ushering/Welcoming/Greeting			Office/General secretarial
		Hospitality			Typing/Computer
		Home for get-togethers			Filing
		Home for home Bible studies			Telephone
		Home for backyard Bible clubs			Sewing/Costume design
		Transportation			
		Loan car/van			
		Lodging			

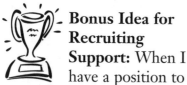

Bonus Idea for Recruiting Support: When I have a position to fill, I invite a member of the congregation to be my prayer partner, praying for the right person to accept the job. I give a prayer reminder card to my partner. It encourages me to have a partner supporting me, and sometimes the partner turns out to be the answer to my prayer! *Elsa Barber, Central Church, Memphis, Tennessee*

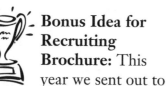

Bonus Idea for Recruiting Brochure: This year we sent out to our contact list brochures with the headline "Someone Just Like You Taught These Children About Christ!" Then we showed pictures of five of our church staff members—one picture as each looks today and one picture as each looked in elementary school. At the bottom of the page we invited people to "Join Perimeter's Children's Ministry Team and help us train the teachers of tomorrow!" *Mike Gaskins, Perimeter Church, Duluth, Georgia*

GOAL 5:
MAKE THE FIRST CONTACT A PERSONAL ONE

A personal meeting with the prospective volunteer provides specific information concerning the position and length of service and the opportunity to ask and answer questions.

People who are recruited in the halls or parking lot of a church may feel as though both they and the job are of less than crucial importance. Setting up a personal interview with a prospect lets him or her know that you consider both the prospect and the position important and that prayerful and serious thought preceded his or her being contacted for a specific task. A personal meeting also allows an unhurried period of time in which you and the prospect can get better acquainted, answer each other's questions and clarify information as needed.

Personally contact the prospect by phone or by mail. Ask him or her to meet at a convenient time and place for the purpose of considering teaching or helping in the Sunday School.

During the interview:

1. Begin by explaining to the prospect why this job is important and why you feel he or she would be effective at the task;
2. Clearly present the position's basic responsibilities, focusing on the program goals and the methods to be used, giving the prospect a written job description;
3. Tell the prospect the specific length of service expected;
4. Show the prospect the resources the church provides for teaching materials, visual aids, supplies, etc.;
5. Explain what the church offers in terms of training and support;
6. Ask the prospect to pray for God's direction in whether or not to accept this commitment and provide the opportunity for him or her to observe a current session where someone is doing the same (or similar) job to the one you are asking the prospect to consider (see Goal 6: Observation—The First Step on page 170).

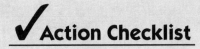

✔ Action Checklist

❑ When a large number of teaching positions are to be filled, consider setting up a display in a well-traveled area of your church. A large, attractive poster will attract attention as will a video or photographs of the program for which you are recruiting. If you want to display a list of jobs to be filled, be sure to show that a significant number of positions are already filled. No one wants to be the first to sign up!

❑ Ask several people (current or former teachers) to come for a "Coffee and Calling Night." Provide a variety of coffees or teas. Give participants a sample telephone script to follow and a list of potential volunteers to call. End the evening with a time of prayer.

Contact Record

Name _____

Date _____

Position (include age level and length of service) _____

_____

Interview Date _____

Job Description Given: ❑ Yes   ❑ No

Observation Date _____

Follow-Up Date and Decision _____

Orientation Meeting _____

Application Received _____

Application Approved _____

Date Service Begins _____

Date Service Ends _____

Comments_____

GOAL 6:
OBSERVATION—THE FIRST STEP

Each prospective volunteer must be given: (*a*) opportunities to observe someone doing the job he or she is being asked to do and (*b*) guidance as to what to look for and questions to ask the person being observed.

Observation of a particular job that one is considering gives a clearer picture of what is expected in that position. Be sure you have trained staff members who are effectively teaching students and following established procedures so that prospects will have positive models to observe. In order to get the most out of the observation, the prospect needs guidance concerning what to look for.

- Meet with the prospect before the observation session to briefly explain what he or she should look for in the class.
- Meet with the prospect after the observation in order to review the class schedule, discuss what was observed and answer questions. Help prospects realize that no one begins a teaching or helping ministry with all the required skills. Training, experience and support from other teachers—undergirded with God's help—all combine to equip Sunday School teachers.
- Following the observation, give the prospect time to prayerfully consider his or her decision. Encourage your potential staff member to review this ministry commitment with family members. Their prayerful support and encouragement is important. At the close of the observation session, set a time, about one week later, when you will call the prospect for his or her decision.

✔ Action Checklist

❑ If teachers are not used to the idea of being observed, distribute a copy of the observation form to each teacher. Ask them to first complete the form about themselves and then about another teacher in their class. You may also use the form to observe teachers not only to accustom teachers to being observed but also as a way of acknowledging and thanking teachers for their efforts.

❑ Make a list of the classes or departments you think would be good for prospective teachers to observe. Talk with the teachers and helpers in those classes or departments about your goals in observation so that they can be thinking ahead and planning for the observation. Develop observation guides that list specific items for observers to look for, based on the topics and training resources you are using.

Observation Form

1. What are three characteristics you noticed about the students or this class that are important for a teacher (or other staff member) to keep in mind?

2. List three words that summarize the role of the teacher.

3. What are two ways the teacher (or other staff member) gives individual attention to students?

4. What are two ways the students are involved in discovering Bible truths and using Bible verses or passages?

5. In what ways are students challenged to put Bible truths into practice in their daily lives?

If applicable:
6. What are two ways the lead teacher keeps the session moving smoothly?

7. What are two ways the lead teacher helps the teachers to be successful in their teaching?

✔ Action Checklist

❑ Maintain a current list of needs in other church ministries and the appropriate job descriptions so that you can connect volunteers with appropriate programs.

❑ Talk with several new volunteers (as well as several people who chose not to serve in your Sunday School or other program) and ask them to evaluate the recruiting process. Look for specific ways to improve the manner in which volunteers are contacted.

 Bonus Idea for Involving People in Ministry: Look for opportunities to have students lead along with you. Develop a pattern of "tandem leadership" that lets students, at any age, begin to experience a supportive model of ministry. *Gina Bolenbaugh, Lake Avenue Church, Pasadena, California*

GOAL 7: FOLLOW-UP

Prompt contact of the prospective volunteer for an answer and gracious acceptance of his or her decision are important.

It's important to be prompt in following up with the prospect at the time you agreed upon. This will let the prospect know that his or her decision is important to you and that you are sincerely interested in helping him or her find an enriching place of ministry.

- If the prospect says yes, express your appreciation for this new step of commitment. Give the volunteer an application to complete and return to you. (See the sample application form on page 165.) Make arrangements concerning preservice training (see Goal 8). And remember to thank God for a new staff member!

- If the prospect says no, avoid the temptation to "twist his or her arm," to interpret the decision as a personal failure or to judge the prospect's spirituality. Be grateful that the prospect withdrew instead of serving only a few months with a minimal sense of commitment. It is better for a person not to be involved than to serve with the wrong motivation. Those who do the latter will often quit at the first opportunity and may tear down the morale of the whole department by their sporadic and unenthusiastic participation.

Remember that since you and the prospect prayed for God's direction in this decision, you can trust the result of His guidance. God may also make it possible for you to be of help to this person in finding another area of ministry for which he or she feels better suited.

GOAL 8:
TRAINING IS THE KEY

New staff members should be provided with well-planned preservice training programs.

When a new volunteer makes a commitment to serve on your staff, the training phase of your recruitment program begins. You can't separate recruiting and training; these elements must be linked in order to make your volunteer's experience positive.

Beginnings are the most important—and probably the most risky—times for a new recruit, so every possible help to assure his or her success is a must!

 Bonus Idea for Getting Teachers to Try New Methods: Don't bother to tell them you are introducing something new. Just model it for them as part of an ongoing training session. If they like it and see the value in what you show them, they will make changes more easily. *Linda Hoover, Calvary Community Church, Westlake Village, California*

 Bonus Ideas for Training New Teachers: In our church, we pair a new volunteer with a teaching "buddy." The buddies walk along side the new teachers and help them learn the ropes! *Karen Perkins, Walnut Creek Presbyterian Church, Walnut Creek, California*

We felt that our new teachers had a hard time learning what was expected of them. So our pastor and I put together a training video. The video walks them step-by-step through a ministry manual. First, we explain all the general information about procedures, security, application forms, etc. Then the teachers can advance the video to the segment about their specific ministries. Teachers can take these videos and manuals home to watch and learn at their own convenience. *Bonnie Aldrich, Pulpit Rock Church, Colorado Springs, Colorado*

 Bonus Idea for Getting Teachers to Come to a Training Meeting: Supply food! *Scott Grabendike, First Presbyterian Church, Palmdale, California*

✔ Action Checklist

❑ Meet with new teachers or helpers to explain the goals, methods, curriculum and organization of your Sunday School. If you have more than one new staff member, communicate this information in an orientation class. You might also consider inviting prospects who have an interest but are not yet ready to make a commitment to serve.

❑ Give each new volunteer a copy of any teacher training material you have available and assign specific chapters to be read. Invite the volunteer to call you with any questions, or set up a time you can meet to discuss the material.

❑ Involve new workers in the classes where they will be serving.

- Provide a copy of the current curriculum materials.
- Arrange for the new person to observe and assist an experienced worker several times. If the teachers in the class are meeting to plan, invite the new volunteer to attend.
- Give the new worker a simple assignment or two as a starter for the next Sunday. For example, a new teacher could assist in a learning activity or guide a small group in a game.
- Observe the new person at work in the class; then offer honest praise for each task done well. Make sincere, kind, specific suggestions for improvement (no more than one or two suggestions at a time).
- Increase the areas of responsibility each week as the new worker shows ability and confidence.
- Continue to observe, evaluate and affirm the new worker.

❑ Outline key topics to present in a basic orientation course: how people learn; age characteristics and needs of learners; policies and procedures that affect your staff (these policies and procedures should be provided in written form—such as in a handbook).

❑ Decide who will conduct the orientation course and how often to provide it. You might set up a regular schedule, such as every six weeks. Larger churches may have enough new teachers that they conduct teacher-training classes as part of their adult education program.

❑ Select training resources to use in the course.

❑ Discuss the preservice program with your current staff. Work with them on ways they can be helpful to prospects and recruits who come to observe in their classes.

❑ Put your preservice training procedures in writing.

GOAL 9:
TIME FOR APPRECIATION

Show your staff they are valued.

Recruiting volunteers and keeping volunteers are not necessarily the same thing! In fact, while most attention is placed in recruiting new leaders and teachers, an equal amount of attention should be given to keeping the volunteers you've worked so hard to get.

One significant aspect of keeping volunteers is to let them know how valuable you consider their time, their ideas and their service.

Bonus Idea for Teacher Communication: All of my staff have E-mail accounts. I send weekly E-mails, sharing what is going on in my personal life. By revealing my inside world, my staff is encouraged. I also praise them for things that I notice. Since the rest of the staff reads it, there are powerful results from this public praise and encouragement. *Eugene Sim, Thanksgiving Church, Whittier, California*

Bonus Ideas for Staff Appreciation Gifts: We like to surprise our teachers with special gifts each quarter. They never knew when they were coming. One fall Sunday we presented each teacher with a caramel apple with a note of thanks. Another time we gave out plastic mugs with packets of hot chocolate, teas and candy all wrapped in a bow with an appreciative note. One Valentine's Day we gave each teacher a red carnation with a heart-shaped note. *Ivy Beckwith, Ventura, California*

Ask community and church members to donate "perks" such as free haircut, dinner out, CD of choice, gift certificate to book or music store. *Yolanda Miller, First Presbyterian Church, Honolulu, Hawaii*

This month we are giving our teachers a package of Post-it Notes with a label that says "Thanks for sticking with us and making this a noteworthy year for the children of Hollywood Presbyterian." *Lisa Herman, Hollywood Presbyterian Church, Hollywood, California*

Bonus Idea for Planning Appreciation Events: We recruited a volunteer who is solely responsible for planning teacher appreciation events. We call this volunteer "The Appreciator." *First Lutheran Church, Fargo, North Dakota*

Bonus Idea for Teacher Recognition: We make special teacher name tags that, in addition to the teacher's name, show our children's ministry's logo and a "Serving Since (year)" line to encourage and support our teachers. *Ty Rose, Saddleback Valley Community Church, Mission Viejo, California*

✔ Action Checklist

❑ At least once a year, or several months after the start of a volunteer's time of service, invite the volunteer to make suggestions for improvement in the program. Ask for specific ideas of actions that could be taken to make the job of the volunteer easier. Let the volunteer know that you sincerely desire feedback about what can be done to strengthen the teaching ministry in your Sunday School. Always convey a sense of partnership with your leaders, teachers and helpers by asking, "What can we do to work together to make our Sunday School better?"

❑ Periodically publicize the names of your staff—in bulletin-board displays, in newsletters, in church bulletins.

❑ Give small gifts on special occasions: holidays, birthdays, etc. Invite students in the class (or parents of children's classes) to make a special snack item to give teachers.

❑ Once or twice a year invite all staff (and their families) to a special appreciation event: pizza dinner, ice cream sundaes, picnic in the park, etc.

 Bonus Idea for Teacher Appreciation Decorations: To remind our teachers—and the church—of our yearlong teaching theme that kids need a lot of love and touch, we hung 400 to 500 yellow smiley faces with teachers' names all over the hallways and from the ceiling of our auditorium. You couldn't get into the room without dodging them! Each teacher came to the front of the room to receive yellow flowers and a personal smiley face as a thank-you. (Another year we did a similar theme with giant price tags saying "Teachers Are Priceless!") *Bonnie Aldrich, Pulpit Rock Church, Colorado Springs, Colorado*

Look to the Future

Duplicate and complete the "Recruiting" worksheet (pp. 178-180) to determine how you can begin working to meet the goals stated in this chapter.

Note
1. *Statistical Abstract of the United States: 1998.*

Bonus Ideas for Teacher Appreciation Events: In the spring, just before the teaching year ends, have a Latte Sunday just for teachers. Invite your teachers to drop into a designated room anytime during the morning. Provide flavored lattes for them to sample, and serve assorted brownies, cookies and fruits donated by grateful parents and students. *Karen Perkins, Walnut Creek Presbyterian Church, Walnut Creek, California*

We did a two-part event that the teachers loved. We served a baseball-theme dinner with vendors serving hot dogs and ice cream. Later we gave a trip to a Red Sox baseball game as our gift to the teachers. We sold extra tickets so that teachers could bring family members. The night of the game we rented buses and all went to the game together. *Grace Chapel, Massachusetts*

In early December, I invite teachers to an appreciation breakfast. Paid sitters provide child care during the breakfast. After breakfast, they can leave their children, so they can have a "day off" during the busy season to do Christmas shopping, wrap gifts or enjoy a quiet day with their spouses. I take the kids on an outing to a park or one of our local free museums. *Vikki Randall, Arcadia Presbyterian Church, Arcadia, California*

At a staff appreciation event, we show a video of what's been happening all year long. The highlight of the video is students from all the classes saying what they like best about their teachers. *Hailey Armoogan, Waterloo Pentecostal Assembly in Waterloo, Ontario, Canada*

One year we invited teachers and their families to an old-fashioned pie social. We served apple pie and ice cream. Cover the tables with red and white checked tablecloths. Make table decorations by wrapping three large red apples in clear cellophane, tying them with red ribbon and tying two or three red helium-filled balloons onto the package. *Eastminster Presbyterian Church, Ventura, California*

We've used a variety of themes for our teacher appreciation events. Bible Baseball and Lip Synch Contests were our two favorites. *Debbie Barber, Central Church, Memphis, Tennessee*

Recruiting

Rate your church's progress toward each goal and then list two or more actions you can take to reach each goal.

GOAL 1: MAKE RECRUITING EVERYBODY'S BUSINESS

Everyone on the Sunday School staff knows about and prays for recruitment needs.

1	2	3	4	5
Need to Start		Fair		Goal Achieved

Actions to Take:

GOAL 2: PLAN POSITIVE PUBLICITY

Create a churchwide campaign to let people know the good things happening in your Sunday School.

1	2	3	4	5
Need to Start		Fair		Goal Achieved

Actions to Take:

GOAL 3: HELP PEOPLE KNOW THEIR JOBS

Write a job description for each position on your Sunday School staff.

1	2	3	4	5
Need to Start		Fair		Goal Achieved

Actions to Take:

GOAL 4: FIND THE RIGHT PERSON FOR THE RIGHT JOB

List prospects for your staff with the goal of helping individuals find fulfilling places of ministry and growth.

1	2	3	4	5
Need to Start		Fair		Goal Achieved

Actions to Take:

GOAL 5: MAKE THE FIRST CONTACT A PERSONAL ONE

Set up a personal meeting with the prospective volunteer to provide (a) specific information concerning the position and length of service and (b) an opportunity to ask questions.

1	2	3	4	5
Need to Start		Fair		Goal Achieved

Actions to Take:

GOAL 6: OBSERVATION—THE FIRST STEP

Give each prospective volunteer (a) opportunities to observe someone doing the job he or she is being asked to do and (b) guidance as to what to look for and questions to ask the person being observed.

1	2	3	4	5
Need to Start		Fair		Goal Achieved

Actions to Take:

GOAL 7: FOLLOW-UP

Contact the prospective volunteer for an answer and accept his or her decision.

1	2	3	4	5
Need to Start		Fair		Goal Achieved

Actions to Take:

GOAL 8: TRAINING IS THE KEY

Schedule well-planned, preservice training programs for new staff.

1	2	3	4	5
Need to Start		Fair		Goal Achieved

Actions to Take:

GOAL 9: TIME FOR APPRECIATION

Plan ways to show your staff members that they are valued.

1	2	3	4	5
Need to Start		Fair		Goal Achieved

Actions to Take:

Chapter Eight

The Basics of Training and Planning

If you want an effective teaching ministry, you need to provide training and planning opportunities. The only questions are, What will you do? How will you get people to come?

What This Chapter Tells You

- Training is more than a one-time event.
- The benefits that result when leaders and teachers plan together.
- Planning together is an essential part of effective teaching and ministry.
- Communication of training opportunities and planning methods helps leaders and teachers make these essential steps to good teaching and ministry a priority.

What This Chapter Shows You

- What to do at training and planning meetings;
- How to encourage busy leaders and teachers to plan together;
- How to create a yearlong teacher training plan.

Where Do I Start?

Look at Where You Are

Duplicate and complete the "Training and Planning" worksheet (p. 183) to take a closer look at how training and planning have been accomplished in your church.

worksheet (p. 183)

> *"If the Church has important business to accomplish, why are we so sloppy about the way we do it?"*
> *Lucien F. Coleman, Jr.*

Straight Talk on Training

Sometimes ministry leaders are so glad to have someone (anyone!) willing to lead a group that they are tempted to forego the steps that are needed to help the willing volunteer become an effective teacher. Just as a flower garden that receives water only once a year is unlikely to produce blooms, a teacher that receives little training is unlikely to experience a fruitful ministry.

Get the Big Picture

Leaders and teachers must receive regular training and plan together in a systematic fashion. In order for training to truly make a difference, it must be an ongoing process. No matter what you call it—teaching enrichment, networking or orientation—the process of building up the skills of your leaders and teachers is a significant part of an effective Sunday School.

Teachers do not automatically know how to guide others in Bible learning. When left untrained, most teachers tend to teach in the way they were taught: good, bad or indifferent. And who among us would accept a new task without the promise of training to help us make a good start?

These are the benefits that will result from a long-term view of training and planning:

- By taking a step at a time, information about teaching methods and program procedures can be absorbed, allowing new teachers to gain confidence to take the next step;
- An ongoing training plan throughout the year makes sure that new staff members are given the thorough training they need, instead of a haphazard, quick orientation;
- When procedures inevitably change during the year, ongoing training means that a plan is already in place to communicate and discuss the changes;
- Veteran teachers will have the opportunity to enhance their skills;
- A sense of fresh enthusiasm is received from participation in a well-run training event.

Consistent planning goes hand in hand with training. Leaders and teachers who meet regularly can encourage and support one another in trying new ideas, evaluating progress, finding solutions to problems and sharing successes.

LOOK AT WHERE YOU ARE

Training and Planning

1. How is a new teacher most typically trained?

2. What training opportunities have recently been offered to the teachers in your program?

   How often do these training events take place?

3. Are the training opportunities instructional, inspirational or both?

4. How and when do most teachers plan together?

   What is done to encourage teachers to plan together?

5. What obstacles keep teachers from attending training events or planning meetings?

Focus on the Goals

GOAL 1:
TRAINING IS A CONTINUAL PROCESS

Well-Planned, Regular Training Is a Necessity for Effective Ministry

Teachers who are highly motivated in their jobs of sharing and teaching God's love to others need the support of a well-planned training program. Just think of the many parts of a Sunday School teacher's job:

- Bible knowledge;
- Understanding of students;
- Knowledge of teaching methods;
- Awareness of church policies and procedures;
- Understanding of communication techniques—to name just a few!

Six Major Characteristics of a Good Training Program

1. **It is related to the age level taught.** While principles of learning are essentially the same for all age groups (see chapter 3), teachers need to know how to apply these principles to the age level they teach.
2. **It is practical.** The focus of any training event should always be on practical ways in which the information being taught can be used in upcoming Sunday School sessions or programs.
3. **It is related to the curriculum.** Teachers should be able to see how their teacher's manual can help them continue to put into practice the information learned at a training event. For this reason, it is ideal when training events provide teachers with time to plan together during or at the end of the event.
4. **It is experiential.** Unless a teacher tries a new skill or method, he or she will probably not feel confident enough to use it in class. Every training event should involve participants in observing and practicing the skills they are being trained to use.
5. **It is regular.** When people are recruited to teach, they should clearly understand how they will regularly be equipped to succeed in their jobs.

6. **It is consistent.** From event to event and year to year, the training being offered is based on the same teaching/learning philosophy (if you didn't read chapter 3 before, read it now!). When all training events are carefully chosen to reinforce each other, you can be sure that your staff is not presented with conflicting educational philosophies and methods, and more than one age level can be trained at a time.

Three Major Types of Training

Training Events

All teachers will benefit by attending training conferences or workshops in which their total teaching ministry can be enriched. Both new and experienced teachers need opportunities to learn new skills, correct mistakes and expand their vision. Many churches find it helpful to plan at least two special training events each year, approximately four to six months apart. More than one such event is advantageous because

- Not all teachers will attend any single event;
- New teachers need significant reinforcement during the first year or two of service;
- New staff members added during the year need special help;
- Improved skills need reinforcement and support.

After any training event, evaluate what learning occurred. Were your objectives for the event met? Have teachers acquired or improved the needed skills? If the answer is yes, concentrate on the next area of need. If the answer is no, consider how you can address the need in a different way.

Class or Department Training

Teachers who meet together for planning can include a time of training in their meetings; then during the next Sunday School classes, they can immediately put into practice new methods or procedures they have learned. Well-attended training and planning meetings keep the entire staff working together and build a sense of teamwork.

Individual Training

In addition to participating in special training events or planning meetings with other teachers, individual teachers can improve their skills in a variety of ways. While doing everything possible to encourage teachers to attend planning and training meetings, also provide ways for teachers to improve their skills on their own.

 Bonus Ideas for Good Planning Meetings: I found that making our meetings really useful and productive motivated teachers to attend. So we plan meetings that include making Bible learning games, preparing transparencies, organizing picture files, singing new songs, preparing lesson materials and/or bulletin boards. *Willamae Myers, Grace Bible Fellowship, Pinellas Park, Florida*

Create a theme for your meeting, promote it well and plan your meeting agenda around the theme as well. For example, "Sail into Summer with C. E." with nautical decorations, blue punch and "sea" food. *Hailey Armoogan, Waterloo Pentecostal Assembly, Waterloo, Ontario, Canada*

Food is the key! Serve significant food—more than cookies and coffee! Our favorites are a potato bar with toppings, a soup and salad, a pizza or spaghetti feed. *Karen Perkins, Walnut Creek Presbyterian Church, Walnut Creek, California*

✔ Action Checklist

❑ Suggest that teachers observe a Sunday School class or other program in action. Choose a class that is functioning well and suggest the following questions as a guideline for the observer to watch for: How did the teacher involve students? How did the teacher achieve the lesson aim? How did the teacher communicate interest and caring for students? It is not necessary that the model class be perfect, as people can learn as much from weaknesses as from strengths.

❑ Provide books, videos or cassette tapes that offer training on a particular skill (discipline, discovery learning, communication skills, etc.). A viewing guide and worksheet are often provided with videos to help teachers apply the skills being discussed and demonstrated. Keep a supply of several such materials to loan out to teachers on a regular basis. Suggest that teachers take advantage of times such as commuting in the car or riding a stationary bike to build their skills.

❑ Post mini-posters in classrooms or teacher workrooms which feature a specific training tip or a particular procedure of which teachers need reminding. Change the posters frequently to keep interest high.

❑ Send a monthly newsletter with a brief article highlighting a particular skill and listing a variety of specific ways to put it into practice. Ask an experienced teacher to write examples of how he or she applies the skill in specific classroom situations.

❑ Contact the supplier of your curriculum to determine what training resources are available that will provide the most help to your teachers in using the curriculum successfully.

❑ Survey teachers to discover specific training needs. Ask each person to indicate topics and skills he or she would like to learn about.

❑ Develop a plan to meet the training needs you discover: What special events do you need to schedule? What individual training opportunities do you need to provide? Putting your plan in writing at the beginning of the school year makes it more likely that the needed training will take place. If your training ideas are written on your planning calendar from the very beginning, they are less likely to be forgotten or crowded out by other events.

❑ Evaluate the training programs offered in your area and then invite all teachers who would benefit to participate. Various denominational and other publishing companies conduct training events to help people use their curriculum materials more effectively. Sunday School conventions are held in many communities. Designate specific workshops or sessions for new teachers who may find it difficult to choose which to attend. Encourage teachers to attend workshops or sessions with their supervisors. Before your staff attends a training event, share your expectations. For example, you might inform participants:
  • "We will schedule a time for those who attend to discuss plans for putting new ideas into practice."
  • "Be ready to tell two or three key ideas you learn at the event."
  • "You can help us implement (feature of training) in our Sunday School."

❑ Conduct your own training courses or workshops, or work with the teachers in several nearby churches to plan a training event together. Schedule these courses to fit your church's needs and circumstances: weekend training (Friday night and Saturday morning or all day Saturday), a training week (four successive evenings) or a training month (one session per week for four weeks). Churches with strong leadership in each age group can have all groups meet at the same time in separate rooms in the church. Other churches may need to focus on one or two age groups at a time. Experienced leaders or teachers from your church or denomination may lead the sessions.

Topics for Teacher Skill Improvement: This list is just a starter! Add to it according to your needs.

Age-Level Characteristics
Discipline
Class Schedule
How People Learn
Learning Activities
Leading Discussion Groups
Storytelling
Sharing the Gospel
Building Relationships
Outreach Ideas
Leading Bible Studies
Listening to Teens
Interacting with Families
Multicultural Ministries
Developing Your Spiritual Life
Finding Balance in Your Life

 Bonus Idea for Busy Teacher Training: Instead of conducting one large training meeting, train facilitators to do a two-hour training session at the leader's home with a pizza supper included. Help the facilitators by giving them an outline to follow or a teacher training video to use and discuss. Make sure they leave plenty of time for team building and discussion of how to take the ideas into the classroom or their ministry. *Ron Richardson, Hillsong Church, Chapel Hill, North Carolina*

A Sample Training Calendar

(Use the monthly calendar form on the following page to create your own training calendar.)

Subject: Teacher Training

September	*Training event at church*
October	*Distribute training videos*
November	*Feature skill improvement in newsletter*
December	*Display mini-posters each week*
January	*Training event at church*
February	*Feature skill improvement in newsletter*
March	*Citywide Sunday School convention*
April	*Distribute training videos*
May	*Feature skill improvement in newsletter*
June	*Display mini-posters each week*
July	*Teacher interview about a skill in newsletter*
August	*Distribute training videos*

 Bonus Idea for Weekly Teacher Training: Each week I give a Sunday Morning Memo to all my teachers. The memo includes some bite-size teacher training helps on one or more topics and current announcements. *Terry Platt, Calvary Memorial Church, Oak Park, Illinois*

Monthly Calendar

January	February	March

April	May	June

July	August	September

October	November	December

GOAL 2:
CONSISTENT PLANNING

Schedule Regular Planning Meetings

There will be some who feel there is no need (or time) for planning together. Many leaders simply give up on the idea of planning because of the seemingly insurmountable difficulties of bringing teachers together. First, let's talk about the reasons planning is needed, what happens at a planning session and some practical ways to make planning happen.

Time for planning is important for the following reasons:

- Communication and coordination among the teaching team is required for lesson aims to be met. Experienced teachers are able to help new teachers grow in their understanding of teaching procedures; even those who teach alone will find it beneficial to talk over lesson plans and brainstorm teaching methods with another teacher of the same or similar age level.

- Planning together makes it possible for each member of the teaching team to work toward the same learning aim and feel supported, which in turn will improve each member's enjoyment of his or her teaching tasks.

- Problem solving and idea sharing are needed by all teachers and are particularly helpful when provided in the context of planning the next lesson.

Each planning meeting should include:

1. **Ministry to each other:** Getting to know each other and discovering ways in which God's Word relates to their lives is an important aspect of ministry and builds a sense of unity and teamwork between teachers. Prayer requests can be exchanged or team members may participate in a prayer time as part of the meeting.

2. **Skill improvement:** Whether through watching and discussing a teacher training video or listing ideas to meet a particular challenge in the class, teachers need to focus on one specific skill or topic each month. In a formal meeting involving a group of teachers, activities and discussion can be done to improve a particular aspect of teaching.

3. **Lesson preview:** Teachers skim through the next few lessons (often called a unit) and familiarize themselves with the Scripture to be studied. Lesson aims are reviewed and learning activities are selected based on the aims.

4. **Lesson planning:** Planning for the upcoming lessons (at least one unit) is completed as a group, determining who will lead each activity, confirming supply availability and reviewing classroom procedures as needed.

 **Look to the Future** Duplicate and complete the "Training and Planning" worksheet (p. 191) to determine how you can begin working to meet the goals stated in this chapter.

✔ Action Checklist

The more often planning meetings are held, the more effective and productive they will be. Here are specific ideas and tips for making planning meetings happen:

❑ If planning meetings have been held irregularly in the past, first ask several key teachers to help you plan the time and frequency of meetings. Then ask all teachers to give your plan a three- to four-month trial period. Then do all you can to make each meeting so helpful to your staff that they will *want* to continue at the end of the trial period. Some churches highlight the importance they place on planning meetings by making attendance a requirement.

❑ Carefully plan the meeting agenda in order to begin and end the meeting on time.

❑ Consider a variety of options in choosing planning meeting times: Weeknight dessert, Saturday morning continental breakfast, Sunday pizza lunch (include all family members for the pizza!) or Sunday during regularly scheduled classes (recruit a one-time team of parent helpers or substitutes).

❑ Set and publicize the date, time and focus for each meeting well in advance; then take the following steps to make them a reality:

- Personally talk to everyone who should attend, letting them know how they will benefit from attending. Publishing a bulletin announcement and/or sending a letter is usually not enough to motivate attendance.
- Provide transportation or babysitting if needed.

❑ Give teachers preparation assignments. For example, you might ask each teacher to read a short article about leading discussion groups and share one idea from it. When teachers come prepared, they bring an attitude of expectancy and their sense of responsibility to be there increases.

❑ One alternative idea is to plan two or three all-staff planning meetings during the year at which all teachers meet together for a time and then divide according to age-level groups for lesson preview and planning. Throughout the year, however, the teaching teams (usually two to six teachers) are asked to meet together for planning on a more frequent basis.

❑ Encourage teachers to meet together informally (two or three at a time)—brown-bagging lunches together once a week; coffee night once a month, etc. The goal is to encourage planning and communication by whatever means possible!

- A time of lesson preview and planning can be followed by a brisk walk in the park while discussing ways to improve classroom procedures;
- A team of teachers can get together once a month for an early morning breakfast before work;
- Two teachers can meet together at one home while a toddler is taking a nap, etc.
- Interview teachers to find out the many and creative ways in which they plan together, and publish your findings in a newsletter as a way of encouraging others to meet on a regular basis.

Training and Planning

Rate your church's progress toward each goal and then list two or more actions you can take to reach each goal.

GOAL 1: TRAINING IS A CONTINUAL PROCESS

Regular training events are carefully planned to provide significant help to teachers in their ministries.

1	2	3	4	5
Need to Start		Fair		Goal Achieved

Actions to Take:

GOAL 2: CONSISTENT PLANNING

Teaching teams meet together for regular planning meetings.

1	2	3	4	5
Need to Start		Fair		Goal Achieved

Actions to Take:

Chapter Nine

MakeRoom for Teaching

Teaching and learning can occur almost anywhere, but the setting where it takes place has a significant impact on every aspect of the process. Facilities can make the teacher's task easier or more difficult. The surroundings can draw students toward learning or distract them from it. Furniture can make a room comfortable so that learning can occur or uncomfortable so that restlessness results. Equipment can help communicate, room arrangements can aid in building relationships, and walls can help introduce or reinforce learning.

What This Chapter Tells You

- A Sunday School needs to provide rooms that meet the unique needs of each age level.
- There are numerous practical ways to adapt inadequate facilities.

What This Chapter Shows You

- How to calculate the amount of space and number of rooms needed;
- How to select and arrange appropriate furniture and equipment for each age level;
- Tips for adapting nontraditional facilities in warehouses, schools, theaters, etc.;
- What to do when facilities are shared with other groups, when facilities do not fit current uses, or when you run out of space.

Where Do I Start?

Get the Big Picture

There are those who say that one hour a week hardly warrants investing very much time, energy or money to improve or expand facilities. Of course, that all depends on what happens in that one hour. When people are being reached, when faith and knowledge are being enriched, when lives are being changed, then that investment makes a great deal of sense.

A Sunday School with facilities planned to accommodate the unique needs of each age level will benefit in the following ways:

- Teachers and students are able to focus on effective learning and building relationships.
- People recognize that the congregation values its teaching ministries.
- Outreach efforts are enhanced when provision has been made for new people to be welcomed and involved.

The church that provides appropriate facilities for the Sunday School also gains ample facilities for a wide variety of other ministries throughout the week.

The goals of your teaching ministry should shape your facilities. Don't let your facilities shape the goals of your ministry.

A Case Study

I stood in front of a group of Sunday School teachers in Russia, distributing sheets of paper with suggested room dimensions and furniture arrangements for different age levels. As these leaders looked through my handouts, it quickly became obvious that my recommendations had struck a nerve. I glanced at Eugene Pavlov, my interpreter, who whispered to me, "Those room sizes are bigger than some of their church buildings."

Some of the recommendations in this chapter may seem as unrealistic to you as they initially did to those Russians who were valiantly striving to build Sunday Schools under extremely difficult situations. But the recommendations in this chapter are valid guidelines for church leaders in any culture, for they describe ways to plan and adapt and improve the places where Sunday School classes meet. In all cultures, similar-size groups of the same age take up approximately the same amount of space when they sit down and participate in learning.

Unfortunately, many Sunday Schools allow the current limitations of their facilities to limit not only their current learning environment, but they also allow them to limit their vision for the future. As I told those leaders in Russia, "If you only learn how to get by in your present circumstances, you will probably stay in those circumstances." This chapter is intended to help you prepare for improvements and expansion in the years to come.

Look at Where You Are

Duplicate and complete the charts in this chapter (General Room Requirements on pp. 197-198, Recommended Sizes for Tables/Chairs on p. 205 and Recommended Furniture by Age Level on pp. 206-207) to take a closer look at how your facilities are aiding or hindering your teaching ministries.

Focus on the Goals

GOAL 1:
FACILITIES

Facilities Need to Support the Teaching/Learning Plan.

The layout and setup of the rooms in a church building reflect the congregation's commitment and approach to learning. The preceding chapters in this manual describe how to build a Sunday School where life-changing learning takes place. This approach to learning has significant implications for the *rooms* where people gather. Consider the impact your facilities can have on reaching your learning goals (see chapter 3) in all of your classes:

1. Since your teaching is centered on God's Word, rooms should reflect the beauty, majesty and importance of the Book we study. Dingy and depressing rooms communicate a lack of caring for what we claim we value most.
2. Since reaching out to others is vital to the health of the Sunday School, space must be provided for more than those already attending. When classrooms are full, motivation to reach others drops.
3. Since the focus of Bible teaching is to meet the life needs of students, facilities need to fit the needs and characteristics of all who attend. Chairs that are the wrong size and bulletin boards that are at the wrong height are too often accepted as normal, causing people to feel they don't belong in groups where they should be nurtured.
4. Since the most effective Bible teaching methods are those that actively involve students, facilities need to allow for learning participation.
5. Space needs to accommodate workable group sizes that allow teachers to efficiently guide active participation in all steps of the learning process.

A Few Factors

The size needed for a classroom and the way you equip it depends on:

- **The age level of the students**: Younger students need more space and more varied furniture than older ones;
- **The number of students**: Larger class sizes need more space and furniture than smaller ones;
- **The number of teachers**: More teachers allows for the creation of more classes, as opposed to larger, more impersonal classes.

 Bonus Ideas for Improving Facilities: In our church, we try not to have any bare walls. We dress up our classrooms with bright wall paint, large posters we order from school supply stores, precut letters and borders for large four-foot-wide bulletin boards. *David Arnold, Parkview Evangelical Free Church, Iowa City, Iowa*

Have teachers walk into the classroom at the height of their students (some will have to be on their knees!) and ask, *What does this room say to my students?* Challenge teachers to make a list of at least five ideas/changes that can be made so that the room says "Something exciting is going to happen here!" *Willamae Myers, Grace Bible Fellowship, Pinellas Park, Florida*

Once a year, have a gift shower for each age level. Display needed items along with their prices (get them on consignment) and invite people to individually or cooperatively purchase them. *Authors*

✔ Action Checklist

❑ Walk through classrooms and rate them with a similar scale to that used in evaluating restaurants (A=excellent, etc.). The Room Evaluation form on page 199 will help you evaluate appearance, age-level appropriateness and cleanliness. Use the completed form to help you compile a dream list of priority projects to improve your facility.

❑ If you're involved in a building program or looking for ways to add life to the facility, plan a field trip or two. Visit several places where people in your community like to spend time—a mall, a community park, an outdoor shopping area. When you visit, notice what parts of the facility invite people to come and stay. Is it a welcoming entrance? Comfortable seating arranged to facilitate conversation? Attractive decorations? Then think about ways you can incorporate one or more of these enhancements to the facility.

General Room Requirements

1. **Ceilings** should be 8 to 10 feet (2.4 to 3 meters) high. Acoustical (nonasbestos) covering helps muffle noise.

2. **Walls** should be painted attractively and be free of clutter or distracting elements. Two or more colors and/or textures on the walls add interest. For example, carpeting the lower section of a wall varies the texture and color while helping to muffle noise and improve insulation. Avoid large murals that leave little space for displaying lesson-related items.
   - **Bulletin boards** or **strips** should be mounted at eye level for the age group using the room.
   - **Displays** should be kept current (changed once a month, if possible), giving priority to those that reflect/support the current Bible learning emphasis.
   - **Early childhood, children's and youth rooms** need durable wall surfaces that can accept frequent touching as well as tacking or taping items to them.
   - **Moveable walls or partitions** should allow for easily changing the function and arrangement of space, opening up a classroom to allow participation with another group or a large assembly. Flexible design of space allows other programs of the church to use space in significantly different ways throughout the week.

3. **Floor coverings** should have subdued patterns. Washable carpet or vinyl tile are best.
   - **Carpeting** provides warmth, sound control and a relaxed atmosphere.
   - **Vinyl floor coverings** may be easier to clean, but an **area rug** may be desirable in children's rooms for activities done on the floor.
   - Consider your **maintenance and cleaning** procedures. Floor coverings are only as attractive and clean as the care they are given.

4. **Lighting** should be semidirect, avoiding glare while allowing ease of reading. At least two intensity settings should be possible, allowing lights to be dimmed (e.g., for viewing video, film or overhead projection) without making a room totally dark. **Windows** should be as large as possible, ideally looking outside at trees, shrubs and/or flowers. Shades or blinds may be needed to cut glare, hide distractions and/or allow darkening the room.

5. **Heating and ventilation** should be easily adjustable to keep rooms at 68 degrees Fahrenheit (20 degrees Celsius) and avoid the air becoming stuffy.

6. **Rest room facilities** should be provided in each building on each floor. It is desirable that rooms for children, especially those under six years of age, have direct access to a rest room (i.e., shared between two rooms). Rest rooms to be used by these children should have fixtures appropriate to their size:
   - **Ages 3 and under**: 18-inch (45-cm)-high washbasins, 10-inch (25-cm)-high toilets
   - **Ages 4 and 5**: 20-inch (50-cm)-high washbasins, 12-inch(30-cm)-high toilets

7. **Electrical outlets** should be the three-prong grounded type with at least one receptacle on each wall to eliminate hazardous use of extension cords. In rooms for young children, outlets should have safety covers and/or be installed out of a child's reach (i.e., above light switches, counters, etc.).

8. **Audiovisual accessories** should be provided for each room, including:
   - **Visual items for all ages**: chalkboards and/or white boards
   - **Visual items for children**: flannel boards, maps, word/song charts, puppet stage
   - **Visual items for youth/adult**: projection screen, flip chart with easel, maps
   - **Audio items for all ages**: CD or cassette players/recorders

9. **Furniture** should be selected to fit the physical needs of the age level using the room and the types of activities being provided (Goal 3). Rooms for early childhood and children's classes should be furnished and arranged to meet the present needs of children, not to imitate adult rooms.

10. **Decor/Atmosphere** should be appropriate to the age group meeting in the room, giving people a sense that this room was prepared for them. Avoid a sterile, structured classroom feel that causes people to think *boring*, *dull*, or *same old stuff*. Something in the room should be obviously fresh or different every week (posters, furniture arrangement, flowers, materials or supplies on chairs or tables, etc.).

11. **Approaches** to the room should help invite people into the room. Building entrances, foyers, hallways and classroom doorways should convey a sense of welcome, helping to build a sense of positive expectation.

12. **Signs** should clearly direct people, never assuming that everybody knows where the youth meet or assuming that visitors will feel comfortable asking for directions. Signs should be
   • Posted high enough to be visible when people fill the area;
   • Placed strategically throughout the campus (i.e., in the parking lot, in common areas, visible when entering or exiting the worship area, etc.).

A sign outside each room should clearly identify the group that is meeting there, not just by the name of the group, but also identifying the age, grade or topic, as well as the time when the group meets.

Room 101

8:30—Single Adults (20s & 30s)
9:45—College/Career
11:00—Young Marrieds (20s)

---

13. **Hallways** should be wide enough (8 to 15 feet [2.4 to 4.5 m]) so that several people can easily pass each other and that stopping for a quick chat will not create major traffic jams.

14. **Meeting spots** should be available throughout the campus, places where people can enjoy standing or sitting for a few minutes of friendly conversation. For example, instead of having the end of a hallway simply be a dead end, arrange a couch or bench next to a planter with an indoor tree or shrub. Evaluate approaches to youth rooms in terms of teenagers' desire to hang out before or after a session. Is an area needed outside the room, or is the room large enough and informal enough to provide for that need inside?

15. **A resource room** stocked with supplies, audiovisual equipment and curriculum resources should be readily accessible to all classroom areas. Most teachers are unlikely to walk very far to pick up items before class, so a large facility usually needs more than one such room.

Room Evaluation Form

	Class Name

Date _____

Evaluated by _____

| | Room |

Put an X in each box where improvement is needed

The Classroom						
Adequate space?						
Quick, easy movement from large to small groups?						
Adequate lighting from windows, fixtures?						
Proper ventilation?						
Controlled temperature?						
Floor and ceiling absorb sound?						
Bulletin boards/wall displays at students' eye level?						
Bulletin boards current and uncluttered?						
Provision for darkening room for videos?						
Electrical outlets accessible/adequate?						
Screen or blank wall available for projection?						
Room attractively decorated?						
Walls clean, cheerful in color?						
Walls need repair/painting?						
Toilet, sink facilities easily accessible?						
Handicap access to room?						
Any doors that could be taken off small rooms to facilitate movement?						
Any walls that could be removed to give more flexibility?						
Adequate storage facilities?						
Floor coverings adequate, clean?						
Classroom Equipment						
Furniture/equipment easily moved to provide flexibility?						
Classroom materials available, so students have easy access?						
Tables, chairs the right size?						
Any excess furniture that could be removed to provide more space?						
Any additional furniture/equipment needed?						
Any furniture/equipment needing repair/painting?						

Bonus Idea for Creating Space: Partitions can be made from multipurpose bins or cabinets—when commercially made partitions aren't available, decorate a piece of cardboard from a large appliance box. If partitions are "tired" looking, glue new carpet squares to them for a fresh, colorful look. *Terry Platt, Calvary Memorial Church, Oak Park, Illinois*

GOAL 2: SPACE

Amount of Space Affects Teaching Procedures.

How much space do we need for our nursery? How big a room should we give our middle schoolers? Why shouldn't adults get the nice big rooms? Preschool rooms are licensed for a maximum number of children; is it OK to exceed those limits on Sunday since it's only once a week and many of the children are here for a short time? These are typical of the questions people ask about the amount of space needed for different Sunday School classes. The answers to these questions are very important, because adequate space makes a big difference in being able to implement effective teaching procedures.

Why Space Is Important

1. Students need space to interact easily with others in the group. When space is limited and people feel crowded, friendly interaction drops.
2. Students need space to work on activities, individually and in groups. When space is limited, so are the possibilities for active learning approaches.
3. Young children are not able to sit still for extended periods and need room to move around.

The Attendance/Space Recommendations chart on page 201 is a useful tool in evaluating the amount of space needed for groups of any age level. The chart has four major columns, each divided into two subcolumns: "Recommended" and "Actual." Duplicate copies of the chart and distribute them to teachers and staff who fill in the "Actual" columns; then compare those numbers with the ones in the "Recommended" columns.

Attendance/Space Recommendations

R= Recommended   A = Actual (what you now have)

	Column 1 Maximum Attendance per Department		Column 2 Optimum Room Dimensions and Approximate Square Footage		Column 3 Floor Space per Person		Column 4 Student Ratio for Small Group Class	
	R	A	R	A*	R	A+	R	A
EARLY CHILDHOOD Ages 0 to 1	12-15		24'x36'=900 sq.ft.		30-35 sq.ft.		1:3 or 4	
Ages 2 to 3	16-20		24'x36'=900 sq.ft.		30-35 sq.ft.		1:5	
Ages 4 to 5	20-24		24'x36'=900 sq.ft.		30-35 sq.ft.		1:6	
CHILDREN Grades 1 to 5/6	24-30		24'x36'=900 sq.ft.		25-30 sq.ft.		1:6 to 8	
YOUTH Grades 6/7 to 12	30-40		24'x36'=900 sq.ft.		20-25 sq.ft.		1:8	
ADULT Ages 18+	30-40		18'x25'=450 sq.ft.		10-15 sq.ft.		1:8**	

Notes

*To figure room square footage, multiply the length of the room by the width.

+To figure floor space per person, divide room square footage (see column 2) by department attendance (see column 1).

**Ratio for small discussion groups.

NOTES ABOUT CHART COLUMNS

Column 1: Maximum Attendance per Department

"Department" refers to classes or groups that meet together for at least part of the Sunday School session. Maximum size recommendations recognize that personal relationships and student involvement diminish as class or group size increases. (See chapter 5 for further explanations of class sizes.)

Column 2: Optimum Room Dimensions

These recommendations are based on classes or groups with attendance at or near the maximum figures in Column 1. Obviously, smaller classes can function very well in smaller rooms. However, smaller rooms will impose growth limits on classes. To allow for future growth, it is wise to build or modify smaller rooms as expandable units of an optimal room. For example:

- A 900-square-foot room (24x36-foot) could be divided into two rooms of 450 square feet each (24x18-foot), housing a youth group of 15 to 20 and an adult class of up to 40.
- The same room could be divided into three rooms of 300 square feet each (24x12-foot), housing a children's group of eight, a youth group of 10 to 12 and an adult class of 20 to 30.

Smaller rooms that you may need to expand in the future to accommodate growth can be temporarily separated either by a nonbearing wall that can be removed when the time comes or by a moveable partition. The latter approach is more costly but allows the flexibility of moving back and forth from a larger open space to smaller rooms.

If your building has small classrooms that cannot easily be expanded, see Goal 3 (Room Arrangements, pp. 212-213) later in this chapter. You will see how a cluster of small rooms can be adapted for use similarly to a single larger room.

Column 3: Space per Person

All age groups can be squeezed into less space per person. Churches do it all the time. But there are negative consequences when these guidelines are violated:

Safety: In most communities, fire departments post maximum numbers of people who can safely occupy a room. Typically, these calculations assume a theater-style seating arrangement, in which adults occupy a chair and the space between it and the chair in front (six square feet per person). When you add in space for aisles so that people can get in and out, area for the teacher to stand and move and place a Bible and notes (and perhaps an overhead projector or VCR and monitor), and one or more tables or desks or counters for supplies and/or refreshments, a bare minimum of 8 to 10 square feet per person is essential just to avoid a visit from the fire marshal, let alone to have a comfortable learning environment!

When state agencies license preschools and day-care centers, their calculations take into consideration that young children need to move often. They are not going to spend a session seated in one place—not if they are going to have a healthful, positive learning experience. Church nurseries that crowd too many crawlers and toddlers into the available space are risking a high incidence of bumps, hurt feelings, tears and even biting and hair pulling among these little ones.

Relationships: With the possible exception of teenagers who tend to look for excuses to crowd together as closely as possible, reducing the amount of space per person restricts positive, friendship-building interaction. In addition to the mechanical problem of taxing even the best quality air conditioning/ventilation system by overcrowding a room, people are less likely to exert themselves to talk with others in such settings. Crowded rooms also pose the following challenges:

- Members who spot visitors on the other side of a crowded room typically assume someone else will make that person feel welcome.
- Seating is usually in rows, leaving people looking mostly at the backs of other people's heads, except for those in the front who only see the teacher.
- Getting people in and out of a crowded room is more like an exercise in crowd control than a friendly gathering—especially for a visitor who feels surrounded rather than welcomed! (Have you ever noticed how uncomfortable most people look getting onto an elevator crowded with strangers?)
- Children view other children as competitors rather than friends, vying for prized chairs, table space to work on, supplies to complete a task, etc. Close proximity of other children can also create overstimulation and behavior problems, often making teachers and children feel like adversaries.

Learning: Crowded rooms force teachers into using performance/presentation methods instead of active/involving methods. When students do not have ample room to engage in interactive group processes, they end up sitting, watching and listening, quickly becoming passive observers.

Column 4: Teacher/Student Ratio

Some people question what these numbers are doing in a chart about space recommendations. The answer is simple. Space is never an independent factor in the total learning process. Simply providing nice, large rooms will not produce learning. Square footage does not change anyone's life. Thus, room size, attendance maximums and space allotments must *all* be considered in light of the people who guide learning in each class or group (see chapter 5).

Remember Lewis Carroll's fantasy story of Alice and how disoriented she felt when the chair was obviously too large or too small for her size? Or Goldilocks's search for a chair or a bed that was "just right"? In real life, who has not experienced the discomfort of entering a room and not being able to easily find a suitable place to sit? While having enough of the right-size furniture seems obvious, there are many important issues to consider in equipping rooms for every age level. Consider these three reasons why having the correct sizes and type of furniture are important to your Sunday School:

1. Students learn best when they are comfortable.
2. Students learn best when they are motivated. Well-planned furniture creates an environment that encourages learning.
3. People want to return to a group where they felt welcome. Appropriate furniture contributes to helping people feel good about a group.

✔ Action Checklist

If your Sunday School does not provide enough space for some of your classes or groups, consider the following options:

- ❏ Swap rooms with a class or group that has too much room.
  Tip: To help the group being asked to give up their larger room, include several people from that group in the planning process. Also, give the smaller room a face-lift to make it appealing to the group moving in.
- ❏ Rent extra space in a nearby school, restaurant, garage or other building, or provide classroom space in buses, trailers or RVs.
  Tip: Assign adult classes to temporary locations to keep the need for better facilities in front of the people who will pay the bill. This may also reduce problems with fire and building code regulations.
- ❏ Clear out any unused or nonessential furniture or equipment (piano, podium, extra chairs, desks, cabinets, etc.), or reduce table sizes to fit groups of no more than your maximum teacher/student ratio. A table that seats 10 is wasting space in a group that needs one teacher for six students.
- ❏ Convert unused or underused space (offices, storage rooms, hallways, etc.) that can be converted to classrooms.
- ❏ Erect temporary buildings in the church parking lot or lawn area.
- ❏ Remodel existing space (remove walls or portions of walls or enlarge doorways) to convert several small classrooms into a more usable large open room (see Goal 3: Room Arrangements).
- ❏ Replace floor cabinets/cupboards with wall-mounted units 50 inches (1.25 meters) from the floor.
- ❏ Consider an additional Sunday School session to expand your usable space with little or no added expense.
  Tip: Providing two or more worship services and two or more Sunday School sessions usually expands available space for all age levels except early childhood. If parents attend (or teach) Sunday School one session and the worship service another session, most churches find they must provide appropriate programs for those children during each session. Other age groups can share their Sunday School space with a group that meets during another session.
- ❏ Divide large groups into two or more smaller groups that fit better into available space.
- ❏ Start a building program to add facilities for Sunday School and other ministries.

GOAL 3: FURNITURE

Appropriate Furniture and Equipment Are Needed.

Remember Lewis Carroll's fantasy story of Alice and how disoriented she felt when the chair was obviously too large or too small for her size? Or Goldilocks's search for a chair or a bed that was "just right"? In real life, who has not experienced the discomfort of entering a room and not being able to easily find a suitable place to sit? While having enough of the right-size furniture seems obvious, there are many important issues to consider in equipping rooms for every age level. Consider these three reasons why having the correct sizes and type of furniture are important to your Sunday School:

1. Students learn best when they are comfortable.
2. Students learn best when they are motivated. Well-planned furniture creates an environment that encourages learning.
3. People want to return to a group where they felt welcome. Appropriate furniture contributes to helping people feel good about a group.

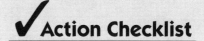 Action Checklist

- ❏ Duplicate the following charts: Recommended Sizes for Tables/Chairs (p. 205) and Recommended Furniture (pp. 206-207). Give a copy to each person involved in evaluating the facilities.
  - Compare the furniture in each room with the descriptions in the charts.
  - Circle the items that need improvement.

Recommended Sizes for Tables/Chairs			
Age Group	**Chair: Height from floor+**	**Tables: 10 inches (25 cm) higher than chairs**	**Tabletops: Durable and washable**
Ages 2 to 5	10-14 inches (25-35 cm)*	20-24 inches (50-60 cm)	Approx. 30x48 inches (75x120 cm)
Grades 1 to 6	12-16 inches (30-40 cm)	22-26 inches (55-65 cm)	30x48 inches (75x120 cm) to 36x60 inches (90x150 cm)
Youth/Adult	18 inches (45 cm)**	28 inches (70 cm)	30x96 inches (75x240 cm) or round tables 6 feet (1.8 m) in diameter

Notes:
+Stackable chairs that do not collapse are preferable to folding chairs.
*In Early Childhood rooms, no adult-sized chairs are necessary, as teachers should sit at child's eye level.
**Chairs with moveable tablet arms are useful in rooms where groups do not sit around tables.

Recommended Furniture

R=Strongly recommended O=Optional, would be nice to have

ITEMS	Early Childhood**			Children	Youth	Adult
	Babies	Toddlers	Preschool	Children	Youth	Adult
Care /Management						
Crib	R	O				
Bouncy seat	R					
Playpen	R					
Adult rockers	R	R				
Wall-mounted storage	R	R	R	R	O	O
Changing table	R	R				
Sink	R	R	O	O		
Drinking fountain			O	O		
Coat rack	R	R	R	R	O	O
Supply table/counter	R	R	R	R	R	R
Wastebasket	R	R	R	R	R	R
Activities						
Rocking boat/steps		R	O			
Child rocker		R	R			
Child stove/sink units			R			
Doll bed		R	R			
Book rack/shelf unit		O	R	R		
Open shelf units	O	R	R	R	O	O
Painting easels			R	R	R	
Lectern					O	O
Tables		O	R	R	O	O
Chairs		O	R	R	R	R

# Recommended Furniture (Cont'd.)
R=Strongly recommended O=Optional, would be nice to have

ITEMS	Early Childhood**			Children	Youth	Adult
	Babies	Toddlers	Preschool	Children	Youth	Adult
Audio/Visual						
Bulletin board(s)	R	R	R	R	R	R
CD/cassette player	R	R	R	R	R	O
Chalk- or white board				R	R	R
Easel for charts				O	O	O
Piano				O	O	O
Overhead projector*					R	R
Projection screen*				O	O	O
VCR/monitor*			O	R	R	R

Notes
*Items can be shared among various classes and need not be provided in every room.
**Corners of all furniture, shelves and counters should be rounded or padded. Furniture and equipment should be light enough that teachers can easily move items to vary the room arrangement.

Room for a Crowd

The room diagrams and space recommendations in this chapter are the result of a commitment to a teaching approach that emphasizes student involvement and personal relationships. Alongside that commitment is awareness that there are times when churches need to bring larger groups together for programs that focus on presentations rather than interaction:

CHILDREN'S PROGRAMS (GRADES 1 TO 5/6)
- Children's Churchtime
- Weekday clubs
- Puppet presentations
- Choirs/Singers/Entertainers
- Vacation Bible School

(**Note:** Rooms for younger children do not need to be expandable unless they are used by other age levels during the week. Children under six should remain in their own classes if at all possible, combining with older children only if the total group remains within the maximum group size for the age level. For example, five-year-olds are better off in a room specifically designed for them than meeting with a large group of elementary-aged children.)

YOUTH PROGRAMS (GRADES 6/7 TO 12)
- Games
- Concerts
- Guest speakers

A building that meets the needs of various ministries usually makes use of at least some movable walls or partitions. There are many ways to design space so that it can be divided or opened depending on program needs. Many large churches provide a bigger scale variation on the old assembly/class design, with "classrooms" built for groups of up to 20 to 30 and the assembly area holding well over 100.

SAMPLE CHILDREN'S COMPLEX

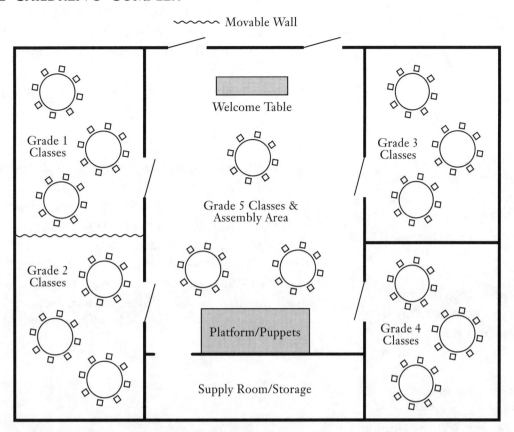

CHILDREN'S COMPLEX: HEXAGONAL ROOMS

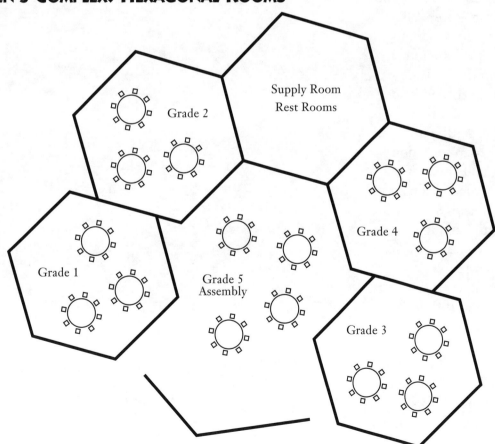

✔ Action Checklist

If your Sunday School does not provide appropriate furniture for all groups, consider the following options:

❑ Analyze your budget for the current year and determine if any money is available to purchase needed furniture and equipment. Also consider next year's budget.
Tip: Set priorities for the most urgent furniture or equipment needs.

❑ Share your needs with church leaders and then with the congregation.

❑ Schedule a workday to build some needed equipment (storage cabinets, shelves, early childhood furniture). Enlist parents, grandparents or retired craftsmen to build items.

❑ Temporarily substitute alternate materials.
Tips: A cardboard box can be used for a doll bed; a half sheet of plywood nailed to a piano bench makes a children's table; a blank, light-colored wall serves as a projection screen.

❑ Carpet squares can be substituted if there is a shortage of chairs for groups.

❑ Tack sheets of paper to the wall or tape it to the floor if there is a shortage of table space for art activities.

A Few Tips

• The main assembly area should be flexible enough to allow one or more groups to meet there when the dividers are closed. If this area is located directly adjacent to the classrooms, it can also serve as a welcome center for students arriving for any of the classes in the group.

• If the combined group requires more than five or six rows, a low platform helps those in the back to see.

• Large groups do generate enthusiasm, but that benefit can quickly wane if students feel lost in the crowd.

• Some children's teachers, youth directors and adult teachers lead Sunday School classes that are considerably larger than the maximum group sizes suggested in this book. (It is sometimes easier to work with a large group than to enlist and train others who could guide smaller groups of students.) Since this results in limited student involvement and personal attention, opportunities for small group/active learning should be provided at other times in the week.

GOAL 4:
ROOM ARRANGEMENTS

How the Room Is Arranged Has Significant Impact on the Atmosphere of Learning.

Facilitate Student Involvement

Having enough space and the appropriate furniture is only part of providing good facilities. How the furniture is arranged in the room has a significant impact on a teacher's ability to engage students in active participation.

Why Room Arrangements Matter

Teachers are more likely to use involving Bible learning methods when it is easy to form smaller interactive groups for part of the session.

- Youth and adult groups need to be able to shift chairs easily, whether focusing toward the front of the room or forming smaller (up to five or six people) groups.
- Children (grades 1 to 5/6) need to physically change locations during a session (i.e., moving from tables to another area of room and then back to tables).
- Early childhood groups need a choice of activity areas/centers for part of the session (i.e., home living, blocks, art, puzzles, books, etc.) and an area to come together for singing, story time, etc.

More time can be spent in valuable learning when the movement between activities can be done quickly and easily. The teaching staff can function more easily as a supportive team and be more flexible and creative in their planning when facilities are arranged in an open manner conducive to varied groupings and arrangements.

It's easier to adjust room assignments as attendance patterns change if all the rooms are planned to allow for varied arrangements.

More Than Just a Room: When students walk into their classrooms, do they feel like they've come "home" to a place that fits them? Our goal in improving facilities is to create spaces in which students feel welcome.

Look for ways students can feel ownership of their rooms—preschoolers can help you arrange the furniture in the home-living center, children can help paint a mural on the wall, youth can help select furniture and decorations, and adults can contribute money or time to buying or making needed furniture. Students who have helped create their place are more likely to look forward to spending time in it, as well as take care of it!

✔ Action Checklist

- ❏ Duplicate the room arrangement diagrams in the age-level portion of this chapter: Early Childhood on pages 222-223, Children on page 224, Youth/Adult on page 225. Compare these arrangements with those in your rooms for each age level. Make a list of suggested improvements that can be made in your present room(s).

SPECIAL SITUATIONS

Fixed Seating

Often adult classes—and sometimes youth and children's groups—must meet in rooms where seats are linked together and cannot be easily moved, if at all. This arrangement makes it more difficult to encourage interaction and build relationships, but a resourceful teacher can work around these limitations.

- **Have groups stand up:** Most discussion and writing activities can be done in small groups simply by having everyone stand and interact with those nearby. People in alternate rows can easily turn around and talk with those directly behind them.
- **Move to open areas:** Rooms with fixed seating usually have at least some areas of open space—aisles, platform, ends of rows, etc.—where chairs can be provided for small groups to sit comfortably.

Assembly Room with Small Classrooms

Many older buildings were designed with very small classrooms (one teacher and a small group of students) opening onto a larger department assembly room.

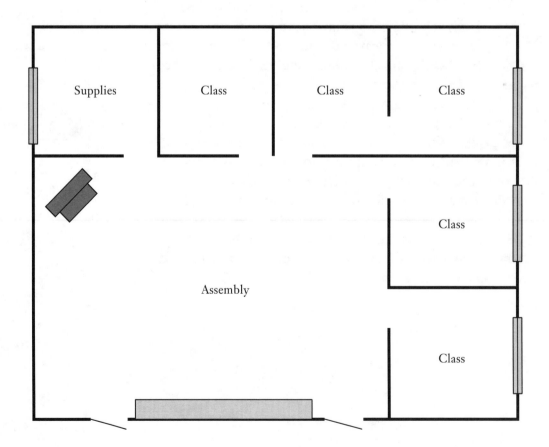

This plan was intended to provide for both large and small group learning. However, the isolation of the small groups in their individual classrooms limited the kinds of learning experiences that could be provided and restricted teachers and leaders from giving support to one another.

The diagram below shows one way to adapt such a facility for greater flexibility and interaction. By removing doors and portions of the dividing walls, the room now conveys to each student "There is something for you to do here. We have planned ways for you to get to know others and work together."

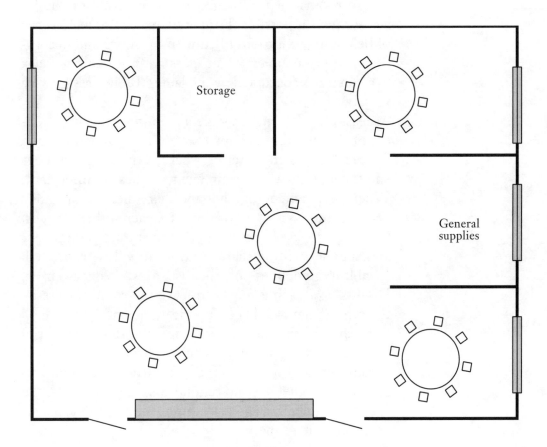

SHARING FACILITIES

Rarely does a Sunday School have the luxury of being the only group to use a room. In most churches, most rooms are used frequently throughout the week. Churches that have a school often find that the group that meets in the room five days a week gradually takes precedence over the Sunday ministries. Churches that rent their facilities from schools, community groups or other churches, face significant challenges in attempting to work in rooms that they do not control.

Guidelines for Sharing Facilities

1. Assign rooms for use by groups of the same or similar age as much as possible. Fifth graders will not feel a sense of belonging in a room filled with furniture and decorations for preschoolers. Teenagers are not likely to relax in a room next occupied by the ladies' Bible class (or vice versa!).

2. At least once a year, schedule a meeting with the teachers of the different groups that use a room. Allow time for each teacher to describe what his or her group does and the reasons why certain facility issues are important. When people meet together and share their visions, they become more accommodating to each other's needs. Come to an agreement on what furniture, equipment and supplies will be shared and what will be restricted. Establish guidelines for the use of shared resources. Discuss how each group is to leave the room for use by the other; then clearly communicate the guidelines to all staff who use the rooms. Mounting a poster with a brief summary of the guidelines is helpful for making sure that substitutes and new staff are informed. Periodically review the guidelines and remind staff about them. If the staff teach the same age level, offer training to the teachers at the same time.

3. Provide adequate storage space for each group's supplies. If this cannot be done in (or immediately nearby) the room, provide portable storage containers (available at office supply stores) for transporting needed items. Provide tables (at height appropriate for age of students) on which supplies can be placed for easy access by students.

4. Provide appropriate display space for each group. It's important for each class or group to have something displayed that's focused on their interests. Some options:
   - Provide portable bulletin boards that can be rolled or carried into a room when needed, or build hinged boards that can be easily turned from one side to the next.

- Mount displays on butcher paper which can be attached to classroom walls for display and then rolled up for storage.
- Request that any displays be limited to seasonal art which is then appropriate for all groups using the rooms.
- Assign specific display space in a room to each group that regularly uses the room.

5. Plan for adequate custodial help to handle movement of furniture and equipment to prepare a room for use by different groups. Each group should provide the custodian with a clear diagram—ideally mounted on a wall—of how the room should be set up. If paid custodial help is not able to handle this on a regular basis, enlist volunteers so that teachers are not burdened with the task and can focus on students. Most teachers are not likely to change a room's arrangement unless absolutely necessary. Changes that would merely enhance learning tend to be viewed as too much trouble.

Problem Solving for Sharing Facilities

1. If a room must have furniture or equipment that is not appropriate for the age group using the room, think creatively of how its use might be adapted to meet your needs. For example:
   - A chair that is too big for a five-year-old to sit on might serve as a shelf for supplies.
   - If small children cannot work comfortably at an adult-sized table while seated, have them stand around it as they work.
   - If desks or other paraphernalia belonging to the school are stacked in an unsightly manner on one side of the room, drape them with colorful fabric.

2. If a teacher brings to your attention that items are not being put away properly in prior programs, quickly meet with teacher of that program to go over the agreed-upon guidelines. Avoid allowing these lapses to become a bone of contention that hinders both programs from being effective. Often a simple reminder resolves the problem (at least for a while), but be open to changing the guidelines if they are proving unworkable.

3. Periodically remind teachers in all programs that sharing facilities requires that some concessions must be made on all sides.

Bonus Idea for Sharing Space: We provide reversible bulletin boards for all our classrooms that are used by two different programs, for example preschool and Sunday School. *David Arnold, Parkview Evangelical Free Church, Iowa City, Iowa*

Nontraditional Facilities

Many new congregations or those that have outgrown smaller facilities find themselves meeting, temporarily or permanently, in buildings that were not designed for teaching ministries. In applying or adapting the information in this chapter, some unique challenges may be faced. For example:

1. **Rooms for similar age groups may be widely separated.** Buildings that were not designed for education ministries may not have classrooms grouped together. In such cases, it is easier for youth and adult groups to be isolated from similar groups than for children's groups. Try to avoid forcing parents to walk from one end of your facility to the other to drop off and pick up their children.

2. **Rooms may have harsh or inadequate lighting.** Rooms that were designed for other purposes may seem sterile or depressing. Many lighting supply stores will send a consultant at no cost to look at your facility and make recommendations. Or enlist an independent lighting consultant for this purpose.

3. **Rest rooms are too far away and/or too small.** This could get costly, but younger children especially need easy quick access to rest rooms. If teachers need to organize time-consuming expeditions to the rest room, irreplaceable teaching time is lost.

Updating Old Facilities

Applying or adapting the information in this chapter to older buildings also raises some unique challenges. While older buildings often have a unique charm, they can hinder efforts to create attractive, functional learning environments. Typical problems and corrections include:

1. **Floor plans are incompatible to current approaches to teaching.**
   - Remove walls or portions of walls, even if posts must be retained within a room. Involvement approaches can easily work around even a sizeable barrier, sometimes taking advantage of it for displaying posters or other visuals.
   - Widen doorways or remove unneeded closets or hallways.

2. **Rooms are windowless, dark and depressing.**
   - Paint the walls and ceilings in fresh, light colors, with some bright highlights on doors, trim, furniture, etc.
   - Install light-colored floor covering, carpet or tile.
   - Update the lighting.
   - Display colorful posters of outdoor scenes.

3. **Rooms are cold and damp.**
   - Check the heating/ventilation system to be sure air-flow is adequate.
   - Check for and repair any water leaks.
   - Carpet the floor and the lower third or half of the walls.
4. **Rooms lack running water.** Bring water for learning activities, snacks or diaper changing, etc. in one of the following containers:
   - A large, unplugged coffee urn (place a plastic bowl under the spout to catch drips);
   - A plastic dishpan placed on the floor or a table;
   - Water bottles with spouts.
5. **Rooms lack adequate electrical outlets.**
   - Recruit an electrician to help with this need.
   - Avoid temporary measures such as stringing extension cords, removing the grounding prong from plugs or overloading an outlet with multiplug adapters. Until a church updates the wiring in old buildings, there is always the risk that someone will plug in a piece of equipment that the old wiring cannot handle, and the results may be tragic.

Upgrading Facilities
Tips for Making Improvements
1. **Set priorities and make a long-range plan.** You probably can't improve everything at once, but you can improve some things now and other things over time. Start with improvements that...
   - You can accomplish without needing approval by 14 committees or resolving a longstanding debate among people with opposing viewpoints.
   - People will notice and can help motivate further improvements (some people want to hold off on purely cosmetic improvements in favor of ones that are practical; however, cosmetic issues often have a very practical impact on people's attitudes, especially on the all-important first impressions made on visitors).
   - Correct safety problems.
2. **Look for ways to use volunteers.** People care more when they have invested their own time and energy into making improvements. While not every church may have volunteers who can install carpets, plumbing or windows, or who can upgrade electrical wiring, there are probably people (parents, teenagers, grandparents, etc.) who can help paint, plant flowers or even knock out a wall or two. Make a workday into a community-building event. Provide refreshments and plenty of encouragement, and make sure everyone gets to know one another.

 Bonus Ideas for Improving an Unfriendly Classroom: In our church a classroom used for storytelling was very boring. So we painted a different scene on each wall: desert, sea, Temple, Bible-times home interior. We added several three-dimensional items to each scene: Bible-times well, sheep, trees, etc. As teachers tell Bible stories, the children sit facing the appropriate scene. *Bonnie Aldrich, Pulpit Rock Church, Colorado Springs, Colorado*

In a classroom for youth, let them make hand- or footprints in bright colors all over their classroom walls. Spice up a classroom for children by having kids trace each other standing in various poses against the wall. Then kids can paint themselves. Repaint every August before the new school year. *Terry Platt, Calvary Memorial Church, Oak Park, Illinois*

Bonus Ideas for Improving an Unfriendly Classroom:

Purchase clear, plastic shower curtains with colorful designs on them and hang them on blank walls, or get yards of chiffon or other light material in bright colors and drape them like bunting across the ceiling and walls for dramatic, quick changes. You can also create murals on walls by projecting transparency pictures onto the wall or butcher paper, tracing the lines and then painting the pictures.

For a less obvious but still significant effect, change the lighting in the classroom. Use incandescent lamps, spotlights, fluorescents, electric lanterns, etc. *Hailey Armoogan, Waterloo Pentecostal Assembly, Waterloo, Ontario, Canada*

3. **Challenge the congregation to value improved teaching facilities.** Many churches think little or nothing about spending substantial sums on certain parts of their buildings. Typically, rooms that are seen and used by everyone take precedence over rooms that are used mainly by two-year-olds or middle schoolers or senior citizens. Most congregations need teachers who will become advocates for investing in the right kinds of places to attract students and teach the faith. Asking for money should not be done apologetically, but boldly presenting the need and the opportunities, calling the church to care for its teaching facilities equivalently to the rest of the rooms in the building.

Providing Outdoor Options

Have you ever noticed that most of the events in the Bible took place outside, yet most of *our* study of the Bible happens inside? Whether that contradiction is significant or trivial, there is often great value (with any age group) in occasionally moving outside the walls of the classroom.

1. **Change the setting.** Every group needs some variety to avoid falling into a rut. Simply moving out of doors can increase students' enjoyment and interest in the same activities they would have done inside.

2. **Tell the story.** Since so much of the Bible happened outside, taking a class outdoors can help students feel more a part of the action.

3. **Pray and meditate.** Even adults can benefit from a walk outside, with time for group or personal prayer to the God who made the world.

4. **Serve a snack.** If hotdogs taste best to some people at a ball game, imagine how good crackers and punch might taste on the lawn or under a tree.

5. **Do an activity.** A wide range of learning experiences can be more enjoyable and thus more effective when done outside: art activities, games, exploration of God's wonders or service projects.

6. **Supervised play.** An outdoor play area for children is a great resource for meeting the need to move and make noise. The two definitely go together. There is also great benefit in children being able to connect their enjoyment in play with the people and place where they learn about God. As children enjoy recess on the playground, teachers are able to informally build relationships with them, improving their ability to communicate about more serious matters.

7. **Make friends—hang out.** The time before and after sessions is often viewed as outside the real teaching ministry, with the space outside the classrooms considered to

be just a means to allow passage to wherever people are going next. Many churches are discovering that the impact of their teaching ministries is greatly enhanced by providing conversation-friendly places, both inside and outside their buildings. Teachers and/or students benefit from continuing to talk about issues and questions that came up during class, as well as simply getting to know one another better.

Outdoor Facilities

Consider providing some of the following features outside your church buildings:

1. **Playground:** Provide areas with age-appropriate equipment for toddlers and twos or threes; threes through fives; and younger elementary children.
2. **Lawn:** An open grassy area provides space for a wide range of activities.
3. **Benches:** People enjoy sitting in partly shaded areas for reading, discussion, prayer, informal conversation, thinking or just resting.
4. **Patio:** Many classroom activities adapt easily to a patio area normally used for meeting and greeting each other before and after sessions.
5. **Water:** Running water can provide a relaxing backdrop and help to cover the sounds of any nearby traffic. Pools and ponds of standing water set a calming tone. (**Warning:** Standing or running water is an attractive hazard to small children. You will need to follow safety measures to avoid unfortunate tragedies.)
6. **Firepit:** Summer evenings become something special with a campfire in the middle of the patio.

❑ Develop clearly defined policies and procedures for regular (a minimum of weekly) maintenance of all rooms. Include such mundane items as:

- Which tasks are to be done by the custodian and which ones by the teachers?
- Who empties wastebaskets? And when?
- What is to be done with leftover papers and student work?
- Who decides when things are to be thrown out? Most churches end up with quantities of outdated materials that people saved because it might be used again someday. Clearly defined guidelines on what to keep and what to dispose of can help reduce clutter.
- How often are floors to be swept/mopped/vacuumed?
- How often are tables and toys to be washed? And with what cleaner?
- Are all nursery rooms equipped with sterilizing solutions that are regularly (after each session) used to clean all equipment, toys and furniture?
- When are buildings and rooms to be unlocked before a session?
- What is the procedure for locking up afterwards?

GOAL 5: MAINTENANCE

Establish Procedures for Systematic Maintenance and Evaluation

Busy facilities require continuous loving care. All the work of improving buildings can quickly be undone by lack of proper maintenance.

Take Another Look

Parents of growing children must periodically review the contents of closets and drawers and replace that which has been outgrown. Similarly, teachers of teaching ministries must periodically review current building usage and make changes to ensure that facilities aid in teaching and growth efforts. Just because the Overcomers Class has always met in Room 101 does not mean they should continue meeting there next year. The charts in this chapter are useful tools to revisit at least once a year to see if changing attendance patterns warrant making usage changes. In most churches, there are always rooms or buildings that need to be updated in some way.

Look to the Future

Duplicate and complete the "Facilities" worksheet (p. 226) to determine how you can begin working to meet the goals stated in this chapter. Refer to the calendar logo for specific actions you can take to meet each goal.

✔ **Action Checklist**

❑ Provide written procedures for reporting damaged equipment or other needed repairs.

- Produce forms people can use to report problems (you might want to adapt the sample form on page 221).
- Identify how and where reports are to be submitted.

Early Childhood Room Guidelines

1. Arrange furniture to prevent hard-to-supervise blind spots.
2. Bolt permanent shelves and cabinets to the wall. Small, portable shelf units must also be sturdy enough that a child cannot tip them over.
3. Attach safety hinges that open and close doors slowly to prevent slamming them on fingers or toes.
4. Place furniture away from windows, protecting children who may climb on it.
5. Observe the ways in which children move from one area of the room to another.
   - **Toddlers to Twos:** Make sure that movement is not impeded.
   - **Threes to Fives:** Avoid creating areas that invite children to run.
6. Include space for teaching staff to safely store their personal belongings (purses, coats, etc.).
7. Do not block any entrance or exit with unused furniture. Every exit should be clearly marked. Contact your local fire department or state licensing agency to help you determine proper placement of fire extinguishers, fire alarms, emergency exits and other safety considerations. For example, all doors, even when locked, should be openable from the inside. Post fire and other emergency (tornado, earthquake, etc.) plans next to every doorway.
8. Avoid creating rooms too small or too long and narrow to be flexibly used as the needs of groups change.
9. **Babies/Toddlers:** Arrange changing areas so that the caregiver is facing out to the room while changing diapers and is in full view of other adults in the room. This arrangement provides protection for children and the caregiver, prevents unwarranted complaints of inappropriate behavior, and allows the adult to keep an eye on the other children.

Sample Report Form

Facility/Equipment Repair Needs

To: _____ Date: _____

Repair need in room: _____

Item to be repaired: _____

_____

Briefly describe problem: _____

_____

Person requesting repair: _____

Room Diagrams

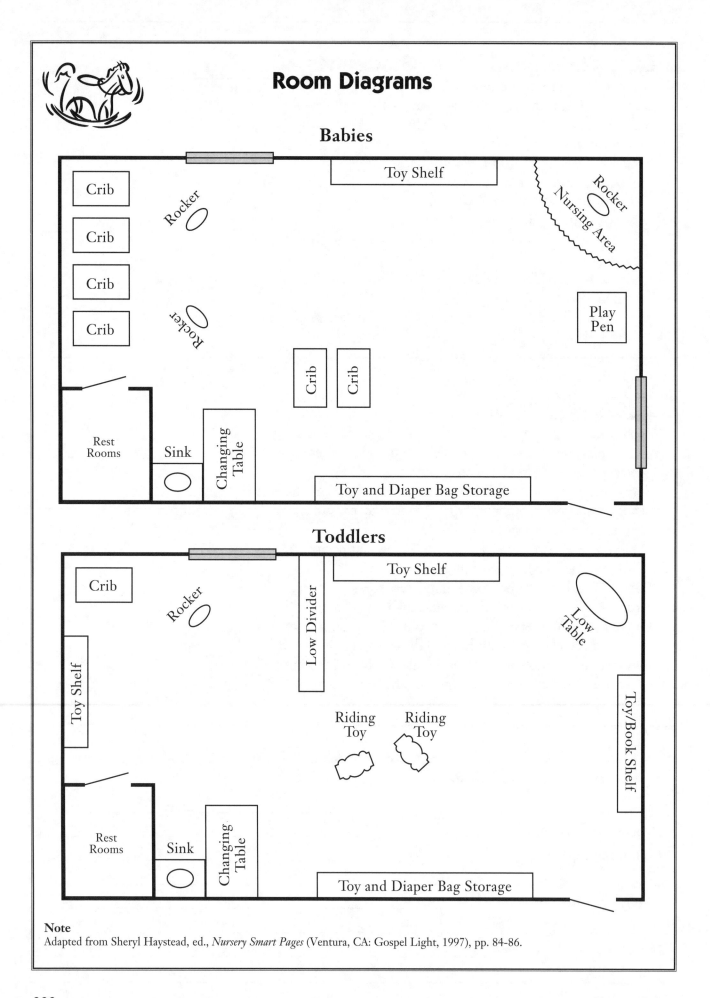

Babies

Crib
Crib
Crib
Crib

Rocker

Rocker

Toy Shelf

Rocker
Nursing Area

Play Pen

Crib
Crib

Rest Rooms

Sink

Changing Table

Toy and Diaper Bag Storage

Toddlers

Crib

Rocker

Low Divider

Toy Shelf

Low Table

Toy Shelf

Toy/Book Shelf

Riding Toy

Riding Toy

Rest Rooms

Sink

Changing Table

Toy and Diaper Bag Storage

Note
Adapted from Sheryl Haystead, ed., *Nursery Smart Pages* (Ventura, CA: Gospel Light, 1997), pp. 84-86.

Room Diagram

Twos to Fives

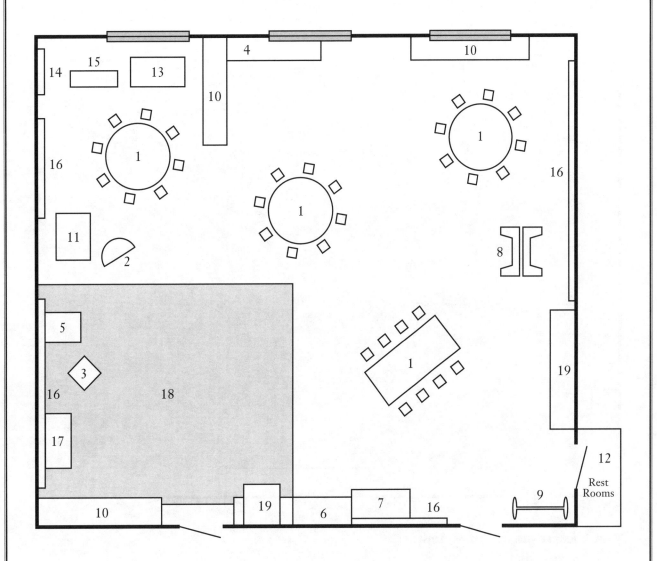

1. Table
2. Child rocker
3. Chair
4. Book rack
5. CD/cassette player
6. Storage cabinet and sink counter
7. Low supply table
8. Chalk/painting easel
9. Coatrack
10. Open shelf
11. Doll bed
12. Rest room
13. Child stove and sink
14. Wall mirror
15. Dress-up clothes
16. Bulletin board
17. Small table for teacher's materials
18. Rug
19. Shelves/table for take-home materials

Note: Rectangular rooms provide maximum flexibility.

Note

Adapted from Lowell E. Brown, *Sunday School Standards* (Ventura, CA: Gospel Light, 1986), p. 119.

Room Diagram

Children—Grades One to Five/Six

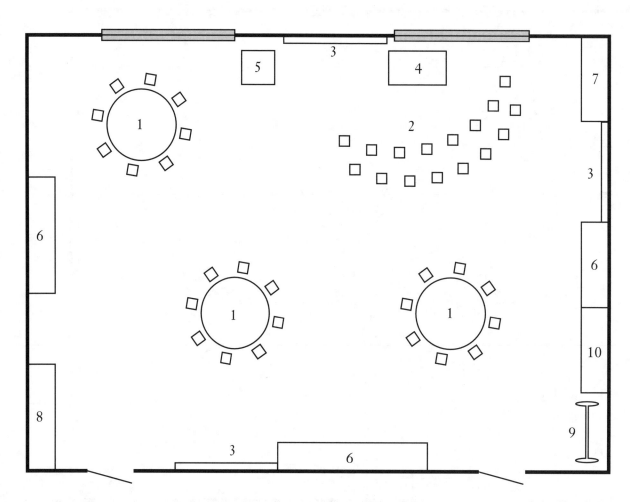

Open Classroom Arrangement

1. Table and chairs
2. Chairs (optional)
3. Bulletin board/white board
4. Small table for teacher materials
5. CD/cassette player
6. Open shelves
7. Bookshelf
8. Storage cabinets and sink counter
9. Coatrack
10. Shelves/table for take-home materials

Note: Rectangular rooms provide maximum flexibility.

Note
Adapted from Lowell E. Brown, *Sunday School Standards* (Ventura, CA: Gospel Light, 1986), p. 119.

Room Diagram

Youth and Adult

With Tables

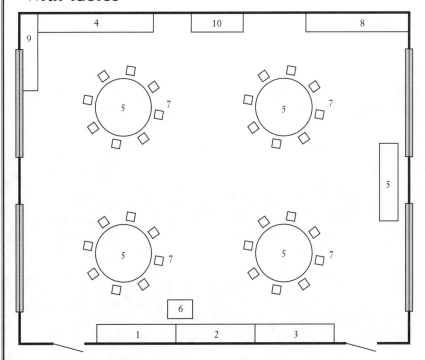

1. Bulletin board
2. White board
3. Screen
4. Supply cabinet/closet
5. Table
6. CD/cassette player
7. Chairs
8. Sink
9. Open shelves
10. VCR/TV cart

If space permits, provide an informal conversation area with comfortable seating (sofas, armchairs, beanbag chairs, etc.)

Without Tables

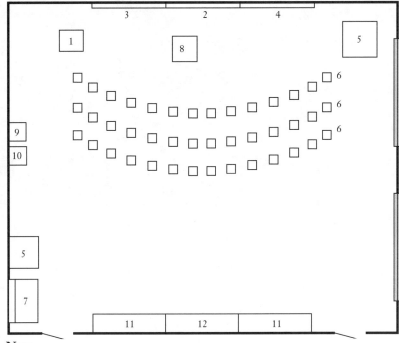

1. CD/cassette player
2. White board
3. Bulletin board
4. Screen
5. Table
6. Chairs
7. Sink
8. Small table
9. Overhead projector cart
10. VCR/TV cart
11. Open shelves
12. Storage Cabinet

Note
Adapted from Lowell E. Brown, *Sunday School Standards* (Ventura, CA: Gospel Light, 1986), p. 120.

Facilities

Rate your church's progress toward each goal and then list two or more actions you can take to reach each goal.

GOAL 1: FACILITIES

Your Sunday School facilities have been designed or modified to support the teaching/learning plan you are implementing.

1	2	3	4	5
Need to Start		Fair		Goal Achieved

Actions to Take:

GOAL 2: SPACE

Each group has approximately the recommended amount of space.

1	2	3	4	5
Need to Start		Fair		Goal Achieved

Actions to Take:

GOAL 3: FURNITURE

Each group has appropriate furniture and equipment to accommodate the age and number of students.

1	2	3	4	5
Need to Start		Fair		Goal Achieved.

Actions to Take:

GOAL 4: ROOM ARRANGEMENTS

Each group has facilities that are arranged to facilitate student involvement in both large and small group settings.

1	2	3	4	5
Need to Start		Fair		Goal Achieved

Actions to Take:

GOAL 5: MAINTENANCE

You have established and implemented procedures for regular and systematic maintenance and evaluation of your facilities.

1	2	3	4	5
Need to Start		Fair		Goal Achieved

Actions to Take:

Chapter Ten

Put Outreach Up Front

Though your Sunday School may be well organized, equipped and staffed, and your teaching plan for Bible study perfect; if your program is not reaching out in love to people beyond your church walls, Christ's great commission to "go and make disciples" (Matthew 28:19) is not being met in your church.

What This Chapter Tells You

- Teachers need a plan for contacting and connecting with unchurched students, visitors and absentees.
- Visitors need to feel welcome and find it easy to learn more about your program.
- Making it possible for newcomers to develop relationships with regular attendees of your Sunday School will help them feel accepted—and encourage their regular attendance, too.

What This Chapter Shows You

- How to develop a plan of outreach that teachers can put into practice;
- How to plan events that will attract unchurched people;
- How to identify and overcome barriers that prevent people from coming to your program;
- How to welcome and nurture visitors;
- How to encourage relationships to be built among newcomers and regular attenders.

Where Do I Start?

Survey Says

"According to a recent survey, 97 percent of the churches surveyed have a Sunday School program, and the pastors of these churches expect Sunday School to be as important—or even more important—to the ministry of their churches than it is today." Barna Research Group's Pastor Poll (January, 1998)

Get the Big Picture

Outreach is more than simply inviting non-Christians to attend your programs; outreach is also making it possible for newcomers to become members of two families—God's and your church's!

You may have heard the prediction that Sunday School is on its way out, and you may even be experiencing a decline in the attendance in your Sunday School. It's interesting to note, however, that at the same time that some Sunday Schools are slowing down, others are experiencing vital growth.

So what's the difference? Studies have shown that the major difference between Sunday Schools that are growing and those that are not is simply a matter of purpose. Most *declining* Sunday Schools (or other educational programs) are inwardly focused—ministering exclusively to Christians who are already attending—with teachers assuming that growth through outreach into the community will happen automatically as class members grow spiritually.

The purpose of *growing* Sunday Schools is focused on reaching out to unbelievers and training and equipping believers for an outreach ministry. The spiritual growth of believers is part of the program, but it is considered a means to an end—not an end itself. These churches consider evangelism and education as two tasks to accomplish one goal: making disciples. And growth is the result, as God gives the increase.

Look at Where You Are

Duplicate and complete the "Outreach" worksheet (p. 232) to take a closer look at how (or even if) outreach takes place in your church.

Will History Repeat Itself?

As we look back over the history of the Sunday School, one thing stands out: Christian men and women who had a vision and who cared a great deal about people, reached out in love to help unbelievers know Christ as Savior and to help believers grow in Him. As a result both the Sunday School and the church grew. And the impact was so great that it actually changed the course of history!

"TODAY'S OUR FIRST SUNDAY. CAN YOU TELL ME WHAT THE KIDS DO RIGHT AFTER SUNDAY SCHOOL?"

"I'M NOT SURE, BUT I THINK THEY MEET THEIR PARENTS SOMEWHERE."

MR. SMITH AND MICHAEL CHOOSE TO GO OUT FOR DOUGHNUTS INSTEAD OF STAYING FOR SUNDAY SCHOOL.

Outreach

1. How do unchurched people most often find out about your Sunday School?

2. Within the last six months, how many visitors have attended your Sunday School or program? Of these visitors, how many have become regular attendees?

3. When a visitor comes, who is responsible for greeting him or her and acting as a host/hostess?

4. How are the students in your Sunday School encouraged to build relationships with newcomers?

Focus on the Details

GOAL 1:
PLAN FOR OUTREACH

Teachers Must Plan to Reach Out to the Unchurched, Visitors and Absentees

Sometimes people think that outreach in a Sunday School just happens, but that's not true! Outreach takes place, and Sunday Schools grow, when there is a plan in place. With a plan of action where each teacher is aware of his or her part, you can be sure that outreach will be consistent and effective.

Four Components of a Meaningful Outreach Plan

1. **Regular emphasis on accurate enrollment and attendance records**

Enrollment is a key factor in outreach. Studies have shown that the average Sunday School attendance will be from 40 to 60 percent of enrollment. As the enrollment goes up, the attendance goes up and vice versa. (See chapter 5 for more information on how to keep good records and the benefits of good record keeping.)

Statistics that reflect who is attending and how often they attend can provide teachers with the information needed to follow-up on all who attend—regularly or not. Sunday Schools that neglect consistent follow-up find that even as they are gaining new members, they are losing others out the back door.

If you recognize that Sunday School classes are not gaining new members, contact teachers and/or members who are no longer attending to determine the reasons for the decline in attendance. You may hear responses such as poor class organization, inadequate teacher training, overcrowded classrooms, not enough staff, lack of visitor and absentee follow-up, lack of transportation, not enough parking, unfriendliness, etc. Plan ways to solve any problems you identify; while every problem may not have an immediate solution, steps for improvement can be taken in any area.

See the ideas suggested for follow-up in the age-level portion of this chapter: Early Childhood (p. 241); Children (p. 242); Youth (p. 243); Adult (p. 244).

Bonus Ideas for Enrolling Students: Early in August, or well before a new class begins at any time of year, give the teachers names, addresses and phone numbers of their incoming students. Teachers write personal notes or make phone calls to students to introduce themselves and invite students to enroll in their class. *Terry Platt, Calvary Memorial Church, Oak Park, Illinois*

We designate one Sunday a year as "Sunday School Sunday" for the purpose of drawing attention to the various adult Sunday School classes. On that day, the various classes invite church members, regular attendees and visitors who do not actively participate in the Sunday School program to come and see what they're missing. Our goal is to plug in those who may have only experienced our church through worship services and who have missed out on significant relationship building as a result. *Don Furuto, Briarwood Church, Birmingham, Alabama*

From Here to There: So what happens after a successful outreach event? What causes people—children, youth or adults—to actually decide to take you up on your invitation to come to Sunday School or some other Bible teaching time? How can you help them make the connection into a program that doesn't have a special music group, a Jolly Jump or other special attraction?

Many times, it helps to have the person who was the emcee of the outreach event also be the teacher of the Sunday School class. A familiar face will help the newcomer feel a connection. For an even better connection, however, make sure that all the leaders, teachers and helpers in a Sunday program attend outreach events, making a special effort to introduce themselves to visitors. Youth Sunday School classes may choose to have students leading parts of the class so that newcomers are more likely to feel comfortable. At all age levels, however, keep looking for ways to help visitors transition from a one-time attendee to a regular attendee.

2. An up-to-date list of potential participants for your program

A contact list can be compiled from many sources, including attendance at an outreach event or Vacation Bible School, recent church visitors, families who have recently moved to your community, people who once attended but now attend infrequently, family members of regular attendees, etc. Systematically make these names available to the appropriate teachers so that they have a realistic number of names to contact.

Contact with potential participants can take many forms: a flyer advertising a special-interest class, an invitation to a party, a phone call to offer information and answer any questions, or a newsletter that describes an activity in which the class just participated in and a teaser notice about an upcoming activity. Holiday seasons (Christmas and Easter), the beginning of the school year or the beginning of summer are all prime times for sending information to potential students.

3. Regularly planned special events or programs that help teachers make contact with unchurched people

People who might never be reached through regular church events and meetings will often respond to events that are planned to meet their particular needs and interests—which gives current Sunday School students an opportunity to get to know unbelievers and build relationships with them, sharing their faith in God.

Planning a wide variety of special events and ministries that attract the interest of many different people broadens the appeal of your church. Each member of your church has individual gifts, abilities and interests that can be used to effectively reach out to others in the community. Offering a variety of events allows for involvement of everyone.

Special events and ministries are generally designed to accomplish several purposes. Although these purposes may overlap in many activities, it is important to identify them separately and make sure they are included in the overall plan of action for outreach.

- **Get acquainted.** The goal of an outreach activity is to help all the participants (especially newcomers) have a good time and to create opportunities for newcomers to get to know class members. It is an opportunity for all participants to get acquainted in a nonthreatening atmosphere.
- **Build a bridge.** An outreach activity may or may not include a time of spiritual input, but it should include an invitation to attend a Sunday School class or other church activity. Many outreach events are largely social but are specifically designed to funnel newcomers into another program. Special events serve as a bridge for newcomers into consistent Bible study.

- **Share the gospel.** In every outreach plan of action there should be occasions when evangelistic outreach is the central purpose of an event. There are many ways evangelism can take place, and the methods you choose will be determined both by the personality of your group and the overall goals of your program. Evangelism will most likely include a verbal and/or visual explanation of what it means to be a Christian.

One of the most important aspects of planning for outreach is a balanced approach. If all your outreach events are fun and fellowship, with no attempt to funnel newcomers into Bible study, your group may not effectively gain the goal of reaching others for Bible study. And if every outreach activity ends with a strong evangelistic appeal, some newcomers will be less likely to return.

In planning an outreach event, it is important to involve as many of your regular attendees as possible. This practice accomplishes several purposes. First, the regular attendees know the interests and understand the needs of their peers and can probably give accurate direction to the event. Second, they will have a stake in the event and will be more highly motivated to work toward its success. Third, they will know precisely what they are inviting their friends to attend and so will not fear being embarrassed by an unexpected or inappropriate event.

See lists of special events in the age-level portion of this chapter: Early Childhood (p. 241); Children (p. 242); Youth (p. 243); Adult (p. 244).

4. One or more people who take responsibility for coordinating an outreach plan of action

It's important to designate someone to coordinate and supervise your overall outreach plan. We all tend to become satisfied with the status quo and feel comfortable with seeing our own circle of friends each Sunday. It's easy to forget about the many people in our community (neighborhood, school or workplace) who still need to know the Savior. Even the most highly motivated staff and students will often lose their enthusiasm and vision for outreach unless there is someone to guide and support their efforts. Also, an uncoordinated outreach program can result in five different people visiting a new family the same week, while other visitors and contacts are neglected.

Depending on the size of your church, you may need to have more than one person coordinating outreach—in order for an outreach plan to be fully effective, every class or age-level program must actively participate in the coordination of the plan.

 Bonus Idea for Outreach Service Projects: Provide a list of user-friendly service projects for classes to work on together: cleaning windshields at a parking lot, giving away a free children's video, giving away chocolate chip cookies at a fair or festival booth, etc. An invitation to your church or special event at your church can be included. *Ron Richardson, Hillsong Church, Chapel Hill, North Carolina*

 Bonus Ideas for Special Event Outreach: Look in your community for apartment complexes for families with children. Invite children and parents to attend a variety of special events: puppet shows, parenting seminars, special-interest classes. During the event, distribute invitations to your church services. *Carl and Christine Franzen, Redeemer Covenant, Carrollton, Texas*

Plan a Family Funfest for the community on a Saturday. Set up lots of fun activities such as Jolly Jump castles, pony rides, minigolf, dunk tank, BBQ, etc. Periodically during the event have a short musical program or a relevant message. *Hailey Armoogan, Waterloo Pentecostal Assembly, Waterloo, Ontario, Canada*

Bonus Idea for Follow-Up on the Go: Keep a small, appropriate gift item for the students in your class (stickers, candy bar, inspirational book, bookmark, etc.) and a class roster in your car. As you run errands in your community and pass near a student's home, stop to say "Hi" and drop off the gift item.

Keep note cards, pens and a class roster in the car. When stopped in unavoidable traffic or when facing an unexpected delay at a doctor's office or mechanic's garage, use the time to write brief notes to the students in your class.

JOB DESCRIPTION

OUTREACH COORDINATOR
Task: To plan, organize and direct the outreach program of the Sunday School
Term: One year, beginning September 1
Supervisor _____ (name)

Responsibilities
- Maintain up-to-date enrollment records.
- Gather names for a contact list and assign names to the appropriate leaders and/or teachers.
- Coordinate follow-up of visitors and absentees.
- Evaluate the manner in which visitors are greeted and involved.
- Plan special events or programs with staff.
- Recruit, meet with and supervise age-level outreach coordinators as needed.
- Communicate regularly with supervisor.

✔ Action Checklist

❑ At least once a year, heavily publicize your Sunday School program and actively pursue students to enroll in the appropriate classes. For example, you might offer an incentive for the first 20 people who enroll in a Sunday School class, such as a free book or gift certificate. Set up tables or videos of current classes in a well-traveled area in the church so that people will be encouraged to enroll in a class. Include enrollment forms in the bulletin and a convenient box in which to place them. Provide a small prize for each person who enrolls. Give a helpful parenting article to each parent who enrolls a child.

❑ Encourage each teacher to contact absentees, visitors or irregular attendees. You may provide already-stamped postcards, prepared mailing labels, and address and phone lists. At a planning or training meeting, interview a teacher about the benefits of follow-up. Make sure the follow-up plan that you expect teachers to follow is included in their job descriptions.

❑ Write a job description for an outreach coordinator; then ask God to send you the person who can develop and coordinate a successful outreach program.

❑ Let others know of your desire for outreach. Ask for prayer partners and recruit others to pray with you.

❑ Look at the list of special events or programs in the age-level section of this chapter (Early Childhood, p. 241; Children, p. 242; Youth, p. 243; Adult, p. 244). While these lists are just a few of the many events and programs possible, take time to consider what events you might be able to do in the near future: check off two events (or add two) you've already done; star the two events you think the students in your class or program would most enjoy; underline one event you think would be fairly easy to plan; circle one event you'd really like to do and write the name of a person or two who might be interested in planning the event with you.

*Sunday School Registration Form for Children
SIGN ME UP!
Name _____
Grade_____ Gender _____ Birthday _____
Parents_____
Address _____
City/State/Zip _____
Home Phone _____ School _____
Special Interests _____
Notes for Teacher_____
Parent Participation: I would be willing to help with…
_____ Snacks   _____ Art   _____ Music
_____ Games   _____ Drama   _____ Transportation
_____ Other: _____

*Sunday School Registration Form for Youth
SIGN ME UP!
Name _____
Grade_____ Gender _____ Birthday _____
Parents_____
Address _____
City/State/Zip _____
Home Phone _____ School _____
Special Interests _____
Something I Hope to Get from This Class _____
_____
_____
_____

*Sunday School Registration Form for Adults
SIGN ME UP!
Name _____
Grade_____ Gender _____ Birthday _____
Parents_____
Address _____
City/State/Zip _____
Home Phone _____ School _____
Special Interests _____
Something I Hope to Get from This Class _____
_____
_____
_____

*Some churches include a medical release form on the back of their registration cards.

❑ Designate one or more people who will be aware of visitors who may arrive. In a small church, one greeter can serve for more than one class, perhaps stationing him- or herself at the entrance of the education building. In a larger church, each class may need to have a greeter. In any size church, if there is no official greeter, one teacher or regular attendee in each class should be prepared to welcome and introduce visitors.

❑ During the busiest times of the year (holidays, special church events), several visitors often arrive at one time. Plan for these possibilities ahead of time so that these experiences are positive ones for visitors. When your church is sponsoring a special event or when holidays come around, plan for extra help in advance! Arrange for additional staff to be present and to be easily identified with a button that says "Ask me" or a ribbon that says "Host" or "Hostess."

❑ Small gifts can be given to welcome visitors (stickers for children, gift certificates for youth, bookmark or small devotional book for adults).

❑ After several visits by a newcomer, make sure that someone in the Sunday School class or other program personally calls to welcome him or her, answer questions and invite the newcomer's continued participation.

GOAL 2:
MAKE THE MOST OF YOUR VISITORS

Communicate Christ's Love by Welcoming and Caring for Visitors

When a visitor appears in the Sunday School door, genuine friendliness and interest in them may communicate Christ's love more effectively than anything else you do.

The goal of a greeter should be to welcome visitors and answer any questions. Equip each greeter with a supply of get-acquainted brochures that not only provide information about your church but also describe the programs available for a variety of ages. In addition, greeters need to be familiar with other age-level programs and locations. For example, an adult visitor may have a teenage child and want to know about the youth program. Or a parent bringing a child to his or her class for the first time will want to know what classes or programs are offered for adults at the same time.

It's also important that greeters be sensitive to the comfort level of a newcomer; some first-timers are looking for a person with whom to connect on a personal level, while other visitors will feel threatened with too much of a welcome.

If at all possible, another goal of a greeter should be to build a bridge between the visitor and someone else in the Sunday School class or program. For example, the greeter in an adult class may introduce the visitor to a friendly regular attender, letting the regular know that this is Mr. and Mrs. Smith's first Sunday and suggesting that he or she can help Mr. and Mrs. Smith find their way around this Sunday. At the youth level, a greeter can find a student who attends the same school or the same grade level as the visitor.

Another way of making your Sunday School class or other program friendly to visitors is to make sure that references to people, places and events within the church are kept to a minimum unless introduced and explained in such a way that visitors will understand. Attractive and current bulletin-board displays, handouts, etc. will help a visitor to feel comfortable. And, of course, the general appearance of the room in which the class meets will encourage visitors to return as much as the words that are spoken. Put yourself in the shoes of a visitor and ask yourself, *What would make me want to return to this Sunday School class?*

Remember, your goal in welcoming visitors is to ensure that every person sees and experiences the love of God. With a little planning, the visitors to your Sunday School will want to return again and again!

GOAL 3:
TURNING VISITORS INTO MEMBERS

The Sunday School Program Must Work Together to Encourage Regular Attendance

Successful outreach requires the personal attention of every staff and church member in meeting the needs of visitors. Since the center of Christianity is a personal relationship with Jesus Christ, outreach efforts must emphasize the individual. Somewhere in the middle of the special events and the weekly classes, each person needs meaningful personal interaction.

The Sunday School's structure of classes grouped by age or grade level makes it an ideal organization for helping new people find a place where they feel comfortable. When students are only in large groups with few or no opportunities for small-group interaction or activities, visitors often feel lost in the crowd and are unlikely to return. In large groups, people find it hard to make new friends, and teachers can overlook newcomers. At all age levels, student interaction in small groups for at least a portion of the session provides the best structure—not just for effective learning but for involving new people as well. (See chapter 4 for help in organizing your Sunday School or other program to incorporate small groups as a regular part of your ministry.)

Space is another issue which needs to be considered for effective outreach. Overcrowded, uncomfortable facilities don't encourage visitors to return. Lack of space discourages teachers and regular attendees from reaching out to invite and involve more students. Overcrowded conditions often discourage teachers from including any small group activities in their program, and as a result the effectiveness of the Bible teaching ministry in the program will decrease as numbers increase.

If you are finding that the people in your Sunday School are saying "We don't have enough room for the people we have now; we don't dare invite any more!" encourage them to ask with you, "What options do we have to increase our space or improve the use of space we now have?" (Read tips for making good use of your facilities in chapter 9.)

A third component of turning visitors into members is to be ready with the appropriate number of staff members. It's not enough to recruit and train staff to meet your present needs. Part of your preparation for outreach and growth should include recruiting and training staff for future needs.

What to Do to Open the Doors to Visitors: At some point, for whatever reason, you may become aware of the fact that visitors to your Sunday School or other programs have a hard time fitting in or making friends with the regular attendees. What can be done to overcome this barrier to becoming a truly welcoming church? Try one or more of the following ideas, depending on the age level in which you serve:

- **Youth/Adult:** Ask one or two of your students to visit another Sunday School to see what it's like to be a guest at another program and to discover ways of helping guests at your own church. Ask them to share their observations with the entire class.
- **All Ages:** Give positive reinforcement (verbal or written thank-yous) to anyone whom you observe making an extra effort to welcome a visitor.
- **All Ages:** Ask the students in your program to pray with you (during class or at a prayer time during the week) for visitors who attend.
- **All Ages:** Invite the students in your program to suggest ways they think visitors could be made to feel welcome.

Bonus Ideas for Reaching People on the Fringe:

1. Do something fun with the whole group.
2. Move the group into your home for dinner, dessert, games, a video, etc.
3. Plan opportunities to hang out with smaller groups (six or fewer) that include some "fringe folk." Keep fun, food and activities as important ingredients.
4. As relationships are built, look for one-on-one opportunities to talk about issues of importance to the individual. *Eugene Sim, Thanksgiving Church, Whittier, California*

Bonus Idea for Helping Group Members Build Relationships:

Divide the class into pairs, asking students to not choose partners they already know well. Allow three minutes for the partners to tell each other as much as possible about themselves. After three minutes, have each pair join with another pair, with each person introducing his or her partner, sharing one piece of interesting information. *Willamae Myers, Grace Bible Fellowship, Pinellas Park, Florida*

Unfortunately, most churches recruit only when there is a shortage. A church with a vision for outreach recruits new teachers *before* they are needed. When new classes or ministries are formed or expanded or when substitutes are needed, you will have already-trained staff available. (Chapter 7 gives ideas for making recruiting and training an ongoing process.)

Look to the Future

Duplicate and complete the "Outreach" worksheet (pp. 245-246) to determine how you can begin working to meet the goals stated in this chapter.

Early Childhood and Elementary Children

Follow-Up

Make It a Habit! While contacting *each* child each week by phone, mail or personal visit may be unrealistic for busy teachers, most can make a habit of contacting one or two children each week.

✔ Action Checklist

❑ Telephone one or more children in the class each week—visitors, absentees or regular members. Children enjoy receiving phone calls. A brief conversation can tell an absent child he or she was missed, encourage a child for good work last Sunday or remind a child of something happening next week.

❑ Send a short note to each child, thanking him or her for something he or she did.

❑ Greet a visitor's parents on the first Sunday, telling the parents about one specific experience their child enjoyed during the session. Teachers can offer to call the parents during the week or give their own phone numbers for parents to call with questions.

❑ Briefly visit children in their homes, taking a sample student's book and/or pictures of Sunday School activities to use in explaining to parents what the children do and learn on Sundays.

✔ Action Checklist

For Preschoolers and Their Families

❑ Ask one or two children to bring some of the equipment or supplies needed for an upcoming week's session: puzzles, play figures, magazine pictures, etc. Children will enjoy sharing with their class.

❑ When a child has been promoted into your class, make a personal contact within a few weeks to help ease the child's transition.

❑ Take pictures of an activity or class. Get double prints and mail out the photos along with a note.

PRESCHOOLERS SPECIAL EVENTS OR PROGRAM IDEAS

"Mommy (or Daddy) and Me" classes

Babysitting co-ops

Bubble Play Day

Children's museum field trip

Family Night Out

Grandmothers'/Grandfathers' Clubs

Kids' Night Out

Mother's Day Out

Parenting classes

Petting zoo

Play groups

Puppet shows

Story times

Children's Follow-Up

✔ Action Checklist

For Elementary School Children and Their Families

❑ Invite several children to a favorite location (park, playground, pizza or other food place, mall, skate park, etc.). Children who have been reluctant to participate in Sunday School or who have been shy or somewhat rebellious in class often undergo dramatic attitude changes as a result of having a good time outside of the classroom with the teacher and a handful of other kids. The advantage of inviting two to six children at a time is that they help entertain each other and stronger friendships are built. Include a child who is less regular in attendance with several children who are regular attendees.

❑ Send flyers to students asking each to bring a particular item relating to the session's topic (nature item, photograph of their family, magazine picture of a certain item, etc.). Students who have assignments involving them in the class are more likely to make an effort to attend.

❑ At the beginning of the school year students are likely to sign up for new activities. Contact them by mail, phone or personal visit.

❑ Take pictures of an activity or class. Get double prints and mail out the photos along with a note.

CHILDREN SPECIAL EVENTS OR PROGRAMS IDEAS

Many of the preschool suggestions would be appropriate as well as the following:

Amusement park trips
Back-to-school parties
Bike and bag trips
Cooking classes
Craft classes
Crazy Olympics
Day camp
Easter breakfast
Harvest parties
Hobby classes
Live nativity scenes

Miniature golf
Performing arts classes
Pumpkin Patch Party
Puppet show presentations
Sports clinics
Summer and winter camps
Play Day
Swim parties
Wacky Wednesday Club
Water Olympics

Youth Follow-Up

✔ Action Checklist

In addition to the suggestions for preschool and elementary follow-up, you should encourage the following:

- ❏ Take at least two students with you when you go places: beach, park, mall, etc. Invite two regular attendees to each invite a friend along. Relationships will be built and students will be encouraged in outreach.
- ❏ Attend sporting, musical or dramatic events in which students participate.
- ❏ Send E-mail messages inviting students to attend Sunday School. Include a teaser note about the upcoming week's topic.
- ❏ Ask one or two students each week to be the greeters for the class or an activity.
- ❏ Send postcards to students, offering a small prize (free ice cream, candy bar, etc.) to students who attend the following week's class and can answer a question designed to introduce the session's topic.
- ❏ Take pictures of an activity or class. Get double prints and mail out the photos along with a note.

YOUTH SPECIAL EVENTS OR PROGRAMS

Backpacking trips	Scavenger hunts
Bike trips	Service projects
Bowling	Skate parties
Concerts	Ski trips
Guys' or Gals' Night Out	Swim parties
Gym nights	Tutoring
Movie nights	Ultimate Frisbee
Pizza parties	Video rallies
Praise and Prayer nights	Water Wars

Adult Follow-Up

✔ Action Checklist

❑ Invite several class members to meet you for a meal, coffee or dessert, or for a fun activity: tennis, hike, sporting event, concert, etc. After modeling these kinds of informal get-togethers for several months, ask class members to initiate their own get-acquainted activities.

❑ Ask one or two current students to serve as the greeters for the class, introducing newcomers to people, including newcomers in conversation, etc. This task could extend into the week by having the greeters contact visitors informally to thank them for coming and to invite them to return. Rotate the greeting task among class members on a monthly basis.

❑ Challenge several group members to invite friends to class in a particular week. Encourage these individuals to ask God for guidance as to which friends to invite.

❑ Ask a group member to contact former class members who no longer attend. Those contacting dropouts should invite them to return and/or try to discover why they dropped out from the class. Even if the dropouts are unable to return, helpful information can be learned that may prevent future dropouts.

❑ When you discover that a particular topic has generated interest, rent a video on a similar topic and show it on a Friday night at your or a class member's home. Invite students and irregular attendees who might be more interested in coming to someone's home than to church on Sunday.

❑ Take pictures of an activity or class. Get double prints and mail out the photos along with a note.

ADULT SPECIAL EVENTS OR PROGRAMS

Aerobics classes

Book or video discussion groups

Coffeehouse groups

Crafts classes

Cultural events (plays, concerts)

Demonstrations (gardening, photography, computers, etc.)

Game nights

Hiking or camping

Informational seminars

Seasonal parties (New Year's eve, etc.)

Silent auctions

Special speakers

Sports teams (softball, basketball, golf tournaments, soccer, volleyball, etc.)

Weekend or miniretreats

Outreach

Rate your church's progress toward each goal and then list two or more actions you can take to reach each goal.

GOAL 1: PLAN FOR OUTREACH

Each teacher participates in a plan to contact unchurched students and to follow up on visitors and absentees.

1	2	3	4	5
Need to Start		Fair		Goal Achieved

Actions to Take:

GOAL 2: MAKE THE MOST OF YOUR VISITORS

Special attention is given to the ways in which visitors are welcomed and cared for.

1	2	3	4	5
Need to Start		Fair		Goal Achieved

Actions to Take:

GOAL 3: TURNING VISITORS INTO MEMBERS

The program, space and staff for your Sunday School all combine not only to encourage nonchurched people to attend but also to become regular attenders.

1	2	3	4	5
Need to Start		Fair		Goal Achieved

Actions to Take:

Chapter Eleven

Taking Sunday School Home

Sunday School's efforts to impact lives must include reaching into the homes of students and supporting families in fulfilling their roles at the center of effective teaching ministries.

What This Chapter Tells You

- The Sunday School, because it touches all age groups, has a unique opportunity among church ministries to contribute to strong Christian families.
- In order for the Sunday School to take its ministry to the various members of a family, it must intentionally nurture an active partnership with the home, seeking ways to work together to build Christian lives.
- Sunday School leaders and teachers must regularly communicate with the home about the goals, benefits and opportunities of the teaching ministry.
- Family ministry leadership needs to be involved in coordinating Sunday School efforts to help families.

What This Chapter Shows You

- A view of the Sunday School and home as allies, not as competitors;
- Family ministry ideas that strengthen both the Sunday School and the family;
- How to plan events that will benefit families.

Where Do I Start?

Look at Where You Are

Duplicate and complete the "Families" worksheet (p. 249) to evaluate the impact of your Sunday School on the families in your church.

Families Together or Separate?

Some people view the Sunday School as having a negative impact on families. The comments sound something like this: "Going to Sunday School 'as a family' just means riding together in the car and then splitting up in the church parking lot as everyone goes to their own class. That sounds like separating families, not uniting them."

That sounds logical, until that hour of separation is looked at in terms of how it can help each person become a better family member. An hour of studying God's Word with a group of peers can give a positive boost to each student's family life. Learning approaches designed carefully for each individual age group ensure that each family member has the opportunity to rejoin family members having gained insights and experiences that make a positive difference.

FAMILY FOCUS

Basically, providing Christian teaching for someone (at any age) without knowing and interacting with that person's family is like pruning a tree without considering the health of the roots and trunk.

Get the Big Picture

When the family and the Sunday School are headed in opposite directions, tensions result and students end up choosing one or the other. But when the family and Sunday School share common goals, they strengthen and encourage each other, combining to make a greater impact than either could alone.

In most churches, students periodically get a new teacher. This happens when classes are promoted, teachers quit, a group begins studying a new topic or the seasons change. There is almost no end to the reasons why teachers come and go. In comparison, family members are much more constant.

Long after students have forgotten the names of previous teachers, family members will remain actively engaged in students' lives. When Sunday School teachers have a vision to help families grow together in Christ, the positive results go on for years to come. To carry out this vision, the Sunday School must seek to:

- Strengthen marriages, providing instruction and guidance at all levels on the values of a Christian home;
- Equip parents to nurture and teach their children, setting positive examples the child can follow;
- Enhance family life through opportunities for growth as individuals and as families in worshiping, learning, serving and playing;
- Welcome and support those whose families are actively involved in the life of the church, those who are the only members of their families who attend and those who are without family support and challenge.

Families

1. What contacts do teachers have with the family members of those they teach?

2. What topics are studied in Sunday School to help students better understand what contributes to strong families?

3. What actions are taken to welcome and include people in various stages of family life?

   • Young married couples

   • Families with young children

   • Families with older children

   • Families of teenagers

   • Couples whose children are grown (empty nesters)

   • Seniors/widowed

   • Singles/single parents

Focus on the Goals

"If only we could get those parents to bring their kids every week."

"If only we could get those teachers to make Sunday School more interesting."

Sounds like an impasse. On one side teachers blame parents for everything from sporadic attendance to behavior problems. At the same time, parents criticize teachers. What will it take to get teachers and parents to join forces in improving the ministry of teaching?

GOAL 1: FAMILY FOCUS

Sunday School Staff Need to Build Partnerships with Students' Families

The typical Sunday School teacher tends to feel that the effort of preparing lessons and guiding sessions is more than enough responsibility. Even a hint that teachers should do something to get to know the family members of students raises the cry: "That's asking way too much. I'm too busy to take on that job!"

I just remembered. It's Parent Open House Day in my Sunday School class.

 Bonus Idea for Family Ministry: Encourage Sunday School or other program teachers to make a list of practical ways in which families need help during crisis situations—death, illness, moving, divorce, etc.—then when a family is in need, it's easy to call them up and offer help in a specific way, instead of a general "Call me if you need anything."

When Sunday School teachers work in isolation from the family connections of class members, they cannot be aware of individual students' life circumstances. Not only do they miss the opportunity to benefit students and their families, but they also

- Reduce their own effectiveness as teachers;
- Lose opportunities to build relationships with family members who could be valuable resources in the classroom;
- Fail to add new friendships to their lives.

Challenging Sunday School teachers to build partnerships with families is not asking them to add time-consuming new tasks to their teaching ministry. Developing a family focus throughout the Sunday School staff is simply asking everyone to expand their interest in their students to include their family members.

Teaching Two or More Generations: Sometimes there is real value in bringing family members together for intergenerational learning experiences. The following guidelines help make these times effective:

1. **Make these times special ones, not every-week occurrences.** The challenges of keeping all age levels productively involved makes it difficult to extend intergenerational groups for very long. Usually, the first ones to want out are the teenagers, followed closely by adults without children of their own. But sooner or later, participants of all ages start to long for a group designed for their own needs and interests.

2. **Emphasize active participation and limit verbal communication.** Children, especially, tend to get restless if anyone talks, reads or prays too long. Many of the learning activities suggested in chapter 4 work wonderfully for intergenerational groups. Adults and teens will often thoroughly enjoy activities in this setting that they might not feel comfortable doing in their regular peer-group classes.

3. **Provide alternate provisions for children who are not ready for what everyone else is doing.** Even with the best of intentions, some group activities do not stretch far enough to comfortably include all of the youngest children. Nothing drives wedges faster than a teacher or parent pointing out "My children always enjoyed being with the grown-ups!" The obvious and unfriendly inference is that there must be something wrong with parents who can't get their children to like it, too.

✔ Action Checklist

❑ Guide teachers in a discussion of the ideas on the "Helping Teachers and Families Connect" handout (pp. 259-260). Brainstorm some additional ways to get to know family members of students. Then have each person choose one or more ideas to begin implementing in the coming month.

❑ Provide regular information to families on the goals and benefits of the Sunday School. Use the ideas on the "Is Your Family Missing Out?" handout (p. 261) to help communicate the value of Sunday School for families.

❑ Encourage families to use Sunday School experiences and materials (i.e., take-home papers, etc.) to stimulate meaningful family interaction. The "Questions for Dinnertime Discussion" handout (p. 263) provides ideas families can use.

❏ Evaluate your Sunday School's ministry to families by asking students of all age groups to complete a survey, either as a class activity or individually. Include questions such as:

  • How does coming to Sunday School help your family?
  • What are some ways our Sunday School could help your family more?
  • If you and your family were in charge of planning Sunday School next week, how might it be different?

❏ Review the job descriptions for all teachers in the Sunday School and be sure there is a clear reference to building partnerships with the families of students.

❏ Plan specific ways that Sunday School teachers can work together with family ministry leaders in coming months.

GOAL 2: FAMILY LEADERSHIP

Clearly Defined Leadership Roles Ensure Family Ministry as a Priority

There is an old saying that "What is everybody's job becomes nobody's job." Sadly, this is often true when it comes to the Sunday School's ministry to families. When teachers are busy doing their own jobs—helping with the two-year-olds, the high school group or the young couple's classes—there is little time left over to implement the ideas for strengthening families.

As a result, it is not uncommon that churches have either little or no family emphasis or they organize family ministry efforts outside Sunday School with great fanfare in the beginning and hit-and-miss efforts over time. The lack of a family ministries organizational structure tends to make continuation of family ministry efforts dependent on an individual or small group, and eventually the size of the task is too big a burden for just a few people.

Family ministry should be made a priority of the Sunday School.

1. Churches that assign family ministry activities to volunteers or part-time teachers should define a means of regular communication between these leaders and Sunday School teachers. It is unlikely that people with only a limited amount of time to give will find it easy to coordinate regularly with leaders of another program unless steps for doing so are clearly defined.

2. Churches that have a pastor/director of family ministries as a full-time leadership position should define a correlation with the Sunday School in the job description for this position. Items to include should be:

   • Directly encourage and support efforts of Sunday School staff to build families;
   • Promote family ministry awareness and activities through Sunday School groups;
   • Encourage participants in family ministry activities to get involved in Sunday School.

3. If no churchwide family ministry exists or if the family ministry leadership is unable to give attention to the Sunday School's role in family ministry, appoint a family ministry coordinator or director who will focus on this important area. This leader would work to encourage and assist the efforts of the teachers in communicating and strengthening families. They would also plan and lead periodic and ongoing family ministry activities and events in cooperation with Sunday School staff.

GOAL 3:
FAMILY EDUCATION

Apply Bible Truth to a Variety of Family Situations

The Bible is the primary textbook for the Sunday School. Students of all ages need to see on a regular basis how Scripture addresses specific issues faced in family living. While psychological theories come and go, a solid foundation in the Word equips a person with the ability to handle a wide range of contemporary family issues.

Three Ways to Address Family Education

1. **Apply ongoing Bible study to family situations.**
   Whether guiding a class of preschoolers, high schoolers or adults, teachers need to help students apply God's truth to circumstances they face in their own families.
   - Lesson materials need to be chosen that direct teachers to make the links between the Scriptures being studied and the situations faced in family living.
   - Teachers need to be reminded to prepare lessons in light of current family issues. In doing so, teachers need guidance to ensure that the meaning of Scripture passages must not be changed to make it fit a family interpretation. Also, teachers sometimes need to be cautioned against using Scripture to drive wedges between students and family members who have not yet decided to follow Christ.

2. **Offer special classes on family issues.**
   Adult classes will often study topics on various aspects of family living, but all age levels benefit from focused attention on life together as a family. Sometimes such classes work well with the regular class groups during the Sunday School session. Classes that require specialized leadership (i.e., therapist, pastor, social worker, etc.) are often more effective at another time (i.e., a weeknight free of weekend conflicts). The following topics may help you get started in choosing topics to offer:
   - Parents and children (periodic, short-term classes featuring active learning for all ages)
   Families in the Bible
   Wisdom for Today's Families
   Jesus Is Coming to Our House!

 Bonus Idea for Family Education: In the fall we communicate to all parents in the church, offering them an opportunity to gain the skills needed to be successful in teaching their own children. We encourage them to commit to 12 hours of ministry for each child. By getting actively involved, we promise that they will discover what to teach kids and how to do it effectively. We stress Deuteronomy 6 and seek to change the attitude from parents just bringing their kids to church to parents fulfilling God's plan for their lives. *Bonnie Aldrich, Pulpit Rock Church, Colorado Springs, Colorado*

- Children
  Why God Made Families
  When Mom and Dad Divorce
  When Someone You Love Dies
- Youth
  Dating, Sex and Marriage
  Choosing a Life Partner
  Looking Ahead to College/Career Choices
  Getting Along with Parents
  When Families Need Healing and Forgiveness
- Adults
  Marriage Preparation (for engaged couples and singles)
  Making Your Marriage Even Better
  Parenting Preschoolers (Children, Youth, Adult Children, Grandchildren)
  Family Finance: Stewardship of What We Have
  Caring for Aging Parents

3. **Encourage and train parents to take advantage of Sunday School resources at home.**
   Lesson materials provided to students contain a wealth of interesting and valuable activities and information. Best of all, they give parents an easy way to stimulate meaningful interaction with children and youth, extending the impact of lessons beyond the walls of the classroom.

JOB DESCRIPTION

FAMILY MINISTRY COORDINATOR
Task: To plan, organize and direct the family ministry efforts of the Sunday School
Term: One year, beginning September 1
Supervisor _____ (name) _____

Responsibilities
- Provide up-to-date student/family rosters for all teachers.
- Encourage leaders to get to know, pray for and communicate with family members of students.
- Coordinate family education efforts of the Sunday School.
- Evaluate the manner in which families are cared for through the Sunday School.
- Plan special events or programs for families.
- Recruit, meet with and supervise age-level family ministry coordinators as needed.
- Communicate regularly with supervisor.

Curriculum and Families: There are three major ways that publishers of Sunday School curriculum structure the content to be taught in Sunday School, in each case with a somewhat different approach to equipping the family with nurturing resources related to what is learned in class.

1. Unified lessons: Every age-level studies essentially the same Bible content. This plan is often advocated as a way to make it easy for families to follow up on the lessons taught each week. Also, the plan is seen as having advantages for administrators who can easily keep track of what is being studied by everyone. Others feel that this plan has the disadvantages of either limiting the topics to be studied or of presenting content that is too simple, too difficult or even irrelevant for some age groups.

2. Themes: Every age level studies Scripture dealing with the same major themes. This plan is promoted as allowing the Scripture passages to be selected to fit the needs of each age level while still having a common theme that families can use in lesson follow-up. Critics of this plan feel that a thematic approach to Bible study too easily results in trying to make Scripture fit into predetermined topics. Also, themes may have little or no meaning to all age levels or may be so generally vague as to have little impact or interest.

3. Graded lessons: Every age group studies Scripture selected to fit their needs and interests. This plan is supported by those who feel the limited time available for a once-a-week program requires planning lessons targeted specifically for each age level. Also, family follow-up with this plan avoids problems parents face when trying to maintain or extend everyone's interest in the same topics. Inviting different family members to share something from their own unique, special lesson is usually easier and more interesting than trying to stretch the same topic to fit the whole family.

(**Note:** In case the above descriptions do not seem totally objective, the authors of this book admit to being partial to the third plan.)

✔ Action Checklist

❑ At a teachers' meeting, ask participants to look through their teachers' manuals for content or activities that can be used to help students apply Bible truth to family situations. After about five minutes, invite volunteers to share items they found.

❑ Regularly remind teachers to look for ways to connect Bible content to the family experiences of their students.

❑ For each age level, identify one or more family-life topics that would be helpful for that group to study. Select capable teachers and appropriate curriculum resources. Decide when to offer the classes and whether such topics would best be taught in
  - The regular Sunday School classes;
  - In special classes during the Sunday School hour;
  - At another time during the week.

GOAL 4:
FAMILY EVENTS

Regularly Provide Special Events or Programs That Attract and Benefit Families

Does anyone remember the Sunday School Picnic? It was the family event of the year! There was that spectacular array of food, topped off with homemade ice cream and a selection of every pie known to the civilized world. Teachers of every age group planned games and races—parents and kids in wheelbarrow runs, three-legged races and egg tosses. And there was always some kid who fell in the creek or pond in spite of warnings from Mom to "Stay away from the water!" Far from being a program that divided families, the Sunday School for generations was one of the few agencies that planned activities that brought families together.

We do not need to get caught up in nostalgia for the "good old days." We do, however, need to consider that families today, perhaps more than in any recent generation, need activities that foster enjoyment in being together. While the Sunday School may be struggling just to fulfill its teaching mission, there is great benefit when the Sunday School gets involved with events for families. The time and energy expended to plan, promote and conduct a family event is really not a diversion from the Sunday School's stated purpose; instead, it is one of the most visible and beneficial ways the Sunday School can show that learning God's truth makes a positive difference in the lives of individuals and families. Some suggestions for events are:

1. **Link family events to the Sunday School.** The best events are those that have carryover—ones where new friendships have the opportunity to grow and new patterns of action are seen as possible. For many years the Sunday School Picnic was effective at deepening friendships between teachers, students and family members. Sunday Schools today should consider getting involved with events that have the potential to build bridges between people.

2. **Provide a wide range of activities for families.**
   - Outdoor activities: picnics, hiking, bike riding, etc.
   - Retreats/family camps: day trip, overnighter, weekend, week, etc.
   - Concerts, puppet shows, film nights, etc.
   - Family Sunday School—Occasional or short-term intergenerational group studies

- Summer evening socials: ice cream social, barbecue, campfire, etc.
- Parents' Go Out/Kids' Eat 'n' Shout: Kids enjoy dinner, games and fun while parents enjoy a date.
- Activity programs: sports, clubs, craft nights, etc.
- Family Heritage Night: Families bring a photo album and a few objects to display as everyone browses what other families brought.
- Service projects/mission trips.

3. **Some activities are best for all families in the church while others for only a selected group of families.**

- **All-church family events:** These are usually easier to provide in a small church. The larger the church becomes, the more challenges are involved in planning and conducting events for everyone in all age groups. In either case, there is great value in events that help people get to know others regardless of age, marital status or children.

- **Family groups linked by children's ages or interests:** Some events are more appealing to families with children in a certain age group. For example, families with preschoolers would thoroughly enjoy a zoo trip or puppet show, while families with teenagers might respond to a concert or game night. Families with children who play soccer might enjoy going to a high school, college or professional soccer match.

- **Involvement of Sunday School leadership:** Events for families with children of similar ages should closely involve the Sunday School leadership for the children's classes. Whether or not teachers become active in planning and conducting an event, they should be consulted in the scheduling and be enlisted to help promote the event to children and their parents. Teachers should also attend the event to take advantage of the opportunity to get to know parents better.

- **Family groups linked by parents' ages or interests:** Families with parents interested in missions would value the opportunity to assist with Vacation Bible School for a mission church. Single parents need the option to do some activities with other single-parent families and some activities with other families. Adult Sunday School classes benefit from a picnic or a fundraising event that involves all family members, not just the adults.

❏ At a teacher's meeting, brainstorm events that can involve the families of the students. After compiling a list, divide it among two or more groups of teachers, asking them to select one or two ideas they feel would most likely benefit the families. Then ask them to select events that could help to build relationships between teachers and families, as well as between the various families participating. Finally, guide teachers in beginning to plan a family event.

❏ Check your church calendar for upcoming events involving some or all families in the church. Share information on these events with Sunday School teachers and encourage them to get involved in promoting and attending the events.

❏ Meet with the church leaders who are responsible for planning family events. Talk with them about ways to link these events to the Sunday School.

• **Family clusters linked by geography, length of time attending the church or other factors:** Families that live in the same neighborhood enjoy hosting a block party or other event to build relationships with unchurched friends. Families new to a church enjoy attending a luncheon or dessert event at which they get to meet each other and church leaders. Or a cluster could just be people who are interested in being part of an extended family of people of all age groups. A family cluster may consist of as many as 20 or 25 people who get together periodically for meals and a variety of activities of interest to the group.

Again, regardless of the event or the configuration of families for whom it is intended, Sunday School leaders and teachers need to be visibly involved, helping to provide a friendly bridge to relationship- and discipleship-building opportunities.

Look to the Future

Duplicate and complete the "Families" worksheet (pp. 264-265) to discover how to expand your Sunday School's ministry to families.

Helping Teachers and Families Connect

SUPERVISING TEACHERS

1. Provide all teachers with up-to-date rosters that list each student's name, address, phone, E-mail address, birthday, anniversary (married adults) and names of family members. Also provide regular attendance information to teachers.

2. Encourage teachers to get to know family members of their students, focusing on students who might need support (i.e., absentees, irregular attendees, those whose family does not attend, etc.).

3. Encourage family members to get to know the Sunday School teachers. Particularly in large churches where no one knows everyone, it is usually easier for parents to approach a teacher than for a teacher to approach parents. A few ideas:

   All Ages
   - Publish a list of all classes and where they meet and the names and phone numbers of the teachers. Include an invitation to call a teacher for information about a particular class.
   - Outside every class, mount a sign with the name(s) of the teacher(s). Also mount (outside or inside the class) a poster with candid snapshots of teachers in action with students. Add labels with the names of the people pictured and update the photos periodically.
   - Distribute blank note cards to the congregation. Invite everyone to write a note to a teacher telling how his or her ministry has helped their family.
   - Invite family members to be prayer partners with a Sunday School teacher.
   - Encourage families to invite a teacher and his or her family for Sunday dinner, a backyard barbecue or for dessert and coffee after an evening event.

   Early Childhood/Children
   - Suggest that parents volunteer to provide and serve a snack for the Sunday School class near their child's birthday.
   - Invite parents to schedule a Sunday when they will observe a full class session with their child's teacher.

   Youth
   - Form a parent support/prayer group that meets together periodically to pray for the young people and their teachers and for each other. Invite teachers to attend or submit requests and praises for parents to pray.
   - Promote some youth staff along with the students each year, providing continuity for teachers, students and parents.

   Adults
   - Encourage class members to invite a teacher and his or her family to participate in a family activity (picnic in the park, overnight camp out, hike in the woods, etc.).

4. Make a list of the teachers for whom each supervising teacher is responsible. Then supervising leaders choose several ways to get to know the families of their teachers—in the same way that they want the teachers to build bridges with families of their students.

TEACHERS

1. In class, talk informally with students about their families. Share information about your own family and invite students to tell you about theirs. (**Note:** Avoid prying or making judgmental comments about family activities of which you disapprove.)

   - **Early Childhood:** The classroom home-living center is a natural place for talking with children about the people in their family and various family experiences. (Some teachers assure parents that they won't believe everything a child says about what goes on at home if parents promise not to believe everything a child says about class.)

   - **Children:** Take advantage of the times when students arrive early to ask them about their week and how family members are doing. When asking questions during the lesson, periodically pose the question: "How do you think your mom (or dad or brother or sister) might answer that? Why might their answer be different from yours?"

   - **Youth:** As so often happens in the teen years, when teenagers start to become embarrassed that they even *have* parents or siblings, they may rarely (if ever) volunteer any information about their families. As young people move toward increased independence, teachers who earn their trust often become "stand-in parents" and are able to say things to the teen that might not be accepted from a parent.

   - **Adults:** Knowing the names of students' family members is as important to adults as to children. Often, asking about a child or grandchild produces far more meaningful conversations than asking about work, the weather or a sports team.

2. Pray regularly, by name, for your students and their families. Share with your students that you do this and invite them or their family members to share items of concern about which you can pray. Keep a prayer journal on your class, updating it with new family information.

3. At church, look for opportunities to talk to family members of your students.
   - Before and after services, use the free time to greet family members.
   - Instead of sitting in your usual place during worship services, look around for students and their families that you do not know well. Sit near them and take advantage of opportunities to speak to them.

4. When family events are planned by your church or when students are involved in community events (sports games, band concerts, parades, etc.), make it a point to attend even if you aren't expected to be there. Your presence speaks clearly of your interest, encouraging students and their families.

5. At least once per quarter, make a personal contact (conversation at church, phone, home visit, etc.) with each student's family. Share positive comments about the student and invite feedback on what the student likes most or least about the class.

Is Your Family Missing Out?

How Regular Sunday School Attendance Strengthens Families

1. Sunday School provides support and encouragement for building relationships and healthy spiritual growth. Imagine, terrific people who have volunteered to spend time every week with your family just to encourage and help you in your quest for the Word and its meaning for your family! Caring and committed teachers support and reinforce positive Christian values—something every family needs in today's often negative world.

2. There's no better place to build quality friendships. Friends wield a powerful influence, for good or for ill. Regular participation in a Sunday School class is a great way to forge friendships with people who also care about Christian values.

3. Sunday School classes study the Bible, God's Word, to guide our lives *today*. When troubled times come, the family with a solid foundation is better prepared to weather the storm.

4. The role models are great! Many people lament the lack of positive role models in sports, entertainment and politics. The family that attends Sunday School together goes home every week with a whole cast of examples worth imitating—some from the pages of our textbook and some here-and-now, flesh-and-blood teachers and friends of true quality.

5. Stimulating lessons add value to family conversations the rest of the week. Families that attend Sunday School have a wealth of experiences and resources that open the door to talking about things that truly matter. If it's been awhile since your dinnertime conversation touched on insights from Scripture, let this week's lessons suggest a few topics worth everyone's time.

Dinnertime Discussions

MOVING FAMILY CONVERSATION BEYOND TV, SPORTS AND WEATHER

A Few Tips for Asking Questions

- Cut apart the questions so that each is on a separate strip. Add additional questions of your own. Place the question strips in a container; then family members take turns, either drawing questions they will answer or ones they will ask of another family member.

- Share your own answers to the questions you ask.

- Avoid "grilling" family members. Your conversation time should be relaxed and enjoyable, not a test that becomes an ordeal.

- Let all family members ask questions of each other.

- Encourage children to have any Sunday School papers handy to refresh their memory and to stimulate further questions.

- Teenagers may resent any "prying" into their affairs and respond to any question with thrilling answers such as "I don't know," "OK," or "I forget."

- Try writing three or four questions on a sheet of paper; then let the teenager select the one he or she will answer in 50 words or more. Then count the words. (There is no money-back guarantee that this will work with every teenager, but it's worth a try.)

Two Questions to Avoid

1. What did you learn in Sunday School?
   Children especially have little awareness of when they are learning. If they know something, they tend to assume they've always known it.

2. What was your lesson about?
   This question usually just draws blank stares.

Questions for Dinnertime Discussions

1. What was one thing that happened in your class?

2. What was one thing you liked about your class?

3. Who did something friendly in your class and what did that person do?

4. What was one thing someone said that would be good for our family to remember?

5. What kind of problems did your class talk about?

6. What person in the Bible did something our family would not like? What did that person do?

7. What person in the Bible did you hear about who did something our family would like? What did that person do?

8. When we pray together, who is someone in your class that we can thank God for? Who can we ask God to help?

9. When have you seen something happen that was a lot like what happened in the Bible story or verses your class learned about?

10. Which of your friends was not in your class this week? What would be a good way to show that you missed him or her?

Families

Rate your church's progress toward each goal and then list two or more actions you can take to reach each goal.

GOAL 1: FAMILY FOCUS

All Sunday School staff members are encouraged to look for ways to build partnerships with the families of their students.

1	2	3	4	5
Need to Start		Fair		Goal Achieved

Actions to Take:

GOAL 2: FAMILY LEADERSHIP

Leadership roles in your Sunday School have clearly defined responsibilities to ensure that ministry to families is a priority.

1	2	3	4	5
Need to Start		Fair		Goal Achieved

Actions to Take:

GOAL 3: FAMILY EDUCATION

Leaders and teachers provide lessons that address a variety of family situations, helping students apply Bible truth to family living.

1	2	3	4	5
Need to Start		Fair		Goal Achieved

Actions to Take:

GOAL 4: FAMILY EVENTS

Your Sunday School regularly provides and/or cooperates with special events or programs designed to attract and benefit families.

1	2	3	4	5
Need to Start		Fair		Goal Achieved

Actions to Take:

Index